— DAVID FISHER —

HARD EVIDENCE

HOW DETECTIVES INSIDE THE FBI'S SCI-CRIME LAB
HAVE HELPED SOLVE AMERICA'S TOUGHEST CASES

SIMON & SCHUSTER
NEW YORK LONDON TORONTO SYDNEY TOKYO SINGAPORE

SIMON & SCHUSTER
Rockefeller Center
1230 Avenue of the Americas
New York, NY 10020

Copyright © 1995 by David Fisher
All rights reserved,
including the right of reproduction
in whole or in part in any form whatsoever.

Designed by Hyun Joo Kim

Manufactured in the United States of America

10 9 8 7 6 5 4 3 2 1

Library of Congress Cataloging-in-Publication Data

Fisher, David, date.
  Hard evidence : how detectives inside the FBI's sci-crime lab have
helped solve America's toughest cases / David Fisher.
      p.   cm.
  Includes index.
    1. FBI Laboratory.   2. Criminal investigation—United States—Case
studies.   I. Title.
HV8141.F527   1995
363.2'56'0973—dc 20
                                                                94-46293
                                                                CIP

ISBN 0-671-79369-1

to my father, Irving Fisher, who

taught me the things that matter

CONTENTS

PREFACE

Perhaps no government agency has been more written about than the FBI. Countless books, movies, and television programs have documented the Bureau's fight against crime. But one important aspect of the FBI's operations is virtually unknown: the extraordinary work that is being done by its forensic department—the FBI Criminal Laboratory.

Several years ago, when I was writing about organized crime, I became friendly with Special Agent Joe Pistone, who is better known as "Donnie Brasco," the guise in which he spent six years working undercover in the mob and was responsible for the convictions of almost one hundred leaders of organized crime. In conversation with Pistone one evening, the subject of the FBI's crime lab came up, and, on impulse, I asked it if was possible for me to gain access. To my surprise, a week later he took me to the FBI Headquarters Building on Ninth Street and Pennsylvania Avenue in Washington, D.C., and introduced me to the fascinating world of scientific crime detection—sci-crime, as I began to refer to it. I spent the next two years exploring that world. This book is the result.

For a writer, walking into the FBI crime lab was like discovering an unexplored gold mine, a mine so rich it was difficult to believe that other people had not been there before me. I spent months inside the lab, learning how the cutting edge of science and technology is applied to the investigation of a crime. I conducted almost two hundred hours of interviews with the men and women who have worked on every major criminal investigation of recent years, including the people who helped uncover the mysteries behind the destruction of Pam Am Flight 103 over Lockerbie, Scotland, and the bombing of the World Trade Center in New York, and the men who did the ballistics investigation in the Kennedy assassination—the first interview they had ever granted a reporter. I spoke to the man who discovered James Earl Ray's identity through a partial fingerprint, and to the people who helped convict the Atlanta Child Killer, Wayne Williams, on the basis of a few slender hairs and fibers. These are the people who often find out what they will be doing at work by reading the morning headlines. As I was told by one examiner, "We have a piece of every major crime in this country."

Few people know about the capabilities of the FBI crime lab. It is, simply, the finest crime lab in the world. And if its work has gone unheralded, it is perhaps because the evidence it has uncovered speaks quite loudly for itself. I was particularly engrossed by the process of detection. How does a partial fingerprint, a spent bullet, a drop of blood, a hair fiber, a piece of bone, a shard of metal or glass, a dab of paint, or an empty bottle lead to the person who committed a crime? The latest and most sophisticated technologies are vital to this process and, as I discovered, many of them were created or adapted to this work in the FBI lab. But ultimately it is the expertise and experience of the men and women who employ these technologies—along with the gut feelings, hunches, educated guesses, and often pure persistence of all great detectives—that have cracked even the toughest cases.

This book is their story: the role their work has played in solving every conceivable type of crime—rapes, murders, serial killings, product tampering—crimes that have made headlines around the world, crimes that might otherwise have gone undetected or unsolved. It is crime detection of the highest order.

CHAPTER

– 1 –

A World of Wonders:

Inside the FBI's Sci-Crime Lab

From a drop of water, the logician could infer the possibility of an At-lantic or a Niagara without having seen or heard of one or the other. So all life is a great chain, the nature of which is known whenever we are shown a single link of it. Like all other arts, the Science of Deduction and Analysis is one which can only be acquired through long and patient study, nor is life long enough to allow any mortal to attain the highest possible perfection in it.

SHERLOCK HOLMES,
In Sir Arthur Conan Doyle's "The Book of Life"

Not long ago investigators had to find the smoking gun to convict a sus-pect. Now all they need is the smoke.

On December 16, 1989, federal court judge Robert Vance opened a small box that had been mailed to his home in Mountain Brook, Alabama. When he lifted the lid the box exploded, killing him instantly and seriously wounding his wife. Two days later Savannah, Georgia, attorney and alder-man Robert Robinson died in his office when a second package bomb ex-ploded as he opened it. That same day a third bomb was discovered during a routine screening of packages mailed to judges in the Atlanta federal courthouse. A fourth package bomb was delivered to a female employee of the NAACP legal counsel in Jacksonville, Florida. She left it on her desk and went to run some errands, intending to open it when she returned later that afternoon. But her car broke down as she drove back to the office and had to be towed, so she went home. On the news that night she heard of the explosion in Savannah and realized that the package on her desk was similar to the one that had killed Robert Robinson. The next morning she called the Jacksonville bomb squad. And she lived.

Fearing a concerted attack on the judicial system of the United States, local, state, and federal law enforcement agencies immediately began intensive investigations of the bombings. The FBI designated the murders a major case, meaning they took priority over all other cases. In the Bureau most cases are referred to by a description number; major cases are given code names to facilitate communications. Because this case began with the murder of Judge Vance by a package bomb, it was known as VANPAC; it eventually became one of the most massive investigations in FBI history, a year-long manhunt that involved hundreds of agents. More than six thousand people were interviewed and millions of documents were examined. But the case was finally solved on the third floor of the FBI headquarters building in downtown Washington, D.C., in the finest crime lab in the world.

The crime lab is that place where science meets murder. It's where the wonders of modern science and space-age technology are used to transform clues into hard evidence. Killers may live to tell their stories; there is only the evidence to speak for their victims. But those often invisible bits of evidence can speak loudly to those who know how to understand them. Dead men do tell tales. No one disappears without a trace. There is no such thing as the perfect crime.

The VANPAC investigation ultimately involved just about every unit in the FBI crime lab, but the head investigator was soft-spoken Kentuckian Tom Thurman of the Explosives Unit. As a first step, the unopened package bombs received in Atlanta and Jacksonville were rendered safe, a nice way of saying that an aimed explosive was fired into the packages to separate the components. They were blown into pieces; essentially the evidence remained but the bombs could no longer function. When Thurman examined the remains of the four bombs, it was obvious to him that the same person had made them.

Each bomb was constructed inside a carton about the size of a shirt box, and each consisted of a steel pipe filled with smokeless powder that would explode when a current generated by two C batteries ran through a light-bulb filament (the bulb had been removed) to a homemade detonator. The only thing that prevented the circuit between the power source and the detonator from being completed was a thin piece of cardboard between two sheets of aluminum foil. When the cover of the box was lifted, a string attached to the lid was stretched taut and pulled out the cardboard, allowing the two sheets of foil to make contact, completing the circuit and triggering the bomb.

Apart from their construction, there were several other similarities between the bombs. Square end plates were bolted to both ends of the pipes. Everything inside each box had been painted with black enamel. The packages had been wrapped in brown paper. And threatening letters were found inside those bombs that hadn't gone off.

Pieces of each package bomb were sent to the various units in the crime lab for examination of any evidence that fell within their area of expertise. The DNA Analysis Unit attempted to develop a DNA profile of the bomb maker from the saliva used to moisten the mailing labels and stamps. The Hairs and Fiber Unit tried to determine where the string had originated, and knots tied in that string were examined by the lab's knot experts to see if they could be associated with a specific profession or region. The Materials Analysis Unit proved that the black enamel paint in each box was identical. It also attempted to identify the manufacturer of the adhesives and determined that ordinary telephone wire had been used in the circuits. The Elemental Analysis Unit was able to make a positive association between the nails used as shrapnel in all four bombs, providing additional proof that they had been made by the same person, and was also able to identify the specific press in Taiwan on which the nails had been fabricated. The Latent Fingerprint Section found a partial print on the letter inside the Jacksonville bomb and began trying to put a name to it. In the Chemistry/Toxicology Unit examiners set out to identify the source of the explosive, smokeless powder, as well as the primer material. The Document Section began a search for the typewriter on which the threatening letters had been written and for the manufacturer of the cardboard boxes. And the Explosives Unit dissected the remnants of the bombs, trying to trace any single piece to a source that might lead to the bomb maker.

Documents made the first hit. The typewriter on which the letters had been typed had a distinctive flaw: at some time in the past a broken type bar had been replaced with the wrong typeface. It was very easy to spot, and since three bombs had attacked the legal system, the judicial files in four states were scoured for documents written on that typewriter. Amazingly, among tens of thousands of pages, examiners at the Atlanta courthouse found what they were looking for: a threatening letter that had been typed on the same machine.

The letter had been written several years earlier by a resident of Enterprise, Alabama. Officers from the VANPAC task force descended on the small town, trailed by newspaper and television reporters, and several lab examiners flew there to look for the smallest clue that would connect this suspect to the bombings. "We searched every square inch of his house and business," Tom Thurman remembered. "We even drained his sewage system to see if he'd flushed pieces of the typewriter down there. But we didn't find a single thing that would connect him to the bombs. The suspect told us he'd sold a lot of typewriters out of his junk store and this had probably been one of them. So we had to start from scratch again."

In Chem/Tox, unit chief Roger Martz quickly identified the explosive used in the bombs as common Hercules Red Dot smokeless powder, but identifying the primer material was much more difficult. "There are as many as a hundred different primers available," Martz said. "The sample we got from the bombs contained two percent aluminum, and in all my research I found only one primer with two percent aluminum. It was CCI primer for small-arms ammunition, and since it isn't commercially available in bulk, whoever made the bombs had to have bought a large number of primers and opened them up by hand to remove the explosive material."

Agents began canvassing retailers throughout the South, looking for someone who might have sold several pounds of Red Dot smokeless powder and a large quantity of CCI primers to an individual in the period just before the bombs were mailed. But the first solid break in the case came from a conversation Thurman had had with an agent of the Bureau of Alcohol, Tobacco and Firearms while the two men were in Enterprise. "He told me that if we couldn't connect the suspect in Enterprise to the bombs," Thurman said, "we should look at a guy named Moody from Georgia. ATF records indicated that Moody had built a bomb in 1972 that had several characteristics in common with the VANPAC bombs. So when the search in Enterprise failed, we turned our attention to Walter Leroy Moody.

"Moody had been convicted of possession of a bomb in 1972, although he had not been convicted of actually making that bomb. He had served time in prison for possession and that could have been when his hatred of the judicial system began. Our investigation now focused on Moody, and we searched his house looking for anything that would link him to the bombs. We even picked up the floor in a room that had recently been totally redone. We didn't find a thing. We found every color and type of paint

imaginable, except the black enamel. We found every type of tool, except what was used to make the bombs. It was as if Moody knew what we would be looking for and had taken those things out of the house. We never found a single thing in that house that we were able to connect to the bombs."

After a long search, ATF found the original photographs of Moody's 1972 bomb. It was a pipebomb with square endplates bolted to it and it was in a corrugated paper box. It was powered by a flashlight battery, the initiator was a lightbulb filament taken from inside a bulb, and it was triggered by opening the box, which tightened a string. A threatening note was included with the bomb, and telephone wire was used for the circuits. In short, the package bomb found in Moody's possession in 1972 was virtually identical to the four 1989 bombs. "One means we use to identify a bomber is through his 'signature,' " Thurman explained. "People learn how to make bombs one way, and no matter how sophisticated they get, they'll continue to repeat certain techniques. That technique is almost as unique as a fingerprint, and it makes very strong evidence that two or more bombs were made by the same person or group. When I saw all this, I smiled and said, 'Yeah, this looks really good.' But before I would testify that the signature of the 1972 bomb compared strongly to the VANPAC bombs, I wanted to do a little more work. I wanted to compare the damage.

"ATF built us a demonstration bomb duplicating Moody's bombs. We constructed a room similar to Judge Vance's office on our range at Quantico. We used bobber targets, cardboard cutouts, to represent Judge Vance and his wife. Then we opened the box. Remotely. It blew our room apart and destroyed the bobbers. You look at the photographs of the bomb scene and compare them with the results of this test and it's about as close as you can get. When I saw this I said, 'Now I can testify that the same person made all of these bombs.' "

Meanwhile, other lab units were also getting results. Agents in Atlanta found the store in which Moody had bought four pounds of Hercules Red Dot smokeless powder and a thousand CCI primers about a week before the bombs were mailed. Had Moody not been identified by his signature as a bomb maker, it is possible he would have been found through this search.

Moody's wife eventually admitted that she had purchased some supplies for him. She also claimed that he had ordered her to drive to Covington, Kentucky, to make copies of his threatening letter. Latent-print examiners in the Identification Division were able to identify the partial print found on one of the letters as that of a part-time employee of the copy shop, made while he was loading the machine. That print supported the rest of Mrs. Moody's confession.

Walter Leroy Moody was convicted and sentenced to seven life terms plus four hundred years in prison. Primarily due to the work done in the FBI crime lab, VANPAC was closed.

Crime labs have existed for more than a century, for most of that time relying on the basic tools of science and technology to provide support for the detective in the field. But in the last two decades this world has been revolutionized, and today the most sophisticated instruments are used to answer the ancient question at the heart of every crime: Who did it?

The crime lab is not a place for testing theories or conducting experiments. It's practical, and it's often brutal. It's a place where every test may change someone's life forever. "We deal in violent crime here," DNA Analysis unit chief Dave Bigbee explained matter-of-factly. "After you've been here awhile you think you've seen every possible thing that one human being can do to another. And then the next case comes in. In one case we got, a woman went out shopping and left her two children with her boyfriend. He raped her twelve-year-old daughter and strangled her to death, then sodomized the nine-year-old boy and killed him by driving tenpenny nails into his skull with a brick." Truly, the lab is not a place for testing theories.

No one knows how many hundreds of years ago the principles of science and technology were first applied to crime solving. But the use of science to develop evidence and solve crimes, which is traditionally known by the rather prosaic term "forensic science," but now might more appropriately be referred to as sci-crime, evolved slowly. Until recently detectives didn't believe in it at all. They wanted the gun and not the smoke; they wanted evidence they could see with their own eyes and hold in their hands.

Investigators would come upon a crime scene and turn on the lights as brightly as possible, literally trying to shed some light on the crime. No more. Since the 1970s the world of crime detection has changed completely and forever. Now these same investigators will turn off the lights at a crime scene and use lasers and ultraviolet and infrared light; they'll conduct chemical tests, and they'll use special vacuums to try to get just a glimpse of the invisible world where a crucial piece of evidence might be found. "Gone are the days when we'd go to a crime scene and pick up whatever we could see," FBI special agent Dale Moreau said. "Nowadays we're more interested in evidence we can't see."

The FBI's Scientific Crime Detection Laboratory, as it was originally known, had its origins in 1928, when scientific evidence presented at a hearing in the controversial Sacco and Vanzetti murder case impressed Bureau of Investigation director J. Edgar Hoover, although by that time the Bureau was already conducting basic handwriting and bullet comparisons and blood-type testing and had established a national fingerprint file. In 1931, Agent Charles Appel reported to Hoover: "The Bureau should be the central clearing house for all information which may be needed in criminological work." On November 24, 1932, the lab was officially opened in a converted lounge, chosen because it had a sink.

The concept of scientific crime-solving immediately caught the public's fancy. "Aroused by the ever-increasing menace of the scientific-minded criminal schooled in the fine arts and inventions of organized crime," reported Rex Collier in the Washington, D.C., *Evening News* three months after the lab opened, "the United States Bureau of Investigation has established a novel research laboratory where government criminologists will match wits with underworld cunning."

Perhaps that was a slight overstatement. Appel was the lab's only full-time employee and the lab was equipped with a borrowed microscope, ultraviolet lights, a drawing board, and a "helixometer," a device that supposedly allowed examiners to look inside gun barrels, but that was used almost exclusively to impress visitors. If the lab needed to examine a package suspected of containing explosives, an X-ray machine was borrowed from another government bureau. Appel soon added a comparison microscope, test tubes, wax and plaster to make moulages (impressions of shoeprints and tire tracks), and what he proudly described as "an X-ray mirror, which is transparent from the back only and is an improvement on the old spy hole system."

The lab grew gradually, adding both equipment and personnel. In 1938, for example, examiners began conducting lie-detector tests on the "newly perfected" polygraph machine. A year later they started doing microchemical and spectrographic exams. "I sometimes wonder just how we were able to accomplish as much as we did," said Dr. William Magee, who joined the lab as its first full-time chemist in 1939 soon after receiving his doctorate, "particularly in light of the fact that we didn't have much scientific backing. By the time I got there, we had a spark-source spectrograph which allowed us to analyze a specimen to find out what it was, and we had the first infrared spectrometer in any crime lab, and a pretty good comparison microscope for firearms and hairs and fibers exams.

"But we made do with what we had. In those days if any guys were doing dynamite work, they would take an extract, put it on an anvil, and hit it with a hammer. If it went poof, it was dynamite. We also had an animal room in the old Justice Department building where we kept the rabbits we used in our blood testing. If we got a questioned blood specimen, we'd mix it with rabbit serum and if the blood was human, within say twenty seconds a cloudy ring would form at the interface of those two liquids. Generally speaking, if it were not of human origin, it wouldn't be of any interest to us."

To Dr. Magee's disappointment, Hoover showed very little interest in the lab except as a public relations vehicle. "I felt he should have had some little feeling about the value of science to crime detection, but he apparently saw otherwise and felt that he could entrust that to some of his lieutenants. I worked there from 1939 and I only saw Hoover twice, once when they brought in the eight captured Nazi saboteurs and then when they were making the movie *The House on 92nd Street*. I just wondered how a guy could be a scientific backer if he didn't know the value of what we were doing to the consumer. Things were as right as they could be under the circumstances, but I'll tell you, it was a lonely time down there."

Crucial to the lab's success has been the ability to evolve as the nature of crime has changed and to find means of incorporating advances in science and technology into its investigative procedures. For many years, for example, Serology was a minor unit limited to determining whether a blood sample had come from a human being or an animal, and if from a human, to which of the four known blood groups the donor belonged. This was "class evidence," meaning it could apply to any one of a large number of people, and had little value to detectives. But the Serology Unit expanded rapidly in the 1970s, when scientists discovered elements in blood and other secretions that made it possible to match a sample to a much smaller number of people. And this once-quaint unit became one of the most important in the lab; the name was changed from Serology to DNA Analysis, when technology made it possible to extract DNA from human cells and link it to a specific person.

In fact, more advances have been made in the past two decades than throughout all of sci-crime history. Twenty years ago there were only three methods of developing latent fingerprints. Today at least forty techniques are used, including lasers and superglue fumes, and prints that once would have remained invisible are now being used to prove that a specific individual was involved in a crime.

From that converted lounge with a single borrowed microscope, the FBI lab has become the single most important law enforcement facility in America. "Almost every case I work is the biggest case, or the most important case, or the most heinous case in the history of that particular community," metallurgist Bill Tobin of Elemental Analysis said. "We get the most visible cases in this country, and we get them every day. If it's on the news, we're probably going to see some part of it in here."

"This is simply the mother lode of criminal investigation," former lab director John Hicks said flatly.

The FBI lab was established to provide impartial investigative services for all federal agencies in criminal and civil matters, and all local and state law enforcement agencies in criminal matters, and to do so absolutely free of charge. There is never a fee for requesting an examination. This is America's crime lab.

There are only two requirements placed on submitting agencies: First, they must accept the results of the examination as final; they can't go shopping for a crime lab that will issue the report they want. So when they submit evidence to the lab, they confirm that it hasn't been examined by another lab and they agree not to take it elsewhere if they are not satisfied with the results. Second, they agree that those results will be made available to the suspect, even if they show he is innocent. "Sometimes we have to tell prosecutors things they really don't want to hear," said Dwight Adams of DNA Analysis. "I did the DNA examinations in New York's Central Park jogger case, in which a young woman running in the park was gang-raped, smashed in the head with a rock, and left to die in the dirt. The NYPD eventually arrested twelve people and submitted their blood samples, as well as semen found on the victim's body and clothing. Well, the result I got eliminated all twelve of them as the contributor of that semen. It didn't mean they weren't there; in fact, some of them confessed and implicated others. It just meant the prosecutor was going to have a much harder time proving they were there. When I called the prosecutor and told her, if you can actually hear silence, that's when I heard it. I'd been told by police that there were more than thirty individuals involved in the attack, so it's likely the semen came from one of those unidentified people still out there. The prosecutor didn't like what I told her, but everybody knows when they submit something to us they're going to have to live with the results."

In some of the lab units as many as a third of all examinations result in a negative conclusion, meaning the suspect can't be linked to the evidence. As Linda Harrison, a chemist in the DNA Unit, pointed out, "Evidence is neutral. If it matches it matches, if it doesn't I say it doesn't. We don't get paid in here based on the number of people we put in jail. I want to see the guilty guy go to jail and the innocent guy go home."

As an additional service to contributors, agent-examiners will testify to their results during the trial, also completely free of charge. Many people in the sci-crime lab have testified several hundred times. "Only once, in all the trials in which I've testified, have I been taken by surprise," Latent Fingerprint chief Danny Greathouse remembered, "and that was the first question I was asked the first time I testified as an expert witness. I'd been in training for several years, I'd been through endless moot court sessions, so I knew I was prepared. But the first question the defense attorney asked me was, 'Mr. Greathouse, can you get a latent fingerprint off a sponge?'

"I knew that question had absolutely nothing to do with the facts of the case, so I assumed it was a trick question and that he was trying to show the jury that I wasn't an expert. But I couldn't figure out what the trick was, so I said, 'Well, I don't know that you can. I don't think it's possible.' He said okay and sat down.

"After the trial he came over to me and explained why he'd asked that question. 'Oh, it didn't have anything to do with the case,' he admitted. 'It was just something I'd always wondered about.'"

From less than a thousand examinations in 1933, by the beginning of the 1990s the FBI lab was routinely handling almost twenty thousand cases annually, consisting of about two hundred thousand pieces of evidence on which almost a million examinations were performed. And all to answer that one question: Who did it?

There are only three possible ways to solve a crime. The person who committed the crime can confess. It happens. The victim or witnesses can identify the person who committed the crime. That also happens. And finally, information can be obtained through physical evidence, hard evidence, that can be used to link a specific person to the crime or the victim. And that's what happens most often.

Hard evidence is the silent witness. It's always there, always. Every lab examination begins at the crime scene, and no investigation can be any better than the quality of the work done there. A crime scene is simply a mystery waiting to be unraveled, a complex puzzle in which, out of a multitude of items, only one thing need be found. It might be as obvious as a bloody palmprint or a discarded piece of chewing gum. It might be a strand of hair, saliva on a telephone mouthpiece, residue on a curtain, a burnt match, a blank sheet of paper. Anything found at a crime scene might provide the single clue needed to break the case.

When Pan Am Flight 103 exploded over Lockerbie, Scotland, killing 271 people, there were millions of pieces of debris; it was a piece of plastic no larger than a thumbnail that led directly to the bombers. The strongest evidence against Atlanta child-killer Wayne Williams was several hairs and fibers. A partial fingerprint on a forty-year-old postcard was enough to prove that a Detroit archbishop had worked for the Nazis during World War II. Several barely visible green specks led directly to a woman who murdered two people by putting cyanide in Excedrin capsules. Michele Sindona, the Vatican's banker, was convicted of the largest bank fraud in American history because he habitually put a dot inside the bowl of the number 9.

The FBI receives so much mail each day that the headquarters building, at Tenth Street and Pennsylvania Avenue, has its own zip code: 20535. On the average, more than six hundred pieces of evidence are submitted to the FBI lab for examination every day. Physical evidence, hard evidence, consists of anything that might help solve a crime. It might be trace evidence, something so small that only traces of it can be found: a speck of paint; lead that a bullet has left on a bone; human cells from a drop of blood. Or it might be as large as a skull, or a chunk of wall that has to be lifted into the building by crane. Once the entire contents of a suspected serial killer's apartment arrived by van. "It's always something different," said Kelly Hargadon, a chemist in the Materials Analysis Unit, "always. You never know what it might be. When I open up a case for the first time it's as exciting as opening up a present."

It can also be very sad. "One submission that'll stick in my mind forever was an ordinary blanket," Ken Nimmich, chief of the Scientific Analysis

21

Section, said. "A murdered child had been wrapped in it, and when I opened it up I could see the outline of the child's body. The decomposition products had stained an outline on the blanket. In here we're used to seeing blankets with bloodstains on them, but this . . ."

The lab issues general instructions to contributors about how to properly wrap and submit evidence: Human organs should be sent in plastic or glass containers by United Parcel Service, private express mail, or special delivery. Bullets should be sent by UPS, registered mail, or private courier. When a submission arrives in the Evidence Control Center, it's logged into a computer and given a number that will identify it as long as it remains in the lab. Major cases, like VANPAC, are given code names. The bombing of Flight 103 over Scotland became SCOTBOM. Depending on the nature of the submission and the type of examination requested, the ECC will designate a primary investigative unit, the unit that will be responsible for the evidence while it is in the lab. The package will be hand-delivered to the unit chief, who will assign it to an agent-examiner.

The agent-examiner runs the case in the lab. He or she may decide to send the evidence to various other units for examination, but just like the detective working the case back at the precinct, he or she makes all the decisions. A single piece of evidence may be examined by six or seven people.

Every examiner is assisted by a physical-science technician, who prepares the evidence for the examiner to conduct the actual testing or examination. The technician may scrape a garment for hairs and fibers, prepare paint samples for microscopic comparisons, even run chemical tests. Many technicians have advanced degrees in their fields, but they haven't completed the rigorous program of study, training, and on-the-job experience that enables them to qualify as an expert in that discipline so they don't testify in trials.

Included with every submission is a letter from the contributor describing the contents of the package, the facts of the case, and what types of examinations are being requested. What do the contributors want to know? What information do they believe will be valuable to their investigation? Typically, contributors ask for an identification, a comparison, or some other information that will allow them to move forward with their investigation. What is this thing? Where could it have come from? What type of gun should we be looking for? Can you determine what make and model of automobile this paint speck, found at the hit-and-run scene, came from? Or they want to know if an item from an unknown source, the Q or questioned item, matches a specimen whose source is known, the K. Is the Q, strands of hair found in the victim's hand, identical to the K, samples taken from the suspect's head? Did the piece of tape used to bind the victim's hands come from the roll found in the suspect's car? Was *this* signature forged by the same person who prepared *those* documents?

Often evidence has to be examined by several different units, and because some tests are destructive, the order in which they are performed is crucial. So part of every examiner's training is learning what all of the other units do, how they work, and what impact their tests will have on evidence. A blood-soaked shirt might be sent to DNA for the primary investigation, but even before looking at it, the DNA examiner will send it to Hairs and Fibers because hairs and fibers fall off easily and important evidence might be lost. A gun might have human tissue in its barrel, so Firearms will send it to Chem/Tox, but people in the Chem Unit know not to clean the barrel with a sharp object because that might destroy marks useful to Firearms. Latent Prints is last, because many of the liquids and powders they use to try to develop prints will destroy the materials needed by other units to conduct tests—blood, for example. So while each unit is independent, the lab really functions as a whole.

The first thing a primary investigator does when he gets a case is read the accompanying letter to find out what the case is about and what the contributor wants to know. "Sometimes they're pretty confused about what they want," Firearms Unit chief Jack Dillon said, "so we'll call them up to find out what they're trying to prove. Often we can suggest some better ways of doing it."

A lot of requests seem to be inspired by TV detectives. Contributors see Columbo getting results from a crime lab and assume that the FBI lab can perform the same miracles. "We got a package of charred bones in here one day," Chem/Tox chief Roger Martz remembered, "and the contributor wanted us to tell him all sorts of things about the victim. These were charred bones, there wasn't much we could do with them, but the contributor had seen Quincy do something on TV so he knew it was possible."

"On TV detectives are always drawing positive conclusions based on information that they couldn't possibly have gotten from the evidence and that wouldn't stand up in a courtroom," Lee Waggoner of the Document Section said. "I wish it was as simple as it is on TV."

"This is where we really become detectives," Agent-examiner Wayne Oakes of Hairs and Fibers said. "Most other crime labs tend to get very straightforward requests: 'This is the gun. This is the bullet from the autopsy. Was that bullet fired from this gun?' But in here it's more often, 'Please conduct all appropriate examinations.' They might ask us to make a comparison, but we're always going to suggest more if we think it's logical. There is absolutely no pressure on us to limit ourselves to examinations requested in the submission letter, and that's precisely where all our training and experience become invaluable.

"For example, I may get pieces of duct tape that had been used to bind the hands of several murder victims with a request that I compare them to see if they came from the same roll. The police want to tie all the killings to the same person. That's all they're asking for. But when I examine the tape I may see some blue fibers the police didn't notice. I'll examine them and call the submitting officer and tell him, 'I just want to alert you that there were a number of carpet fibers on that tape you sent me. Here's what I'm guessing might have happened. I can't testify to this, it's just a gut feeling based on my experience. But I'm seeing blue carpet fibers on two pieces of tape that match. They're tri-lobel nylon carpet fibers, the type usually found in automotive carpets. My guess is that the man you're looking for has used this roll of tape and he's laid it on the floor of his car. So I'm guessing your suspect has a blue car. Don't dismiss a good suspect because he's driving a brown car, but this makes sense to me. When you develop a suspect, make sure you get me a known carpet sample.' After doing this every day for more than ten years, I'm not afraid to give the guy my gut feeling, but I always remind him it isn't an affidavit, it's a lead."

The first investigators hired to work in the lab were scientists, given the title "examiner." During training they were known as junior examiners. But as the lab expanded in the late 1930s, it became difficult to recruit qualified people, so rather than hiring scientists and training them to be detectives, the Bureau assigned agents with scientific backgrounds to the lab and taught them the necessary skills. Until recently it was strict Bureau policy that every examiner had to be an agent and had to have worked in an FBI field office for several years before joining the lab. But as the science and technology needed in the lab have become more complex, that requirement has been relaxed, and experts from a variety of fields are being brought into the lab.

While the examiners work as scientists, they think like detectives. "Before I look at the evidence, I'll read the facts of the case, then sit back and think about it," said mineralogist Chris Fiedler of Materials Analysis, one of the first non-agent examiners in the lab. "I'll try to get a feel for the case. For example, if I know the crime took place in a certain type of physical environment, I'll think about what I should be finding even before I open the evidence. If I don't find it, then I know something's wrong and we get started on a whole different track."

There are more than three hundred county, city, state, and federal crime labs in the United States, serving more than a million law enforcement officials. Most of these labs perform basic examinations and are staffed with criminalists—people with expertise in several sci-crime disciplines—rather than specialists. But FBI lab philosophy is that the more experience you gain in one area, the better you get at it. The more bombings you investigate, the better you will understand bombs. As Bill Magee remembered, "When I got here in 1939 there was one other chemist, but he was one of those jack-of-all-trades types. The decision was made right about that time that we weren't going to operate that way, we were going to specialize. Even in those days we believed we really couldn't do metallurgy one day and hairs and fibers the next."

"It's really necessary to specialize," Documents examiner Jim Lile said. "I know a lot of smaller labs can't afford it, and some of them do excellent work as far as they go. But the scientific knowledge we need to have is growing daily, and even when you're working in only one area, it's sometimes difficult to keep abreast of it."

In every case the objective of the work done in the lab is to use evidence to prove a crime was committed, to associate a known suspect with the victim or the crime scene or prove his innocence, or to develop information that will help law enforcement agents identify a suspect. That's the lab mission, a benign, almost ordinary one. And the lab itself is a quiet place, where efficient people go about their daily business as they might in any large corporation. Visitors walking through the lab might see men and women wearing white lab coats and staring intently into sophisticated microscopes, or mixing chemicals, or preparing samples for some of the most sensitive instruments of modern science. They might see people standing around a coffeepot and laughing softly, or sitting in small groups discussing a problem. On the surface, the place would look and feel like a research laboratory with a thousand different experiments in progress.

But this is a crime lab. And the things examiners see when they look into the microscope make it very different. The examiner leaning over the comparison scope might be looking at a bloody bullet taken out of the President of the United States. Some of the chemicals might be used to analyze specimens in the rape and murder of three Oklahoma Girl Scouts. The samples being prepared for the mass spectrometer might be slices of the liver of a Miami man who went into convulsions and died after drinking a cocaine-laced bottle of a popular malt liquor.

"Every day we get bloody clothing with bullet holes or stab wounds, rocks covered with blood and hair and brains, bloody cinder blocks that were dropped on people, not to mention the bloody weapons," Dave Bigbee said. "You just can't imagine what we get in here. A broomstick that was crammed up a rape victim's vagina all the way to her throat. We had a case in which a young girl was kidnapped by a motorcycle gang, tied to the back of a motorcycle, and dragged around for a while, and then they killed her by pouring sulfuric acid down her throat. We got her torn shirt that was covered with acid burns, and as I held it, I couldn't help thinking that there was a human being in it not long ago. So I can't help wondering how people can do this to other people. I wonder about it every day.

"I got a call from a prosecutor who wanted us to expedite a rape case and I caught myself asking him, 'Is this a normal rape?' Of course it wasn't; no rape is normal. People call us and tell us it's a homicide, it's very important, and we have to tell them, 'Okay, we'll put you over there in the 'expedite' stack with the other five hundred homicide cases we're working."

"What gets to me is not so much looking at the bullet," Gerald Wilkes of Firearms said, "but that the transmittal letter will have a synopsis of the case. Some of them you just never forget. I worked a Florida case in which two guys killed four people in two different pizza-shop holdups. One of these guys eventually confessed. He said that they'd taken three people in the back of the place, raped the woman in front of her husband and then killed her, and then his partner had put the gun up to the guy's head and told him, 'Smile if you see this coming.' Then he shot him in the head. No matter how many homicides you work, you never, ever get insensitive to that."

Linda Harrison of DNA refused to see the motion picture *The Silence of the Lambs*, even though its hero was a female FBI agent. "Once you've worked on a case in which you cut out blood mixed with semen from Pampers that came off a two-month-old baby, you don't want to see that kind of stuff. I do this every day; I don't need to be reminded of it."

This is the world of the crime lab. But, oddly enough, while examiners might get deeply involved in a case, and while the work done in the lab might lead police to a suspect or might enable a prosecutor to get a conviction, quite often examiners never find out how the case was resolved. They don't know if the crime was solved or if a suspect was convicted. Results like that are just not part of the process. Submissions come in, examinations are made, submissions go out. Next case. Unless an agent testifies in a trial, there's rarely any communication from the agency or prosecutor reporting the results of the case.

But even with all that brutality, most of the people working in the FBI's sci-crime lab find it extremely rewarding. "Every day is different," Firearms Unit chief Jack Dillon said. "Every time the phone rings it could be a drop-everything-and-go-for-it case that no one could have anticipated."

Metallurgist Bill Tobin of Elemental Analysis has turned down offers of as much as three times his civil service salary to work in the lab. "Money isn't everything," he said, "and this is just such an exciting and stimulating place to be. Even when I was working in the field, I found that maybe two out of every ten cases would be good ones, the other eight would be dogs. Here, when I watch the television news at night, I see what we're going to be doing in here the next day."

Or, as former Firearms Unit chief Bob Frazier said, "This is the place where you get the case of a lifetime every week."

CHAPTER
- 2 -

The Little Green Specks of Death:
The Chemistry/Toxicology Unit

Having sniffed the dead man's lips, I detected a slightly sour smell, and I came to the conclusion that he had poison forced upon him.

SHERLOCK HOLMES,
in Sir Arthur Conan Doyle's A *Study in Scarlet*

A baby is dying and no one knows why. A severed head arrives with rotting tissue clinging to it: How did this person die? An airplane carrying sixteen parachutists dives into the ground: Murder, or mechanical failure? The last tears of a murder victim are collected in a vial: Were drugs involved in this killing? Why did two people die minutes after taking a common pain reliever? A small trunk washes up on a deserted beach: Is the caked white residue inside it the remains of a man who disappeared five years earlier? Several hairs are taken from the head of the mayor of Washington, D.C.: Has he been using cocaine?

Deadly things often come in very small packages—sometimes things one five-thousandth the size of the period at the end of this sentence, yet powerful enough to kill within seconds. Things that by virtue of their size and nature are intended to remain secret. Sci-crime chemists are detectives who search for clues that will never be seen, and the FBI's Chemistry/Toxicology Unit is where investigators in search of hard evidence literally analyze the thin air.

Sci-crime chemistry began a thousand years ago, with the search for a reliable means of detecting the presence of poison in a body. For a time it was believed that the heart of a person who had been poisoned would not burn. Even as late as the beginning of the nineteenth century respected scientists believed that the body of an arsenic victim would not decay. It wasn't until 1840 that American courts even permitted the introduction of scientific testimony, finally deciding, "[The chemist's] opinion is in fact his testimony to a law of nature."

Sci-crime chemistry was very much an embryonic science when the FBI lab was founded 1932. It was six months before the lab even conducted a chemical examination. The Physics and Chemistry Section, as it was then known, did mostly bloodstain and firearms exams. They used rudimentary instruments: simple microscopes and ultraviolet lamps. Small animals were kept in an animal room and used to provide blood samples needed to make sera for testing. It was the most basic chemistry, and only rarely did chemical evidence play a pivotal role in an important investigation. Typical of the kind of examinations done by the Chem Unit was a Camden, New Jersey, case in which a commercial laundry was suspected of defrauding the government by charging the Navy for dry-cleaning blankets while simply tumble-drying them. To prove his case, the lab's first chemist, Dr. William Magee, marked several blankets with invisible chemical "tags" that were sensitive to chemicals used in the dry-cleaning process. When the blankets were returned these tags were still there, proving that the blankets hadn't been dry-cleaned.

During World War II the entire Chemistry Section, basically Dr. Magee, was active in espionage and sabotage cases. When eight Nazi saboteurs were caught through tips provided by an informant, Magee figured out how to materialize invisible writing known to be on their handkerchiefs, writing that provided the names and addresses of other German spies.

Probably the first significant criminal case in which sci-crime chemists provided vital evidence was the November 1, 1955, bombing of United Airlines Flight 629. Forty-four people died instantly when, for no apparent mechanical reason, a plane leaving Denver's Stapleton Airport exploded eleven minutes into its flight. Although sabotage was suspected, there had never been a confirmed case of sabotage of a civilian aircraft in aviation history, and no one knew how to prove that there had been a bomb aboard that airplane.

Smoke was still wisping out of the engines when Dr. Magee arrived at the crash site. "After examining literally thousands of tiny pieces of wreckage," he remembered, "I found that some of the small pieces had an unusual appearance—they were kind of a blackish-gray color. What I couldn't figure out was why only these pieces. I packed up a box about the size of a small coffee table and shipped them back to the lab. When we analyzed them we discovered that these deposits consisted primarily of sodium carbonate, along with small amounts of nitrate and sulfur.

"We had no idea what the heck they were doing there. Sodium carbonate is normally found in scouring powder. There was no logical reason for it to be on those parts of the airplane. So we sat down and tried to reason it out. We began by asking ourselves what we were looking for. If there had been a bomb on that airplane, what type of explosive might have been used? And what evidence of that explosive might we find? Gradually, things began to make sense. When dynamite explodes the heat of the blast frees sodium atoms. Sodium atoms like to combine with something—something like carbon dioxide, to form sodium carbonate. Once we'd figured it out, it seemed so obvious. We were looking at the residue of a dynamite explosion; we were holding in our hands the proof that there had been a bomb on that plane.

"Today, the first thing investigators search for when an airplane goes down or a bomb goes off is explosive residue. But we were working on the first case of sabotage in modern aviation history. We were the people who discovered it would be there."

McGee also found traces of manganese dioxide, which could not have come from any parts of the plane. He surmised that it had come from the battery used to detonate the bomb. Tiny pieces of battery wire found in the wreckage were later matched to wire discovered in the home of a suspect named Jack Gilbert Graham. Graham had purchased several large flight-insurance policies for his mother, who had perished in the crash. McGee's work contributed to the arrest and conviction of Graham, who was executed in 1957 in Colorado's gas chamber.

Working in a sci-crime chem lab is rather like searching through a million-piece jigsaw puzzle to find the one piece that doesn't belong. The search may take a lifetime and never be completed; or, with the proper equipment, it can be done in minutes. There are literally ten million organic chemicals, and each of those ten million can be combined with one or more other chemicals to form an infinite number of mixtures. And at some point every case will require that a specimen be analyzed and its composition determined. Once, the lab was limited to those examinations that could be conducted with a microscope. But now, using an array of sophisticated instruments, much of the work is done on samples so small they can't be seen even with the most advanced optical equipment. Generally a hundred-nanogram specimen—a nanogram is one-billionth of a gram—is sufficient for the lab to identify an unknown substance or detect the presence of a specific drug or chemical. In fact, because cocaine has become so ubiquitous in American society, these instruments were finding drug residue on almost all currency submitted to the lab for testing. So the Chem Unit was actually forced to make these instruments *less* sensitive to the presence of cocaine, meaning more of the drug has to be present to obtain a valid positive result.

The sci-crime community is far too small to support the development of specialized equipment for its unique needs, so almost all of the instruments used in the chem lab have been adapted from other industries. The instrument that revolutionized sci-crime chemistry and toxicology is the mass spectrometer, which was developed for use in the petrochemical and pharmaceutical industries. The mass spec gave the lab the ability to analyze smaller samples than had ever before been possible. Every one of those ten million organic chemicals has a unique structure, meaning that each consists of a different combination of basic elements. By measuring those properties, the mass spec is able to provide a molecular "fingerprint" of an unknown substance, making it possible to identify every chemical present by comparing these results to known "fingerprints."

The thing that sets the FBI's chem lab apart from all others is that the work done there has a direct impact on someone's life or freedom. If the chem lab makes a mistake, people may die. So the only rule about equipment is that examiners use whatever it takes to get the right answer as quickly as possible. In several cases, doing that has meant adapting a tool to a purpose for which it had never been intended.

A new kind of deadly crime, product tampering, dominated the headlines in 1982 when seven people in Chicago died after taking Tylenol tablets that had been laced with cyanide. Throughout the country extortionists began threatening manufacturers, warning them that unless they made substantial payments their products would be poisoned. Most of these threats were never carried out, but in New York City investigators discovered several bottles containing poisoned Tylenol capsules. Merchants immediately took thousands of bottles of Tylenol off their shelves, but it

31

would have taken months to examine every single bottle to find those that contained poison. A quick, simple, and perfect method had to be devised to check the bottles, and none of the sophisticated instruments in the lab was capable of doing that job.

"We needed a quick way to scan those bottles," said Roger Martz, who joined the Chem Unit in 1974 and became its chief in 1989. "The answer came from basic chemistry. Potassium absorbs X rays, so potassium cyanide, the poison, would show up on an X ray, while acetaminophen, the main ingredient in Tylenol, would not. So I suggested we just use an X-ray machine. We didn't even have an X ray in the Chem Unit, so I dummied up a bottle with cyanide and brought it over to our mail room, where all incoming packages are screened. Sure enough, the cyanide showed up inside the bottle as a big black blob. It was very easy to pick it out.

"The biggest X-ray machines anybody knew about were the screening devices used at airport security checkpoints. Roger Aaron, the unit chief at the time, flew up to New York and set up the screening process at the airport. We were able to examine thousands of bottles in a matter of hours, and found several other bottles that had been poisoned. So we may have saved some lives, but we were never able to find the person who'd done it."

Desperate situations call for unique and creative measures. The Chem Unit faced a somewhat similar problem in 1990, when a young man in Miami collapsed after drinking a bottle of a popular coffee-flavored soft drink named Pony Malta. He was rushed to the hospital, but he lapsed into a coma and never regained consciousness. Tests showed he was suffering from acute cocaine poisoning, and an examination of the residue in the bottle proved the Pony Malta had been laced with cocaine. Apparently drug smugglers had dissolved cocaine and brought it into the country as part of a large shipment of the soft drink. After the shipment had cleared customs they planned to reclaim the bottles and chemically transform the contents back into crystal cocaine. Each bottle had a street value of almost $5,000. But something had gone wrong, and the poisoned bottles of Pony Malta had been mixed in with ordinary bottles and delivered to stores throughout the Miami area.

No one knew how many bottles contained a lethal dose of cocaine or where they were. The problem was how to pick out those bottles from the thousands of bottles in warehouses and on bodega shelves. In this case X rays wouldn't help, because they cannot distinguish between Pony Malta and liquid cocaine.

The unit got help from Dean Fetterolf, a chemist working in the lab's research unit in Quantico, Virginia. Fetterolf suggested they try a device called a dielectrometer, which is used primarily by engineers to locate imperfections in materials or beams inside walls. A dielectrometer works a little like a microwave; it sends out an electronic impulse and records the amount of energy that is absorbed. It doesn't matter how much energy is absorbed; as long as the reading remains constant, the substance it is examining is uniform. But when there's a change in that substance, when the impulse hits a wall beam or a hollow spot in a concrete block, the reading changes. It won't identify what's there, just that the substance has changed. Fetterolf believed that those bottles of Pony Malta laced with cocaine would have a different density than those with plain soft drink. And he was absolutely right. Within days thousands of bottles had been scanned and forty-five poisoned bottles had been found. Once again, lives had been saved. In this case though, the drug smugglers were captured.

As sophisticated as many of the lab's instruments are, they are only as good as the people who use them. Machines can only answer those questions that are asked, and the most important aspect of identifying an unknown substance is posing the right question to the right instrument.

The chem lab staff has grown to match the capabilities of their instruments. Currently there are six agent-examiners and seven chemists. "We don't prize formal education as much as an individual's ability to think creatively," explained Agent-examiner Tom Lynch. "We do things here that nobody has ever tried to do before, and a lot of times we're very successful."

While everyone in the unit is capable of doing traditional sci-crime chemistry, just about everybody has a specialty. Unit chief Roger Martz is the virtuoso of the mass spectrometer, creating new ways of exploiting its capabilities. Bob Forgione decided to become a toxicologist when he realized he couldn't hit a curveball. Tom Lynch has a doctorate in bacteriology and does most of the unit's work with microorganisms and cell cultures. Ron Kelly is an expert on explosive residues. Jordan Burnett specializes in ink analysis. Debbie Wang has become an expert on sugars in all forms. Brian Donnelly and Henry Schlumpf are expert toxicologists. And Pete Lewis, who joined the unit in 1959, before any of the fancy machines showed up, works the arson cases.

To each other, they are "Bub." No one remembers where that nickname came from, or even what it means, but if you work in the Chem Unit you're a Bub.

Every case begins with a delivery to Roger Martz from the Evidence Control Center. Depending on the facts of the case, Martz assigns it to the proper person. After that, there is no specific or best way to work. The investigators open the packages and just look at the submissions. They see what there is to see. They look for anything unusual, anything unique. They begin at the very beginning.

They simply look at it; they never touch or taste it. "When I started here in 1972," Bob Forgione remembered, "I didn't even use bulbs to suck up biological fluids. I'd just stick a straw in it and suck it up halfway, then transfer it to different funnels for testing. I tried to be very careful, but that's the way it was done. There's a word I would use today to describe that method: risky."

There is potential danger in every submission. Just after Tom Lynch joined the unit he received what appeared to be ordinary white powder, from a Florida police force. Vandals had thrown plastic eggs against the wall of a McDonald's, and when a worker began cleaning up the mess he was burned. The police wanted to know what the powder was. "I must have touched it with my hand, then wiped my eye," Lynch said, "because the next thing I knew my skin was stinging, my eyelid was burning, I'm turning beet red, and I can't stop coughing. I ran to the sink and doused my head in cold water. I later found out this powder was solid tear gas. Solid. Ordinarily tear gas is diluted in an aerosol, but this stuff was pure. I'm lucky, it could have been a lot worse."

The Chem Unit staff would prefer not to smell submissions either, but sometimes that's not possible. Body parts are supposed to be shipped to the lab frozen in dry ice, but on occasion they have thawed out before getting there, and the stench of rotting tissue permeates the lab for weeks. Besides, catching the scent of a case can prove to be the beginning of solving it. In arson cases, for example, the smell of fumes is often the first clue to the presence of an accelerant. Certain poisons and pesticides have readily identifiable scents. And there are cases in which the lab is specifically requested to identify an unknown odor.

Weeks before Christmas in 1989, a strong odor was detected coming from Cabbage Patch Kids dolls being sold in California; a local laboratory identified the smelly substance as a potentially very dangerous organic pesticide. Suddenly, terrified parents became convinced that their children were being poisoned by their dolls, hundreds of which were delivered to the Chem/Tox Unit to be examined. The lab overflowed with Cabbage Patch dolls, their insides hanging out, their heads gone, sitting on closet shelves or hanging upside down. A row of smiling heads lined a long shelf.

It was quickly determined that the odor came from the dolls' stuffing. They had been made in Taiwan, and their manufacturer, rather than using the high-grade filler mandated in the United States, had stuffed them with shredded rags that had obviously been used to clean up grease and oil. The odor came from these rags. But tests proved that they were perfectly safe, and that children couldn't have been poisoned by the defective dolls.

Sometimes just looking at a submission provides a vital clue. One of the most important cases worked in the Chem Unit began in 1986, when a Seattle housewife named Sue Snow woke up one morning with a headache and took two capsules of Extra-Strength Excedrin. Within seconds she was unconscious; within minutes she was dead.

Initially doctors believed Sue Snow had died of natural causes, perhaps a brain aneurysm. But during the autopsy the assistant medical examiner, Janet Miller, detected a faint aroma, a smell that reminded her of bitter almonds. It was the telltale scent of cyanide, a fast-acting poison that kills by locking oxygen out of the blood cells. Detecting this aroma requires a certain genetic sensitivity; Janet Miller was the only person in the room able to smell it. Samples of Sue Snow's tissues were sent to a local toxicologist, who found evidence that she had died of cyanide poisoning.

Detectives searching her home found several more poisoned capsules in the Excedrin bottle. Consumers were immediately warned to stop taking any Excedrin capsules. Four years earlier, when seven people were poisoned in Chicago, people had been told to flush their Tylenol down the drain— and when they did, all the potential evidence went down the drain with it. This time police began collecting Excedrin bottles from a four-state area. Eventually 740,000 capsules were turned in. Using the experience gained in the New York City case, these capsules were screened at an airport security gate X-ray machine. Two more poisoned bottles were discovered.

While this frantic search was going on, a second victim was found. After Sue Snow's death was reported, an apparently distraught woman named Stella Nickell called police and told them her husband had died a week earlier—just moments after swallowing several Extra-Strength Excedrin capsules. Bruce Nickell's death had been attributed to emphysema, but when authorities tested a sample of his preserved blood serum they found evidence of a massive dose of cyanide. Bruce Nickell had been the killer's first victim.

Two additional bottles containing poisoned capsules were found in Stella Nickell's trailer home. The contents of all five poisoned bottles were examined by a Seattle chemist, who found noth'ng beyond the cyanide in the capsules, then sent them to Roger Martz in the sci-crime lab.

"We knew the poison was cyanide," Martz remembered, "so our objective was to try to give the agents in the field a clue as to where that poison might have come from, or if they'd developed a suspect, find a way to link it to that suspect."

Other lab units examined the bottles for fingerprints, toolmarks, anything that might provide a lead. They found nothing. Martz began his examination by pouring the contents of each capsule into a beaker, and just looking at it, seeing what he could see. "I immediately noticed several small specks of a green material that didn't seem to belong there," he explained. "I found those specks in all five bottles. Identifying the cyanide was basic chemistry, and there was no way to trace it to a source. But these green specks were unique. I wondered what they were, I wondered what they were doing there, and I wondered what they might tell us about the killer."

Incredibly, the examiner in Seattle who had first looked at these capsules couldn't possibly have seen the green specks: he was color-blind.

Martz found that 99 percent of the green specks consisted of sodium chloride, common salt. That didn't surprise him; many consumer products use compounds like sodium chloride to add bulk and carry the active ingredient. It was the mysterious 1 percent that intrigued him.

Analyzing that 1 percent on the mass spectrometer, he discovered that it consisted of four relatively common chemicals, but he couldn't figure out what those four chemicals comprised. Even a new computer program that listed the chemical composition of thousands of products failed to identify it. "I couldn't find a single product that consisted of just these four chemicals. But what I did find out was that they were all herbicides. Herbicides in Excedrin?"

While Martz couldn't identify a specific product, with the help of Debbie Wang he learned that two of the chemicals were used almost exclusively in algicides, products that killed algae in fish ponds and aquariums. But what were they doing in a poisoned bottle of Excedrin? For a time he suspected these green specks were the killer's signature. In many cases criminals want to claim credit for their work, so they leave the same sign at each crime they commit.

Meanwhile, Seattle investigators began focusing on Stella Nickell. They discovered that three life insurance policies had been taken out on Bruce Nickell's life the previous year, policies that would pay Stella Nickell $175,000 if her husband died accidentally. Insurance companies consider death by poisoning to be an accident.

Martz finally became convinced that those green specks, whatever they were, came from an aquarium product. So in his free time he began going to pet stores and reading the labels on their fish tank cleaners. Many products contained one or more of the chemicals, but none included all four. Then, one Saturday afternoon, Martz picked up a package of an expensive fish-tank algicide named Algae Destroyer. "And there were my four chemicals," he said. "I opened up the package, and it was full of green tablets identical in color to my specks. I just stood there staring at those green tablets. I immediately notified our field agents what to look for."

When an agent in Seattle read Martz's report, he remembered something he had seen in Stella Nickell's trailer: a large fish tank. Agents descended on pet stores throughout the Seattle area carrying photographs of several women, one of them Stella Nickell. A clerk in a suburban shop immediately picked out her picture and remembered that he had special-ordered Algae Destroyer for her. And then the clerk remembered something else; in addition to the algicide, he had sold Stella Nickell a mortar and pestle to mash the tablets into tiny green specks.

The evidence against Stella Nickell was adding up. She failed a lie-detector test. Agents in the lab's Identification Section found her fingerprints in several books about poisons she had taken out of a local library. The Document Section found that Bruce Nickell's signature on two of the insurance policies had been forged.

Stella Nickell had murdered her husband by putting cyanide inside Excedrin capsules. But when the coroner mistakenly ruled that he had died of natural causes, depriving her of the accidental-death benefits in his life insurance policies, she had to kill someone else to make it appear that a cold-blooded killer was on the loose. One *was*: Stella Nickell. She had prepared the poisoned capsules in the mortar and pestle she had previously used to pulverize the algicide, unknowingly providing the evidence that linked her to the killings.

Nickell became the first person in American history to be convicted of murder in a product tampering case and is currently serving a ninety-year sentence.

Poisoning cases are the most dramatic and, in many ways, the most difficult of the crimes worked on by the Chem/Tox Unit. What makes them so difficult is the extraordinarily large number of readily available toxic substances. The first rule of toxicology is that the dose is the poison. A poison is simply anything that's harmful to the biological system. In sufficient amounts, that can include just about anything. Water can be "toxic," for example: people drown. Household painkillers like aspirin are fatal in large doses. But generally when a poison is used for criminal purposes it's disguised in food or drink, and it's usually given in small doses.

Most units in the sci-crime lab deal with the evidence from crimes already committed. The person has been killed or the money has been stolen. But the Chem/Tox Unit gets cases in which people are dying, and the ability to determine what's killing them can make the difference between life and death. Lives really are at stake. In a California case, for example, two infant children of a foster mother had died mysteriously, and the third child was very sick. And no one could figure out why. After extensive testing, the only clue the hospital could find was the extremely elevated sodium content of the baby's urine. A nurse became suspicious when the foster mother insisted on preparing the baby's formula, and she submitted a sample of it to the Chem/Tox Unit.

"We had a baby dying for no apparent reason," Bob Forgione remembered. "I was not sure where to start. Should I look for arsenic? Cyanide? Drugs? Maybe pesticides? All we knew was that too much sodium was coming from somewhere, so I began by trying to figure out where. I took five grams of the formula and added an acid to it to see if it contained any toxic metals. What happened was totally unexpected. It started foaming up all over the place. Well, that told me there was a carbonate in there. I thought, I know I've got sodium and I know I've got a carbonate; maybe it's something as simple as baking soda, sodium bicarbonate. It's not a drug, it's not a metal or a volatile, it's not cyanide or pesticide, but in sufficient amounts even baking soda would kill a baby.

"I did a dialysis, a separation technique, until I got a crystalline material.

I looked at it under an X ray and, as I suspected, it was baking soda. It was simple and clever; the baby would drink it and excrete the carbonate, leaving nothing but an excess of sodium. The police immediately took the child away from the woman—that probably saved the baby's life—and indicted the woman. I believe she was prosecuted and convicted but, you know, sometimes we never find out exactly what happened in these cases."

Poison has long been a choice weapon for killers. It's simple to use, very effective, difficult to detect, and often impossible to trace back to the killer. In France, white arsenic was once so popular among the rich and powerful that it became known as "inheritance powder." Poisons kill in two ways. "Acute" poisons are substances, such as cyanide, that are toxic enough to be deadly in one small dose. "Accumulative" poisons, such as arsenic and thallium, are not fatal in small amounts; but the body is unable to eliminate them, and those small doses eventually add up to a lethal amount.

Normally, the first clues to the presence and the type of poison are the victim's symptoms. For example, stomach cramps and vomiting might indicate the presence of a heavy metal like arsenic. Dizziness and nausea are symptoms of a volatile compound, perhaps carbon monoxide. Someone who is comatose, with no signs of an external injury, might have taken a sedative or depressant. A maniacal state can be caused by iodine or PCP, angel dust. People who kill with poisons are often aware of these telltale symptoms and try to disguise them.

In a classic eighteenth-century New York City murder case, the killer poisoned his girlfriend with morphine, a narcotic that is easily identified because it causes the pupils of the eyes to contract. He then attempted to hide this symptom by putting drops of atropine in her eyes, a drug that causes the pupils to dilate, or become enlarged. So the easily recognized symptom of murder by morphine was not present, and the attending physician attributed the woman's death to a stroke. But the curiosity of a reporter and the existence of a witness who had seen the killer putting something in the victim's eyes led to an autopsy, which revealed the murder.

Almost a century later in New York the former chairman of a college anthropology department devised a seemingly foolproof plan to get even with a federal judge who had sentenced him to prison years earlier for making drugs in a college laboratory. John Buettner-Janush sent the judge a box of expensive chocolate candies, candies that would kill. He filled several pieces of candy with atropine, which in addition to dilating the pupils will also cause a very rapid heartbeat, and others with pilocarpine, which regulates the heartbeat. If the judge ate both pieces, he would be dying of atropine poisoning, but would have a normal heartbeat, making proper diagnosis very difficult. Buettner-Janush sent the candy to the judge for Valentine's Day; the judge's wife ate a piece filled with atropine and collapsed. Fortunately, hospital technicians noticed that her pupils were dilated and were able to save her life. The box of candy was sent to the Chem/Tox Unit.

Nick Vertullo and Bob Forgione got the case. "I like to feel that if it comes across my bench," Forgione said, "I'll not only detect the poison, but I'll tell you how much is in there and what was the intent. Was it to kill, or make someone sick, or just someone clowning around?

"When I broke open the candies, I saw what looked like a lump of gooey white filling. I wondered, had the poison been added to that gooey white stuff, or was that gooey white stuff the poison? Sometimes things are so obvious we tend to overlook them." Using an infrared spectrometer, an instrument that measures the ability of a substance to absorb energy as a beam passes through it, then identifies it by comparison to known standards, Forgione discovered he was looking at a large lump of poison.

The Latent Fingerprint Section was able to lift a partial fingerprint from the box, and by comparing it to the prints of felons previously sentenced by the judge, they were able to identify the suspect. In Buettner-Janush's home detectives found several boxes of the expensive chocolates—and equipment for manufacturing his own candy. It turned out to be more than enough evidence to persuade Buettner-Janush to plead guilty to two counts of attempted murder.

Sometimes the key clue is revealed in the letter written by the submitting agency outlining the facts of the case. In a North Carolina case, for example, an emergency room nurse would bet his colleagues on heart attack calls that the victim was not going to survive—and he won too many bets. Part of this nurse's job was preparing the adrenaline solution injected into a heart-attack victim's heart to restart it. A sample of this solution was sent to the Chem/Tox Unit with a letter asking that it be analyzed to see if it was composed of the prescribed mixture. Using liquid chromatography, a technique in which the different chemicals in a compound are separated by being adsorbed in other solutions to which they have a greater affinity, it was shown that there was absolutely no adrenaline in the original solution. It was just plain water. So each time one of the other nurses thought they were giving someone a potentially life-saving injection, they were inadvertently allowing him to die. The suspect was convicted of murder and given the death sentence.

Submissions in cases where poison is suspected come in every conceivable form. When a real estate agent was accused of murdering his elderly clients to gain control of their property, the unit received a half-eaten jelly doughnut. It turned out to contain a lethal dose of thallium. In a particularly gruesome case, the submission came in labeled "Q1 chainsaw, Q2 victim's head." But the most common submissions are the "biologicals": blood, urine, and, if the victim has died, body parts. A sample might be several hundred grams of brain. A chunk of liver. A slice of lung. The best place to find a poison is in the liver, the so-called garbage pail of the body, but because that organ is available only after a victim has died, tests have been developed to identify poisons in blood samples. A poison can also be detected in urine, but it's difficult to determine the amount of the poison present in the system as a whole.

Although cutting human body parts into thin slices for testing sounds kind of gory, for the Bubs in the Chem/Tox Unit it's just part of the job. "If a person has been murdered," Bob Forgione explained, "then we're his last resource. If we don't find out what happened, the truth is going to be buried with that person." Body parts generally arrive frozen, because they decompose rapidly after death and chemical changes can mask the presence of certain poisons. In a 1975 case, for example, a nurse in a Michigan veterans' hospital was accused of poisoning patients by giving them lethal doses of pancuronium, a muscle relaxant, through their intravenous tubes. Several bodies had to be exhumed. As their coffins were being opened, Forgione remembered, "All the scientific training I had meant nothing, because the first thing I looked to see was if there were fingernail scratches on the top of the coffin."

Forgione and Roger Aaron spent the next six months in the lab trying to isolate pancuronium from the numerous other chemicals present. After many attempts to separate the poison failed, they decided to try thin-layer chromatography. This is a technique based on the principle of migration. As water will move slowly up your pants if you stand still in a puddle, a chemical will move from a beaker up a plate of metal or glass coated with a solution for which it has an affinity. Each chemical will stop at a certain spot, and by comparing this "band" to known results, the examiner can separate, then identify a chemical. The pancuronium wouldn't migrate. Perhaps it wasn't present. So the technique was reversed. Every other

41

chemical in the beaker was made to migrate, leaving the pancuronium at the bottom. Its presence was readily confirmed by several sophisticated techniques, proving that these patients had been murdered. The nurse was indicted for murder and found guilty, but that conviction was reversed on appeal. These murders remain unsolved.

Some poisons are much easier to find in human remains. The heavy-metal poisons, for example, can be found in bone, hair, even fingernails, hundreds of years after the victim's death. When historians suspected that President Zachary Taylor, who died in 1850, had been murdered with arsenic, his body was exhumed to be examined by a private toxicologist. Reporters asked Roger Martz what the FBI intended to do if these tests indicated that Taylor had been murdered. "Piece of cake," Martz responded. "If tests show he was poisoned, what we'll do is dig up the suspects and give them polygraph tests."

The tests indicated that Taylor had not been poisoned with arsenic.

There is no prescribed testing procedure to follow if the symptoms or clues don't indicate the presence of a specific type of poison. "You start with common sense and intuition," Roger Martz said.

"You start by ruling things out," Brian Donnelly added. If, for example, a body is found in a forest, it doesn't make sense to begin by testing for carbon monoxide.

A complete screen usually begins with a test for common volatile compounds such as alcohol, methanol, chloroform, Freon, and anesthetics—about fifty of which can be found in products from dry-cleaning fluid to airplane glue. When teenagers die suddenly and seemingly for no reason, volatiles are often the cause. Different volatiles actually become fads as young people discover new and inexpensive ways to get a druglike high. For a while, the volatile of choice was airplane glue. More recently, teenagers were killing themselves by spraying Pam into a plastic bag, then inhaling it.

After volatile compounds, the next chemicals tested for would be easily obtainable poisons, the inorganic ions like cyanide. Then come tests for heavy metals—poisons like arsenic, mercury, lead, copper, and cadmium. No single test or instrument will identify every unknown, so dozens of tests are conducted over periods of time as long as several months.

Assuming there are no volatile or obvious poisons or metals, the next test might be for the presence of carbon monoxide, a common, silent killer. Following that, the lab would test for the whole class of drugs: the opiates, narcotics like heroin, which produce a state of calm; stimulants, like cocaine, which produce a rush of energy; hallucinogens, like LSD and designer drugs; and ordinary household medications.

The list of potential killers grows longer. Not a drug? Then there are the herbicides, pesticides, and rodenticides—weed killers and bug poisons and rat killers. And finally, if every test is negative, if there is absolutely no evidence that a poison is present, a sample is fed to the house mouse. The "mouse spectrometer," kept in a tidy cage near the front door of the lab, is particularly useful in product-tampering cases, where an unusual substance that might not show up in a general screen has been used. Most of the white mice have died peacefully of old age; only once in fifteen years has a mouse died from an undetected poison.

In many tampering cases the extortionist will put a common rodenticide into a package, then reseal it and threaten the manufacturer. Rodenticides are generally green pellets and are easy to spot, so their purpose in a product is to show the manufacturer he is vulnerable, rather than to hurt anyone. To test for the presence of a rodenticide after it has been ingested, the gastric contents of the victim are ground up, put through a chemical process to isolate and concentrate the active ingredient, then presented to several instruments equipped to recognize them. That's the way it's supposed to happen.

But it didn't. In a bizarre extortion case, an executive at a major commercial food supplier received a letter warning that rat poison would be put in the company's products if they didn't cease using animal fats. To prove he was serious, the letter writer included samples of the poison he intended to use. Debbie Wang had the case. The sample consisted of several green pellets and they appeared to be a rodenticide, but every test proved negative. "I'd tested for every known rodenticide, I'd searched our computer files, but we'd never seen this one before," Wang said. "I didn't want it reported out of the lab as a negative so I decided to feed it to the mouse. I expected the mouse to die, but I knew its death would justify the extensive exams that were required."

Four days after being fed a sample, the mouse did die. Working with the field agent assigned to the case, Wang contacted governmental and private-industry experts on pesticides. Because rodents quickly develop an immunity to most pesticides, new products are continually being developed. An expert suggested one of those new products, Quintox, and the manufacturer supplied a sample. As Wang discovered, the active ingredient in Quintox, the chemical that actually killed the mouse, was vitamin D_3, which produces test results similar to cholesterol. In fact, the D_3 had shown up in tests, but had been ignored because it was not harmful to human beings.

Most of the submissions to the Chem/Tox Unit are identified rather easily, and sometimes the work becomes routine. But the universe in which this unit explores is ten million organic chemicals large, and occasionally a small package arrives containing something that has never been seen before, something that can kill people. Then the routine is forgotten, and all the sophisticated instruments and the combined years of experience are put to work identifying this "Q," this unknown. The people who work in the lab are chemists, applying the principles of science, but they are also detectives.

Occasionally the Chem/Tox Unit works espionage cases for government agencies. One morning a syringe containing a blue liquid arrived. The accompanying letter asked the same question asked every day: What is this stuff? But what made this stuff different was that it had been used in an assassination attempt.

Whatever the stakes, the procedure is always the same. Start by looking at the sample. See anything unusual? This was a blue liquid. Apply common sense: The case isn't one of a housewife attempting to kill her husband, so the substance is probably more exotic than a rat poison. Use the instruments. Sometimes everything proceeds smoothly, everything works just the way it's supposed to, and the identification is made quickly.

A small amount of the blue liquid was evaporated and left an oily residue. The mass spectrometer identified the residue as a compound called fluoroacetic acid. Fluoroacetic acid, with minor additions, is known by the trade name Compound 1080 and is an extremely toxic substance. This was a highly concentrated poison. The unknown blue liquid had been positively identified in about half an hour.

But most of the time it isn't quite that easy. In 1982, a gravely ill Florida man named John Wesley Gentry was rushed to the hospital. Although Gentry's illness was never identified, he recovered. But several weeks later, he returned with the same symptoms. Trying to find the source of his illness, the hospital analyzed all the medication he had been taking at home. Among the assortment of pills were some vitamin C tablets that had been given to him by his live-in girlfriend, a woman named Judy Buenoaño. The hospital tests produced an odd result. Whatever these tablets were, they weren't vitamin C. In fact, they weren't any easily identifiable chemical.

The tablets were submitted to the lab with a request that they be identified.

Roger Martz began his examination by running the standard screen for all unknowns. The Chem Unit maintains a database of 65,000 mass spectrum "fingerprints." Whatever it was, it wasn't one of those 65,000 common chemicals, yet it was something a woman in Florida could easily obtain. After additional testing, Martz suspected it might be a polymer, a substance made by linking similar molecules. The most common polymer is probably polystyrene, which is used to make everything from coffee cups to insulating packing material. To identify a polymer examiners break it down to individual components; this is a difficult process.

It took Martz a week to identify the substance. It was a polymer, paraformaldehyde, something he had never seen before. The questions then became, Where did it come from? and, more important, Could it be linked to a specific person?

As Martz worked in the lab more facts about the case began to emerge. Somebody certainly wanted Gentry dead. After the poison had failed to kill him, a bomb blew up his car. He'd been seriously injured, but had survived. And Judy Buenoaño, who had given him the paraformaldehyde, had a deadly past. One of her children, a paraplegic, had drowned in a canoeing accident. Both her husband and another boyfriend had died mysteriously. In all three deaths Buenoaño had been the beneficiary of large life insurance policies. And four months before Gentry became ill, Buenoaño had insured his life for $500,000.

Linking the paraformaldehyde to Buenoaño meant finding the source. Florida investigators began by searching her home and sending Martz the twenty-five beauty products they found there. Martz tested every one; none contained the polymer. Then detectives went to the beauty salon where she worked and emptied her shelves. And there they found a bottle clearly labeled "Poison." It contained tablets used to make the disinfectant in which combs and brushes were sanitized. Paraformaldehyde. It had been right there in front of them all the time, clearly marked. Fortunately for Gentry, Buenoaño had been putting the powder in 250-milligram capsules, not a large enough dose to kill anyone. Buenoaño had made a common mistake. She had ignored the very first rule of poison: The dose is the poison.

Although poisons are often used to contaminate consumer goods in product-tampering cases, not all contaminants are poisonous. Everything from ground glass to razor blades has been found in products. In product-tampering cases the first thing the lab has to do is identify the substance found in the product to determine if it's dangerous. If it is, the public must be warned immediately and the product must be removed from supermarket shelves. But if it isn't, law enforcement personnel can quietly follow through on the extortionist's demands and try to break the case.

Because product-tampering cases endanger so many people, when they come into the lab they are given priority attention. There's a lot of pressure on everyone to identify the contaminant as quickly as possible. While one agent-examiner is officially assigned to the case, everybody knows what's going on and contributes to the effort. Several people go to lunch together in the Bureau cafeteria almost every day, and their conversation often focuses on difficult cases. It was over such a lunch one day that a particularly baffling case was solved.

A large supermarket chain in Kansas City had received a neatly typed, well-written letter from an extortionist threatening to inject mercury into produce unless he was paid a substantial amount of money. To prove he was serious, he told the supermarket chain where to find a grapefruit and an orange that he had poisoned with mercury. These fruits were flown to Washington by Kansas City agents and hand-delivered to the Chem/Tox Unit for examination.

The letter stated that mercury had been injected into these fruits. Bob Forgione examined them—mercury can easily be identified with a scanning microscope—and found a hole slightly larger than a pinhead in each one. There were faint marks around these punctures; when he cut open the fruits, he noticed a long red stain inside. Something *had* been injected into them—but, to his surprise, tests showed that it wasn't mercury.

Forgione was perplexed. The extortionist had specifically written that he was using mercury. Everything else in his letter had been precisely as he had stated. So why wasn't the mercury showing up in tests? Forgione explained his problem at lunch. After thinking about it, Henry Schlumpf suggested, "Maybe he's using the red mercury from a thermometer."

That didn't seem to make sense. Wherever it came from, the mercury still would have tested positive. Then Debbie Wang corrected Schlumpf. "They don't use mercury in thermometers anymore," she said. "It's just a red dye in some sort of carrier."

Forgione returned to the lab and broke open three ordinary thermometers, draining the red liquid indicator out of them. He ran the standard test for a volatile substance, putting the liquid in a closed container and heating

it, then analyzing the escaping gases on the gas chromatograph. The red liquid turned out to be a kerosene-based product containing a red dye. Forgione then tested the unknown liquid and got the same result. The extortionist had used the red liquid from an ordinary household thermometer, mistakenly believing it was potentially deadly mercury.

There was no way to trace that liquid to a suspect, but the knowledge that it was not dangerous gave law enforcement officials time to try to develop a case without worrying that an innocent person might die. In this case that extra time didn't matter; the extortionist was never heard from again.

The Chem Unit works a lot of drug cases. Drugs can be the cause of a crime, and the unit is often asked to determine whether a suspect might have been under the influence of drugs when a crime was committed. Or drugs can be the motive for a crime and may be present on some item connected with the crime. In every case the objective of the Bubs is to determine whether any drugs are present, and if so to identify them.

Usually this is a time-consuming but not particularly difficult task. Finding and identifying a drug, like finding and identifying any other chemical, is a matter of separating it from other chemicals and then presenting it to the right instrument. The best place to find evidence of drug use is in blood or urine, but the presence of a drug can be detected in every tissue in the body. One day, for example, a human skull arrived from Alaska. A farmer's dog had found it in a field and brought it home. It was actually only a partial skull; the jaw and teeth were missing, and it had no hair and almost no skin covering, although there was some frozen tissue clinging to it and a patch of mummified skin around the base. From experience, it was assumed that animals had attacked the body and carried away the pieces. This was all that had been found. Alaska police wanted any information that might help them identify the victim or determine how he or she had died.

There wasn't too much to go on. It was a partial skull with only a bit of tissue. It could have been anyone, it could have been lying frozen for years. The tissue was thawed, liquefied, and tested. And it contained a substantial amount of cocaine—so much, in fact, that it was probable that this person had died of a cocaine overdose. That turned out to be vitally important information. Police in the area had suspected that a couple rumored to have hosted several large drug parties was involved in the death. At least partly on the basis of the lab report, these people were questioned extensively, and they eventually admitted that the victim had indeed died of a cocaine overdose, and that they had disposed of the body by dumping it in the woods, assuming the animals would find it and devour it.

Sometimes the unit doesn't even need tissue samples. For example, insects feast on dead bodies, leaving only bones. But Brian Donnelly, working with Wayne Lord, an agent and noted entomologist, developed a mass spec method of identifying the drugs that had been in a victim's body by examining the insects that ate it. In a Connecticut case the partially decomposed mummified body of a woman had been found about a year after her death. Using dead maggots, beetle fecal material, and fly pupa cases removed from the site, Donnelly was able to confirm the presence of antidepressants, antihistamines, and cocaine in her body.

In the "Q1 chain saw, Q2 victim's head" case, a woman in Houston, Texas, had been raped and murdered, and her body had been cut up with a chain saw. Decomposing pieces had been found in several locations. Houston police knew the identity of the victim; what they needed was confirmation of an informant's claim that she had taken a large amount of cocaine shortly before her death. They submitted both decaying body organs and vitreous fluid from her eyes to the lab. If a body has been embalmed or exhumed, if it has decomposed, or if it has been burned, sometimes the only viable source for drug testing is this liquid from the eyes. It's always a very small amount, but it doesn't decompose and the presence of drugs can be detected in it. In the Houston case the lab was able to confirm the presence of a high level of cocaine, allowing police to link the victim to a group of men attending a drug party that had gotten out of hand.

The primary method of detecting drugs in a living person remains urinalysis, although that test can detect most drug use only within the previous seventy-two hours. But in 1987 Roger Martz got a San Diego case in which a suspect was caught driving across the Mexican border with a substantial amount of cocaine hidden in his trunk. The suspect claimed that he had been asked by a friend to drive the car to San Diego, knew nothing about the cocaine in the trunk, and had never personally used cocaine. The Hairs and Fiber Unit was able to associate several human hairs in the trunk with the suspect. San Diego police wanted Martz to prove, by finding evidence of cocaine in the suspect's hair, that the man was lying about his drug use.

There had been some research done into extracting drugs from human hair, but no one had been able to develop a method of finding cocaine in a single strand. By adapting several different mass spectrometer techniques, Martz was able to identify the presence of cocaine in the suspect's hair. Since hair grows approximately half an inch monthly, he was also able to prove that the suspect had been using cocaine for a long time, thereby destroying his defense.

No one yet knows how long cocaine residue will remain in hair, but using Martz's method the Smithsonian has found cocaine in the hair of a five-thousand-year-old mummy. Certainly the most publicized case in which this method was used was the arrest of Washington, D.C., mayor Marion Barry on drug charges. On tapes made before Barry was arrested, an associate was heard to warn him, "If you ever get caught, say that you didn't inhale, say that you blew it out. They can't prove otherwise." In fact, urine testing could prove that Barry had used cocaine within the past three days, but it was important to show that he was a habitual drug user, not simply a man who had gotten caught in the wrong place at the wrong time. The only way to prove that was to examine his hair samples.

Within an hour of Barry's arrest, urine and hair samples were delivered to the lab. Tom Lynch and Henry Schlumpf did the actual examinations. "Usually by the time we analyze a submission, the person has been in jail or in the hospital for a few days, and we don't find too much," Schlumpf said. "We rarely get clinical samples. So this was the biggest positive we'd seen in a live person. More than one political career hinged on this exam, but as far as the chemistry was concerned, it was done exactly the same way as we would work any other case." The urine sample confirmed that Barry had used cocaine recently—and, perhaps more important, a segmental examination of his hair showed he had been using cocaine regularly as long as the hair on his head had been growing. There was no question of a political setup; Barry was an habitual cocaine user.

The largest number of different drugs the Chem/Tox Unit has thus far identified in one person was fourteen, which included everything from codeine to cocaine. In that case the probable cause of death was ruled a drug overdose. But in many criminal cases, defense lawyers will claim that their client acted under the influence of drugs, and was therefore incapable of understanding what he or she was doing. So in drug cases the Chem/Tox Unit runs a general screen, and reports both the drugs that the suspect tested negative for—the drugs that weren't there—and those that were present. For example, the only drug John Hinckley was taking when he attempted to assassinate President Reagan was Valium. And when Charles Manson's disciple Lynette A. "Squeaky" Fromme tried to shoot President Gerald Ford, the only drug found in her system was an antihistamine, which would not have affected her actions at all. But in the case of one killer, it was the absence of drugs that proved to be most important.

On Memorial Day, 1989, a New Jersey man taking therapeutic drugs prescribed by his psychiatrist went beserk. The night before he had seen the movie *Field of Dreams,* in which the main character believes that a voice is giving him instructions. The New Jersey man heard a voice, too, only it didn't command him to build a baseball field. He believed that God was telling him to prove how much he loved his mother by killing her. And God also told him that if he did this, God would protect him by making him invisible. So he stabbed his mother to death.

The suspect's brother came home and saw what had happened. The killer was shocked by the fact that his brother could see him—he was supposed to be invisible—and stabbed his brother to death. After that he went on a rampage, running through backyards, stabbing his neighbors. When he was captured, he told authorities the entire story. He was sane enough to realize that if he could be seen, perhaps God hadn't really spoken to him, and he was crazy.

Obviously his defense was going to be insanity. He was under psychiatric care and was supposed to be taking tranquilizing drugs. The question of whether he was in fact taking those drugs when he committed the murders became significant. If he had been, it would be difficult for his attorney to plead insanity. In this case it was the absence of drugs that was important. In addition to blood and urine samples, the police even submitted a partially eaten powdered doughnut to the Chem Unit, believing that the white powder on top might be a hallucinogen.

This was a complex drug analysis because therapeutic doses are generally so small they won't show up in standard screens. So the unit had to create new standards; they had to determine the minimum amount of a drug that can be detected in blood. Tests can detect as few as five nanograms of a drug per milliliter. In this case a screen sensitive enough to detect one nanogram per milliliter was developed. And found nothing. There were no drugs of any kind in the killer's system when he committed the murders. In this case it was the absence of the drugs that controlled his behavior that made him crazy.

While the bulk of drug tests conducted by the Chem/Tox Unit focus on human drug use, examiners are often asked to try to find drug residue on objects or assist in finding new methods of detecting hidden drugs. For example, drug dealers often keep their records in complex codes, basically long lists of numbers. Sometimes the only way to connect these written records to drug transactions is to actually vacuum the papers and find excessive drug residue on them.

Drug smuggling is probably the most common and profitable of all major crimes, and smugglers have become extremely sophisticated in their methods. Drugs are chemicals and can be treated like any other chemicals. Chemists working for drug dealers—so-called jungle chemists—have succeeded in adding liquefied cocaine to other chemicals to make plastic, then molding it into common items. The cocaine becomes part of the chemical structure of the item. Theoretically, smugglers can mold any item at least partially out of cocaine. For example, plastic plumbing fixtures, identical in appearance to normal fixtures, were found to consist of 20 percent cocaine. It normally costs dealers approximately $5,000 to ship a kilogram, 2.2 pounds, of cocaine into the United States. But dealers were able to ship 350 pounds of plumbing fixtures, which included about seventy kilograms of cocaine, for about $100. Once these fixtures had cleared customs, drug chemists here would have simply reversed the process, liquefying the fixtures to extract the cocaine. Dealers have impregnated large fiberglass bathtubs with cocaine, and in 1991 plastic dog cages were found to have cocaine incorporated into their chemical makeup. Cocaine could just as easily be part of the chemical makeup of the foam packing chips in a box—or, for that matter, part of the box.

Drug-sniffing dogs can't detect drugs being smuggled this way. Standard chemical tests won't find it. But the Chem/Tox Unit has helped refine a sort of miniature ion spectrometer—an instrument originally developed by the U.S. space program to analyze alien atmospheres—so that it can be used in the field to detect drugs, explosive residue, and even environmental pollution. This instrument, which weighs about seventy pounds and costs about $70,000, vacuums particles off the surface of an object and can determine within four seconds if cocaine is present. It will even find the drugs in dust.

As the capabilities of the Chem/Tox Unit have expanded, so has the variety of cases in which it has been asked for investigative assistance. In a Tennessee case, for example, a paralyzed, elderly woman in a hospital was raped and sodomized by two men visiting a patient in another room. The only evidence to connect anyone to the crime was spittle found on the floor by a nurse. Two suspects were arrested in the hospital parking lot and a pouch of mentholated chewing tobacco was found on one of them. Tom Lynch was able to confirm the presence of mentholated tobacco in the spittle, and while it wasn't possible to connect it directly to the suspect, he was able to state that it was consistent in every way with the tobacco found in the suspect's pocket. It made very strong circumstantial evidence.

In another rape case the victim said that during the struggle the rapist had spilled Coca-Cola on the floor mat of his car. Three months after the crime was committed, the police developed a suspect and submitted a floor mat from his car to the lab to see if it could find any evidence of Coca-Cola on it. Fortunately, the Bubs had been saving soft-drink cans for recycling. By testing the residue in some of the older cans, examiners were able to show that the stain on the mat was consistent with Coca-Cola, providing important supportive evidence for the victim's testimony.

Several times every year the unit gets cases in which a woman claims that a man gave her an aphrodisiac, then raped her. The submitting agency wants the lab to identify the substance she was given. Whatever it turns out to be, it's never an aphrodisiac. Thus far there is no such thing, although in one case the Chem Unit did identify a very rare chemical, an extract of the blister beetle, which has been used as an aphrodisiac in animals because it irritates the skin on contact. Of course, it's also highly toxic.

There is no such thing as a magic elixir to cure cancer either, although in an age-old scam a self-proclaimed guru was selling his homemade medicine for a thousand dollars a bottle, claiming it contained ground-up diamonds and pearls. How do you prove that something is nothing? By identifying what it is, and showing that it is a common substance with no medicinal powers. Gem experts in the Materials Analysis Unit found neither diamonds nor pearls, but didn't know what the bottles contained. Tests in the Chem Unit identified the "medicine" as a food product consisting of sugar and carbohydrates; this magic elixir was probably apple butter. Very, very expensive apple butter.

And, so far at least, there are no fuel additives that will allow you to drive a hundred miles on a gallon of ordinary gas, although there always seem to be people willing to invest in such a product. To support fraud cases, the Chem Unit has to identify the components of the substance and verify that it will not do what promoters claim.

Although investigation of airplane crashes is the responsibility of the Federal Aviation Administration, on occasion the Chem/Tox Unit will be asked to analyze a substance to help determine the cause of a crash. When an airliner taking off in a snowstorm crashed into Washington's Fourteenth Street Bridge in January 1982, for example, there was speculation that the crash had been caused by ice on the wings. The Chem/Tox Unit, given a sample of the antifreeze used to de-ice the wings, provided the FAA with its chemical composition. This was simply a matter of determining the percentage of antifreeze in the mixture, important information for the FAA. In 1989 when a Drug Enforcement Agency plane crashed into a mountain in Peru, sabotage was suspected, so Roger Martz joined officials from several federal agencies on a journey to the crash site, a fourteen-thousand-foot-high mountaintop. Generally, sci-crime chemists wouldn't be involved in this type of investigation, but Martz was asked to search for any evidence that the fuel had been contaminated or that the pilots had been drugged. Martz was unable to find anything wrong, and the crash was eventually attributed to pilot error. But the investigation of a crash in Georgia provided very different results.

Sixteen members of a parachuting club were killed when their plane crashed, and after a Georgia laboratory reported finding sugar in the fuel tanks, the FBI was called in. The pilot was believed to have been connected to a drug-smuggling operation, so the possibility of sabotage was very real. Sugar in an engine might cause an in-flight failure by clogging filters and starving the engines of fuel, causing the plane to crash. Tom Lynch, who is a pilot, was sent to Georgia to investigate. "The case agent who drove me to the site told me that his SAC [special agent in charge] wanted to know what had caused the plane to crash by the end of the day," Lynch remembered. "I sort of laughed to myself and told him I really didn't think that was possible."

The fuel ports had been smashed, so Lynch had to cut a hole in the wing tank. Using a pipette—a long glass tube with a rubber bulb on top to create suction—he drew a sample. "As soon as I looked at it, I could see something was wrong. I saw two distinct layers; one layer appeared to be fuel, but the layer beneath it looked like water."

Lynch learned that the plane was used almost exclusively to take up parachutists and then land. The pilot usually carried the minimum amount of fuel required by the FAA for this type of flight. Although the plane could carry as much as 360 gallons, he rarely put more than sixty gallons in his tanks. Each time he landed he would replace the fuel he had consumed from fifty-gallon barrels kept at the field. Lynch focused on those fifty-gallon drums. "I had to use long tubing to get to the bottom of the barrel, and as soon as I started pumping out liquid, I realized I was pumping water. I don't know how many gallon jugs I filled until I finally got to fuel. I didn't know if there was sugar in there or not, but once I saw what was there, I didn't think it really mattered.

"Oil floats on water. So all the fuel was at the top of the barrel. The bottom third of the drum was filled with water. So it was pretty clear in my mind that water was a major factor in this crash. From witnesses I learned that the plane had climbed steeply up to about fifteen hundred feet, and then suddenly nose-dived straight into the ground."

The drums had been carelessly maintained. Some were incompletely covered or had holes in their lids. Water, Lynch believed, probably rainwater, got into the drums and sank to the bottom. Someone lifting the lid to inspect the contents would have found the drum filled with fuel. But the airplane's tanks were filled from a hand pump that took fuel from the bottom of the barrels. Without anyone realizing it, a substantial amount of water was being pumped into the tanks. The plane had sufficient fuel for takeoff, but eventually its turbines were getting water rather than aviation fuel from the fuel lines, and flamed out. The passengers, the parachutists, were standing in the aisle because they would be jumping within minutes. When the engine stalled and the nose dropped, the parachutists fell forward toward the cockpit, changing the plane's center of gravity. Even if the pilot had been able to restart his engine, he probably wouldn't have had time to pull the plane out of its fatal dive. The disaster was an accident.

Lynch didn't even need the entire day to tell the agent the cause of the crash.

While most of the other lab units make cases by linking hard evidence found at the crime scene to a specific suspect, the Chem Unit is rarely able to do so. This is because of the unstable nature of chemicals, which change as their environment changes. Although it's almost impossible to trace a drug sample to its source, for example, occasionally the Chem/Tox Unit can prove a small amount came from a large cache by comparing the type and percentage of the other substances mixed with the drug. And on occasion the unit has been able to match substances on a chemical level. In those cases it isn't even important to identify the substance, simply to be able to positively associate a sample that can be linked to a suspect to a sample found at the crime scene. For instance, a poacher in Alaska was shooting legally protected animals from a plane, then landing to retrieve their carcasses. Alaskan police obtained a sample of engine oil the plane left in the snow, and asked the lab to match it to oil obtained from the suspect's plane. In this case it was possible to make a positive match because the oil was unique; it was a home blend, a mixture of a synthetic oil and a natural oil, and was not commercially available in this mix.

Sometimes it's an additive or pollutant that makes it possible to match oil to a specific vehicle. Oils may be pure when they are put into an engine, but they change rapidly. If an engine is dirty there is a buildup of nitrates, or the owner might alter the composition of the oil by mixing it with additives. So it's possible to match two samples of oil from the same engine if the car hasn't been driven too far between the times the samples are obtained. In several rape cases, for example, the Chem Unit has been able to show that oil found on the street in front of the victim's home came from a specific car. In a hit-and-run case the suspect claimed that his car had been in the shop having the oil changed. On the basis of nitrate accumulation in that oil, Roger Martz was able to prove that it hadn't been changed in at least four thousand miles, thereby destroying the suspect's alibi.

Even under ideal conditions it's difficult to match oil to a source unless it contains something unique. Again in Alaska, thieves were hooking up their own oil tankers to the Alaska pipeline and stealing thousands of gallons of oil. Authorities asked the Chem Unit to add a unique chemical, a "tag," to this oil that could be used to positively identify it. Martz told the agents to add a halogenated compound called chlorobenzene, which is never found in oil and could be identified on the mass spectrometer. Agents dumped several gallons of this chemical into the oil, then waited. Eventually a drop in pressure at a specific point indicated oil was being siphoned from the pipeline, and police arrested a suspect after he had driven away. They took a sample from his truck and sent it to the lab for verification that this was the stolen oil. It seemed like a simple case.

"And that's when I learned that most halogenated compounds can be detected on the mass spectrometer," Martz remembered with a bit of embarrassment, "but not all of them. Not chlorobenzene, for instance. This is what's called a real dilemma. One of the sayings in our unit is that the only exact science is hindsight. So after trying to figure out what to do, we tried to rig up another instrument, an electron capture detector, to identify the chlorobenzene. That piece of equipment wasn't intended to be used that way, but we had no choice. We had to make up a whole new set of standards, then we said a lot of Hail Marys and turned it on. Fortunately, it gave us outstanding results. The oil in the truck was identical to the oil in the pipeline. There was no question about it: this was the guy."

The ability to trace a specimen to its source by comparing their chemical components also provided important evidence in a civil rights case in which a police officer was accused of kicking a suspect. Debbie Wang was able to positively identify a smudge found on the victim's clothes as black shoe polish, strongly supporting the victim's statement.

Perhaps the most publicized case in which the Chem/Tox Unit was able to trace a submission to its source was the controversial Tawana Brawley case. In 1987, a black New York State teenager named Tawana Brawley claimed she had been kidnapped and raped by several white police officers. Soon after she was reported missing, she was found by residents of her family's former apartment complex, partially clothed, with feces smeared on her body and racial epithets written on her torso and clothing. The case immediately attracted national attention for its racially sensitive, as well as sensational, nature.

From the beginning of the case Tawana Brawley was protected by advisers, including the Reverend Al Sharpton, who refused to let her testify before a grand jury. Without her cooperation, law enforcement agencies were limited to the physical evidence, and there was very little evidence to support the girl's story. Initially the Chem Unit received a standard "rape kit"—physical evidence taken from the victim's body in the hospital. Nothing in that kit proved sexual intercourse had taken place, although it was certainly possible that the rapists had used condoms. But within a few weeks a substantial amount of additional evidence was submitted to the sci-crime lab. Working with examiners from the Hairs and Fiber Unit, Tom Lynch was able to identify the fecal matter found on Brawley's clothes as coming from a dog. But then he was asked to identify the substance used to write racial slurs on her body and clothing.

Using infrared spectrophotometry, Lynch was able to identify the substance as charred cotton, which could have come from anywhere. Then, working with Dennis Ward of the Elemental Analysis Unit, he began comparing the particles found on her sweatshirt, the charred cotton, with a variety of items found in the family's former apartment. Eventually the investigators were able to show that these particles came from a cotton washcloth that had been burned. But much more important, identical particles were also found beneath Tawana Brawley's fingernails, as well as inside a pair of gloves found at the scene. Dog fecal matter was found on the outside of those gloves.

Using all that information, Lynch helped piece together a probable scenario. Testifying to the grand jury, he said that the particles from the towel found beneath Tawana Brawley's fingernails indicated that she had written on her own body, then put on the gloves—that was where the particles found inside the glove came from—and spread feces on her clothing. "I can't state positively that it happened this way," Lynch concluded, "but the evidence would be consistent with this."

Only after Lynch's testimony was made public did Reverend Sharpton claim that Tawana Brawley's kidnappers had forced her to write on herself. "When I heard that I knew we'd hit the nail right on the head," Lynch recalled with great pleasure. "I always have doubts, I'm not God, I follow my instincts and I follow science, but I wasn't there so it was impossible for me to know for certain what really happened. But when Sharpton made this statement, I just knew we had it right."

Sometimes the inability to make a positive comparison becomes important evidence. In a Providence, Rhode Island, civil rights case, prison authorities claimed that a man returned to his cell after being fingerprinted, made a noose, and hanged himself. If that was true, the Chem/Tox Unit should have been able to find some ink residue on the noose. A detailed examination for ink turned out negative. There was no ink on the noose, and that made it extremely unlikely that the prisoner had tied his own noose and committed suicide.

From the early days of the sci-crime lab, when the primary function of the one chemist was to analyze gunpowder residue, the responsibilities of the Chemistry/Toxicology Unit have expanded to include all the natural sciences, including biology and bacteriology. If a case involves something that once lived, it will eventually come to this unit. In the notorious "Sea Will Tell" case made famous by writer and lawyer Vincent Bugliosi, an elderly couple disappeared while sailing the world on their yacht. Eventually a younger couple was found sailing the boat. They were convicted of theft, but for five years there was no trace of the original owners. It was as if the sea had swallowed them up. And then a trunk was found on a deserted beach. Circumstantial evidence connected the older couple to that trunk. Several bones were found nearby, and prosecutors needed proof that the body had been inside that trunk. Hairs and Fibers was able to find several human hairs in the trunk, but there was no way of proving when or how those hairs got there. Then the trunk was sent to the Chem/Tox Unit with a request to find whatever there was to be found.

Roger Martz, pleased that "once in a while I get to use my biology degree," found a small amount of a white residue in the trunk. It was caked into a corner and there wasn't very much of it, but it shouldn't have been there. After running numerous tests, he was finally able to identify it as adipocere, a product formed when fatty tissue decomposes under anaerobic conditions—that is, in a place without oxygen. Under the sea, for example. This finding proved that something that had once been alive had been in the trunk; the presence of cholesterol proved that it hadn't been sea life, but a human being.

But that wasn't all. Working with experts from the Smithsonian, Martz was able to identify material found on the bottom of the trunk as the shell of a worm that grows only on the underside of a submerged object, a worm that lives six months before shedding its shell. Martz testified in the murder trials of both the young man and woman, explaining to the jury how he had proved that the trunk had been in the ocean for at least six months, and maybe as long as five years, and that it had served as the coffin for a human being. The man was convicted of murdering the older couple. The sea had told its story, but the Chem/Tox Unit had served as its translator.

CHAPTER
- 3 -

Putting the World Back Together:
The Explosives Unit

Anyone's safety depends principally on the fact that nobody wishes to kill them. . . . We have come to depend on what has been called the good will of civilization.

AGATHA CHRISTIE, *Murder Is Easy*

This is how a bomb works: A power source causes an initiator, which might be heat, shock, or friction, to start a reaction in an explosive substance. With a flash and a bang the explosive substance breaks apart its chemical bonds, releasing gases that take up a much greater space than the original solid or liquid. This detonation begins the instant the circuit between the three components—power source, initiator, and exposive substance—is completed, and takes only a microsecond. All other bomb parts—the casing and timers and relays and switches and shunts—are simply used to control the time and the place of the explosion.

This is how a bomb causes damage: The gases are released as a powerful pressure wave, which rips apart anything that confines it. The positive phase of this wave moves as fast as thirty thousand feet per second until it's equalized with the surrounding pressure. It smashes through anything in its path. This positive phase creates a vacuum, which draws the gases back as a negative phase. (Thus, there might actually be more shattered glass on the same side of a window as the bomb than on the far side.) Many more people are injured by fragments and debris from materials destroyed by the pressure wave than by the explosion.

And this is the power of a bomb: "Moments before the bomb went off the husband of a World Trade Center employee had dropped off his wife and their infant son outside the building," said Agent-examiner Dave Williams of the Explosives Unit, describing the force of the thousand-pound bomb that tore through five levels of the trade center's parking garage and came close to knocking down one of the tall towers. "When the bomb went off, the pressure wave ripped out a three-foot-long section of guard rail from the first basement level, mangled it into a twenty-five-pound metal ball, then flung it more than three hundred yards up the ramp and up Vesey Street. It shot through the rear window of [the employee's] car on the driver's side. It hit the infant seat where the baby had been seconds earlier, and if he'd still been there it would've killed him. It veered off between the bucket seats and embedded itself in the dashboard. If it hadn't hit the infant seat first, it would have taken the driver's head right off. The force of that bomb was phenomenal."

It is the bomb, more than any other weapon, that makes you vulnerable. Unlike a firearm, a bomb doesn't have to be aimed. Unlike poison, it doesn't have to be administered. The bomber doesn't have to be near you. Bombs are weapons of chance as much as choice: the victims are simply in the wrong place at the wrong time. Bombs kill randomly, making them the perfect terror weapon, and they have changed the way we live.

Bombs, or explosive devices, can be as simple as an M-80 firecracker or as complex as a nuclear weapon. The size of a bomb is much less important than its placement. In 1986, a Molotov cocktail, a bottle filled with gasoline and set afire, killed ninety-seven people when it started an inferno at the DuPont Plaza Hotel in San Juan, Puerto Rico. A bomb that weighed no more than fourteen ounces and was concealed inside a portable radio killed 271 people when it blew apart Pan Am Flight 103 over Lockerbie, Scotland, in December 1988. Almost exactly one year later federal judge Robert Vance was killed when he opened up a package bomb in the seeming safety of his own home. Incredibly, no one was even injured when a thousand-pound bomb put in place as part of an extortion scheme blew up Harvey's Wagon Wheel Casino in Lake Tahoe, Nevada, in 1980. And only six people died when another thousand-pound bomb almost knocked down the World Trade Center and Vista Hotel in New York City in February 1993.

Once, bombings were relatively rare and were usually aimed at specific targets. In the Roaring Twenties simple "infernal devices," consisting mostly of a few sticks of dynamite, were used by political anarchists against the wealthy and powerful, or used in the deadly battles to establish the rights of unions. In the 1930s gangsters used stench bombs, or stink bombs, to persuade owners of restaurants and movie theaters to sell their businesses to the Mob, and explosives if they refused. But the general public had little to fear from bombs, and when the FBI crime lab opened in 1932, the sum total of its explosives work consisted of using a borrowed X-ray machine to examine suspicious packages.

Bombs began changing the way we live on November 1, 1955, when United Airlines Flight 629 took off from Denver's Stapleton Airport and eleven minutes later exploded in midair, killing forty-four people. Although a bomb was suspected, no one knew how to prove that a bomb had gone off on that plane. On five tiny fragments of sheet metal that did not come from the plane or its cargo, sci-crime lab chemist Bill Magee found residue left by a dynamite explosion. This was the first time residues had been used to identify an explosive substance. (Subsequently the presence of residues became the primary means of proving an explosion had been caused by a bomb, and then determining the type of explosive used in that bomb.) In addition to the residue, one of these fragments was identified as a portion of a commonly available six-volt battery. Evidence of a power source and an explosive had been found in the wreckage of Flight 629, proving it had been destroyed by a bomb.

Investigators discovered that a man named Jack Gilbert Graham had recently purchased several large travel-insurance policies on the life of his mother, Daisie King, who had died in the crash. During a search of Graham's home a piece of copper wire with yellow insulation was found in the pocket of his work shirt; this was exactly the kind of wire that had been found at the crash site and determined to have been part of the detonator. A store clerk remembered selling dynamite and blasting caps to a customer who looked like Graham. And while Graham denied putting anything in his mother's suitcase, his wife admitted he had put a small gift—supposedly, a set of artist's tools—in the luggage as a surprise. Finally, Graham confessed, telling psychiatrists, "The number of people killed made no difference to me. It could have been a thousand." Although he later recanted this confession, he was found guilty of first-degree murder and died in Colorado's gas chamber.

The world was suddenly and forever a less safe place.

In the 1960s rudimentary bombs were used by segregationists fighting integration in the South. In a particularly heinous crime, six little girls were killed when a black church was bombed in Birmingham, Alabama. It was to investigate these bombings that an explosives unit was created in the Firearms Unit. While the primary job of its members was to develop evidence against bombers, they also actively participated in "substitutions," undercover operations in which dummy materials were substituted for real explosives. "What they'd do," explained Chris Ronay, who served as chief of the Explosives Unit for seven years beginning in 1987, "was dig up caches of dynamite and take it to a garage somewhere, and Fred Smith, who was the lab's explosives expert, would empty out the real powder and replace it with a mixture of peanut shells and anything else he could find, smooth out the wax cover with an iron, then rebury it and begin surveillance. They made several good cases that way."

The bombs became more sophisticated in the 1970s, but the technique remained the same. Ronay remembered working a covert operation against the terrorist group FALN one cold Chicago night. "We went into one of their safe houses and replaced about two hundred detonators with sugar. Those people never knew we had been there until we testified against them at their trial."

The Explosives Unit became independent in 1972, primarily in response to the growing number of terrorist and antiwar bombings. While on occasion the unit will still perform covert operations, its primary objective is to develop evidence from bombs that can be used to identify and convict the bomb maker. The FBI retains jurisdiction in all cases of terrorism against Americans and when bombs are used against federal employees, on federal property, or in federally insured banks. Members of the unit don't work on bomb detection, they don't disarm bombs, and, except for demonstration purposes, they don't detonate bombs. They rarely see a live bomb at a crime scene, and if they encounter a live bomb they are supposed to contact a police bomb squad to dispose of it. Their job is simply to find the guys who make the bombs.

No university teaches explosives; there are no degrees in this subject. The only way to learn is through experience. Examiners study old cases and learn from the people who investigated them; they go to bomb scenes and blow up things in a controlled area to see what type of explosive causes what kind of damage. "You learn by trial and error," Ronay said, then added with a smile: "Although hopefully not too much error."

"If you want to know what certain explosive charges will do to an automobile," explained Fred Smith, the unit's first chief, "then you blow up a lot of automobiles."

The Explosives Unit is one of the smallest in the lab, comprising only seven agent-examiners and an equal number of technicians, but in their investigations these "bombers," as members of the unit refer to themselves, often rely on the talents of other lab units, from chemistry to fingerprint identification.

Each investigation begins with the discovery of a bomb. Surprisingly, it doesn't really make too much difference whether the bomb has gone off, although the job gets a lot more complicated after the bomb has blasted itself into pieces. There are basically four paths to follow in a bombing case: Identify each of the components of the bomb and try to associate them with a specific individual or individuals who bought them or made them. Compare the way the bomb is constructed—the bomber's signature—with bombs found in the past that have been linked to known individuals. Identify evidence found with the bomb that is not actually part of it—the van used to transport it, perhaps, or a latent print found on wrapping paper— and trace that to the bomb maker. Or find the motive for the bombing— perhaps revenge or extortion—and use traditional crime-solving methods to develop a suspect and link him to the bomb.

When a bomb is found intact it's simple to prove that it's a bomb: if an object has a power source, an initiator, and an explosive charge, it's a bomb. But after an explosion has occurred examiners often have a very difficult time proving it was caused by a bomb. Explosives explode, sometimes by accident. So the first determination that has to be made after an explosion is whether it was an accident or a crime. In 1947, for example, the French freighter *Grandcamp*, which was filled with the fertilizer ammonium nitrate, exploded in the harbor of Texas City, Texas, killing 561 people and injuring another three thousand. An investigation revealed that a fire had started in the cargo hold and the ship's hatches had been shut to deprive it of oxygen. Instead, this trapped the escaping gases, and the pressure continued to build up until the entire ship was turned into a huge bomb and exploded, virtually destroying the entire city. In 1989, as a United Airlines jumbo jet took off from Honolulu, the baggage compartment doors suddenly blew off, leading to speculation that a bomb had been hidden in a suitcase. In fact, the latches had simply failed to secure the door.

It's the firm policy of the FBI not to declare that a bombing has taken place until they can prove it. Tom Thurman, who headed the American team investigating the bombing of Pan Am Flight 103 on December 21, 1988, recalled in his soft Kentucky drawl, "When we first heard about it we might have believed it was a bomb, but until we had proof we couldn't say it. I remember asking someone from the National Transportation Safety Board, 'Has there ever been an instance where a commercial airliner with a proven track record has essentially disintegrated at cruising altitude for no apparent reason other than a bomb?' I pretty well knew the answer, but I wanted to make sure that everybody understood that before we could say there was a bomb, we had to prove it.

"We spent that first day walking over the hillsides through the mud. At the end of the day we had a meeting. People were reporting in from various sectors what they were doing and what they'd found. As I walked into the operations center someone handed me a piece of broken metal maybe three inches wide and eight or nine inches long, and asked me if it had any meaning. I knew instantly. It had what we call pitting and cratering. These are marks that look like inverted mushrooms and they're made in metals by superheated gases when an explosion occurs. That's the only time you see them. I took one look at this piece of metal and said, 'Okay, now we know we had a bomb.' "

After a bomb has gone off it's imperative that the bomb scene be preserved. The clues that may eventually lead to the identification of the bomb maker are right there; it's just a matter of picking up all of them. As a British police inspector ordered at Lockerbie, "If it's not a rock and it's not growing, put it in the bag."

Every bomb scene is unique. Debris from Pan Am 103 rained over 845 square miles of Scottish countryside. A French DC-10 exploded above the Sahara Desert in 1989, scattering wreckage over 265 square miles, and every inch had to be searched in heat that reached 142 degrees. In 1976 a car bomb blew up former Chilean diplomat Orlando Letelier right in the heart of downtown Washington, D.C. The World Trade Center was crippled by a bomb that destroyed five levels of the parking garage, knocked out all power to the buildings, and left huge slabs of concrete hanging precariously above tanks filled with potentially explosive Freon.

Somewhere in the Scottish countryside, or in the sweltering Sahara, or in the rubble-filled crater, are the remains of the bomb. There is a common misconception that the bomb destroys itself in the blast. Not true. As much as 95 percent of a bomb will survive detonation, although it will be shattered into thousands of pieces. And finding those pieces is often the key to solving the crime.

The investigation can only be as complete as the crime-scene search.

Finding out what type of explosive was used, the size of the bomb, where it was placed, and how it was transported are the first steps toward discovering who made it and who planted it. Everything found at a bomb scene can help answer those questions. How far certain objects are found from the seat of the explosion might help determine the size of the bomb, and the size of the bomb would limit the means used to transport it to the scene. Everything matters: the sound of the explosion, the color of the flash and smoke, the smell in the air, the direction of the soot on the walls, the type and extent of the structural damage.

"I knew within two hours after entering the World Trade Center what type of bomb we had and how big it was," recalled Dave Williams, who was in charge of the investigation at the scene. "I was able to determine where the seat of the explosion was from the way debris had been thrown, the type of damage done to the concrete and steel, the pitting and cratering, the fact that there were flash burns on one side of a pillar but not on the other. You have to look at everything and put it all together.

"The extent of the damage told me, from experience, that the velocity of the explosion was somewhere between 14,000 to 15,000 feet per second. Different explosives detonate at different speeds. Anything faster or slower would have done a different type of damage. C-4 or TNT would have shattered the steel, for example. So, from the velocity, I knew it pretty much had to be a fertilizer-based product.

"We're pretty familiar with the capabilities of fertilizer-based explosives, so from the extent of the damage I was able to estimate that we had about twelve hundred pounds of explosives. So how do you get a twelve-hundred-pound bomb into that building? It isn't going to fit comfortably inside a car. The height of the garage door limited the size of a truck. So we guessed it had to have been carried in a one-ton van or truck. That gave us a direction: it told us we should be looking for the remains of that type of vehicle in the crater."

Much valuable information can also be learned from the damage done to the bodies of the bomb victims. For example, when a car in which two civil rights workers were riding suddenly exploded on a suburban Maryland street in the late 1960s, the initial assumption was that they had been murdered. But the passenger's arms had been blown off from just below his elbows and his legs had been shattered, while a wide strip of skin across his groin was almost untouched by the effects of the blast. Those injuries told a story. Imagine yourself sitting in a car and leaning forward from your waist. As you do, a protective area is formed in your midsection. So from this body damage it seemed obvious that the passenger was leaning forward, his arms down in front of him—perhaps trying to pick up the bomb—when it went off. The bomb had to have been in plain sight, so the people in the car knew it was there, which suggested that rather than being victims, in fact they were transporting this bomb.

Almost precisely the same type of body damage made it clear to lab examiners that a bomb had caused the crash of a commuter airplane in North Africa in 1988. Twenty-eight people had been killed when the plane crashed less than three minutes after takeoff. Because several Americans were among the victims, the Federal Aviation Agency and the NTSB had investigated, but neither agency had been able to determine the cause of the crash.

By the time examiners from the Explosives Unit arrived in North Africa, every victim had been identified—except one. One man couldn't be identified and his body had not been claimed. He had made his reservations under a fictitious name. No one had reported a friend or relative missing. And when lab examiners looked at the body the reason for that became frighteningly clear.

The body had been torn apart symmetrically. Both arms were severed inches above the elbow. Both legs were gone from slightly below the pelvis, but the femurs showed pressure coming up from underneath and slightly behind the legs. There was no damage to the chest area and the penis was still there. That was significant. Previous exams done on individuals known to have been bending over bombs as they detonated had shown that the belly had hung over and protected the penis. So in this case that made it obvious that this unidentified person had been right on top of the bomb.

His head was missing, with the exception of his scalp from the top all the way down the back. Both ears were still there; it was perfectly symmetrical, meaning he was looking directly at the bomb when it went off.

This person has never been identified. But shortly after the lab determined that the crash had been caused by a bomb, a terrorist orgaization claimed responsibility. While it's not possible to determine if this was a suicide-bombing or an accident, there was no question that the individual was carrying a bomb. And the likelihood exists that this was one of the first suicide-bombings of an airplane in history.

When one of the big guns aboard the battleship U.S.S. *Iowa* exploded while being test-fired in 1989, killing all forty-seven members of its crew, a

Navy investigation concluded that a homosexual sailor despondent over the end of a love affair had planted a bomb in the gun, although there was very little substantive evidence to support that conclusion. In fact, the explosion also could have been caused by what is called an overram, in which powder is pushed too far into the breech. If the explosion had been caused by a bomb, the crew would have had no warning; if it had been caused by an overram, they probably would have heard a crackling sound, like hot oil being poured into a frying pan, seconds before the gun blew up, and would have had a chance to react. Indeed, a split second before the blast the turret commander had reported, "We've got a problem here." In the explosion his lower jaw had been completely severed by a swinging chain, indicating his mouth was open, perhaps shouting an order; this meant he was aware of the situation. The body of the sailor who purportedly had planted the bomb was found with his upper torso and face missing, indicative of the fact that he had been looking directly into the gun barrel, just about the last place he would have been looking if he had known there was a bomb there. Although there was no way of proving conclusively that the blast had been caused by an overram rather than a bomb, the Explosives Unit could not affirm the Navy's conclusion, and after an additional investigation, including work done by the Elemental Analysis unit, the Navy officially withdrew its report and issued an apology to the family of the accused sailor.

At the beginning of a bomb-scene search the entire blast area is divided into numbered grids, and each piece of debris is tagged to indicate exactly where it was found, then either discarded or bagged for further inspection. Large rolling magnets and vacuum cleaners are sometimes used in searches, but inevitably the work comes down to people crawling through the scene and sifting through tons of debris by hand. Three mesh screens of increasing fineness are set down, with the coarsest screen on top, and the debris is shoveled through. Before a bomb-scene search is concluded, every single piece of debris will be looked at to determine if it was part of the bomb or was close to the center of the explosion.

Because any single piece can be the one that leads directly to the bomb maker, no piece can be overlooked. When Orlando Letelier was murdered in downtown Washington, D.C., for example, fire trucks raced to the scene to extinguish his burning car. So, later that night, lab examiners went to the firehouse and inspected the truck tires for debris they might have picked up. Jagged fragments from the car and bits of a tin pin that had been taped to the underside of the car body to hold the bomb in place were found wedged into the treads. Other tiny fragments found at the scene were identified in the lab as being part of a paging-system receiver, meaning the bomb had been detonated by remote control. That directed the investigation toward bomb makers known to use radio-controlled devices.

Separating the remains of the bomb and pieces that had been close to the bomb from the millions of tiny fragments of metal and plastic and electronic components found when a plane crashes or a car explodes is extremely time-consuming but not, according to Thurman, as difficult as it might seem. "Explosive damage has a very distinct look," he explained. "Bomb fragments will have jagged edges and they might be coated with residue or soot. Depending on the force of the explosion, they'll probably be a little smaller than debris resulting from a crash. If people know what to look for, bomb damage isn't hard to identify."

Without question the largest, the most complex, and probably the most successful bomb-scene search in history was conducted in the area surrounding Lockerbie. The work done on the ground in the months following the explosion of Flight 103 led directly to the identification of the people who put the bomb on that airplane. And the most important piece of evidence turned out to be a tiny fragment of that bomb, about half the size of a thumbnail, that was found among the millions of pieces of wreckage resulting from the crash.

"Paul Schrecker of this unit and I arrived in Lockerbie thirty-six hours after the plane hit the ground," Thurman remembered. "Everybody in this business has his own way of starting an investigation. I like to walk through the scene, just looking, trying to get a sense of what happened. It looked like a war zone. There were still a lot of bodies in the fields, some of them still strapped in their seats. The plane had blown up at thirty-one thousand feet and we had crosswinds of a hundred and thirty miles per hour up there spreading wreckage over eight hundred and forty-five square miles. I've been at a lot of bombing scenes. One of the most important things you have to do is maintain complete professionalism; you don't want to focus on the human tragedy. But this—four days before Christmas, these people just trying to get home—it was impossible not to be affected by it."

That piece of metal, found the first day, turned out to be half of the skid rail of the luggage container in which the bomb had been planted. It was taken to a lab outside London, where a chemist found unconsumed residues which he identified as the explosives PETN and RDX. The only explosive in the world known to contain a combination of PETN and RDX is called Semtex. In the past Semtex has been used mostly by terrorists, so this led Thurman to believe that the bombing was a terrorist act rather than murder for revenge or personal gain. Investigators couldn't eliminate that possibility entirely, but when they found the Semtex they began concentrating on terrorists.

"The search continued Christmas morning," Thurman remembered. "It was very foggy and as we walked through the fields we could barely see ten feet in front of us. But incredibly, one of the guys found the other piece of the skid rail that had been ripped apart by the bomb. The odds against us finding those two pieces so fast can't be calculated. It can't happen. What was so important about it was that it told us that the bomb had been in the baggage area rather than in the passenger cabin. The next thing we wanted to find out was exactly which luggage container it had been in. Knowing that might tell us where it had been put aboard the airplane.

"Almost immediately we started putting the airplane back together. In a hangar at Farnborough Royal Air Force Base south of London, a wire frame had been set up, and as each piece arrived from Lockerbie it was hung where it belonged. And gradually the plane came together. As more and more pieces were hung, we started seeing some abnormal bending and crunching of the metal around the baggage area. Then, about seven hundred inches back on the left side of the aircraft, we could see soot and residue, and finally there was a big hole.

"From Pan Am's cargo manifest we learned that Container AVE4041PA had been right where the hole was. At the Longtown Army Depot in northern England the baggage containers were reconstructed. The sides of these containers had identification numbers stenciled on them, so it was easy to identify AVE4041PA. Its sides were badly fragmented. All the bases were recovered, and they were all ripped and torn. Like the others, the base of AVE4041PA had a hole in it, but what was different about it was that the sides of this hole were bent down at almost a ninety-degree arc. So within a few weeks we knew what type of explosive had been used, the container in which it had been planted, and where it was on the airplane."

While investigators were reassembling the baggage containers, they found a small piece of plastic circuit board that had been damaged by explosive forces rather than in the crash. Eventually they learned it had come from a radio that had been made for European frequencies. "That didn't surprise us," Thurman continued. "We'd been expecting to find it. Several weeks before the bombing, the West Germans had raided an apartment being used by a terrorist organization known as the PFLP-GC, the Popular Front for the Liberation of Palestine–General Command, and arrested thirteen people. In the trunk of the leader's car they found a quantity of Semtex and a Toshiba radio equipped with an altimeter fuse—and the only place an altimeter fuse is any good is on an airplane. When the plane reaches a certain altitude the bomb is detonated. Information gathered from members of this terrorist cell indicated that several other bombs had been made—and no one knew where they were. When this plane blew up it was natural to assume that one of these bombs had been used. So almost all of our attention was focused on the PFLP-GC."

The bomb that had been found in the trunk had been built inside a Toshiba radio. Investigators took the piece of circuit board recovered at the crash site to Toshiba and the company confirmed that it had come from one of their radios, but not the same model as had been used in the other four bombs. "That surprised us," Thurman explained. "The PFLP-GC had used a large radio with one speaker; this fragment had come from a cassette radio that was long and narrow. It was completely different. But that still didn't stop us from believing that the PFLP-GC might be involved in this. It just seemed like too much of a coincidence.

"We knew the size of the radio and, from suitcase fragments found in the wreckage, we knew exactly what type of suitcase it had been put in. What we did then was try to recreate the damage done to the container by the bomb. That would tell us exactly how much explosive was used and specifically where the bomb had been in the container. Under the same conditions explosives will act pretty much the same way every time; they'll cause the same damage. In this case the size of the bomb was limited by the size of the radio. So we got several baggage containers from Pan Am, suitcases—identical to the one in which the bomb had been carried—from Samsonite, and radios from Toshiba that we packed with Semtex. We filled these containers with luggage that we got from Pan Am and other airlines, bags that were lost or never claimed. If you've ever lost a piece of luggage on an airplane, there's a chance either we've blown it up or somebody else has. This gives us a random collection of baggage that's as close as we can come to what probably was in the actual container. Then we blew them up, two at a time.

"We were trying to come as close as possible to duplicating the damage to the actual container as well as the one next to it. That means breaking the lower skid rail in the same place, creating holes in the sides about the same size, and inflicting comparable damage to the neighboring container. To do that we bracket the explosions; it's just like targeting a mortar. We try one thing and if we get too much damage or too little, we add or subtract until we arrive at exactly what happened. It took us fewer than ten tests to reach the point at which we were satisfied we'd come as close as possible. And we felt confident that we were able to determine within two or three inches precisely where the bomb was located in that container. Knowing exactly where it was on the plane made us believe that the bomb had originally been aboard Air Malta Flight KM-190, which had connected with Pan Am 103 in Frankfurt, Germany."

At that point the forensic work was being done in England. After several months of work investigators felt they knew the size of the bomb, how it had gotten on the plane, and where it had been located. Then things slowed down: there wasn't too much else to be done. But in Scotland, examiners continued to go over every item found at the bomb scene.

Early in 1990, more than a year after the crash, an English detective examining the clothing that had been in the suitcase with the bomb found a tiny piece of green circuit board, maybe half the size of a thumbnail, embedded in a shirt. In an explosion fragments travel very fast and get very hot. When they hit a fabric such as polyester, the fabric will melt right around it and form sort of a protective cocoon. Investigators in England compared the fragment to the Toshiba radio and realized that it did not come from there. At that point, they determined that this piece had probably come from the timing mechanism used to detonate the bomb.

"From the millions and millions of pieces into which that plane had been shattered we finally had a piece of the bomb," Thurman remembered with satisfaction. "It was the only piece of the bomb we ever recovered. Investigators in Europe tried hard to figure out where this circuit board had come from but couldn't make a positive identification. So they sent us a photograph of it. It was made of fiberglass, and a circuit pattern was printed on it. The first thing I noticed when I looked at it was that it had an unusual curved notch in it. I knew from experience that a lot of travel alarm clocks have a similar notch, which allows some component to fit in snugly.

"I'd investigated several cases in which bombs had been triggered by alarm clocks, and to me, this looked like it might have come from that type of timer. I asked an agent on Malta to buy one copy of every travel alarm clock he could find and send them to me. I got about twenty clocks, plus some other hard devices, but none of them matched up. Truthfully, we were at a standstill.

"We asked other resources in the Washington area knowledgeable in bombing investigations to try to identify that circuit board. Someone I knew at one of these resources told me that the construction reminded him of the timers used in two bombs recovered in the African nation of Togo in 1986 after a failed coup attempt. 'You have them here?' I asked. He went into their files to check and returned a few minutes later carrying two bombs. When we opened up the back of one of the timers, the first thing we saw was a green circuit board. We checked the circuit patterns and they matched pretty closely. I was trying very hard not to get too excited. 'You got a microscope and a screwdriver?' I asked.

"We took the timer apart and examined it under a microscope. Bingo! Professionally, this is the greatest feeling I've ever had. Finally, finally, we had something substantial that could lead us to the bomb maker. I immediately called the case agent, Ed Marshman. 'Ed,' I told him, trying to be as calm as possible, 'you're not going to believe this, but we've identified the timer. I'm holding an identical timer in my hands right now.'

"We'd found the needle in an 845-square-mile haystack. Now we had to exploit it. I took the timers back to our lab to see if we could identify the maker, and under very high magnification, on a second circuit board I found some printing that had been scratched out. Jerry Richards, in our Special Photography Unit, was able to bring it up a little with infrared photography. We could read the letter 'M,' then either a '5' or a 'B.' I thought it might be 'M580,' which is a type of circuit board. But when we checked with the manufacturer in Japan, we were told it wasn't their product. Eventually we learned about a Swiss company, Meister et Bollier, known as MEBO AG, that makes very high-quality timers for many different and legitimate purposes.

"MEBO's managing director positively identified that piece of circuit board from the photograph. Between 1985 and 1986, he told us, MEBO had delivered twenty of these timers to a Libyan official." Then in December 1993, he changed his story, claiming that he had been mistaken when he told investigators that these timers had been delivered only to Libya. In addition to the timers supplied to Libya, he said, several more were sold to

East Germany. The Stasi, East Germany's secret police, were known to have extensive contacts with Syria-based Palestinian terrorists. This led to speculation that the United States ignored possible Syrian involvement in the bombing to secure that country's cooperation in Operation Desert Storm and in the release of hostages being held in Lebanon.

But once the initial connection was made between the timers and Libya, substantial additional evidence was developed that further implicated Libyan intelligence agents. "Some of the items of clothing recovered from the Samsonite suitcase were traced back to a clothing store in Sliema, Malta, named Mary's House," Thurman continued. "Mary's House was located just a few feet down the block from the Libyan embassy on Malta, and the owner identified photographs of a known Libyan intelligence agent named Abdel Basset Ali Al-Magrahi as the person who'd bought the clothing found in the suitcase. He remembered one pair of pants in particular, he said, because they were so ugly. He remembered Abdel Basset so well because he'd bought a lot of unrelated clothing. He didn't even care what size they were. Obviously he wanted to make sure the suitcase looked legitimate in case it was opened up and inspected."

Agents on Malta learned that Abdel Basset had arrived on the island on December 20, the day before the bombing. He was met there by a second Libyan intelligence agent, Lamen Khalifa Fhimah, who had been the station manager on Malta for Libyan Arab Airlines. That position gave him access to the airline baggage system, allowing him to bypass normal security checks. Investigators eventually obtained Fhimah's diary, in which he had written, "Abdel Basset is coming from Zurich. . . . Take tags from Air Malta." In retrospect, the meaning of that reminder seemed ominously clear: the bomb would be put aboard an Air Malta flight that connected to Pan Am 103.

Basset and Fhimah were indicted in November 1991. Even in the face of worldwide economic sanctions against his country, Libyan ruler Mu'ammar Gadhafi has refused numerous requests from Western nations that he allow these men to be extradited for trial. "I don't think anyone will really be satisfied until they've been tried," Thurman concluded, "but we feel very comfortable with our conclusions. This was entirely a forensically driven investigation, made possible by the fact that two pieces of plastic, neither of them longer than two inches, were found among literally millions of pieces of debris in the largest crime-scene search ever conducted. That eventually led us to the clothing, which was key to ID'ing the suspect."

. . .

Being able to specifically identify a component of a bomb allows investigators to link it to other bombs, often in seemingly unrelated cases—an important step in tracking down the bomb maker. To assist in this identification the Explosives Unit maintains an extensive Explosives Reference Collection, perhaps the most complete collection in existence of bits and pieces that might be used in an explosive device.

When the unit was established in 1972, the entire collection consisted of one four-drawer file cabinet and about twenty items found on German saboteurs who landed on Long Island during World War II. It has since expanded to fill dozens of large cabinets and includes two computer databases. The physical collection consists of samples of any type of device that might be used in a bomb: common and exotic batteries from around the world; detonators and detonating cords; inert fireworks and road flares and dynamite wrappers; all types of blasting accessories; shunts and plugs and relays and delays; timers and locks; wires and tapes; road flares, which are often used to simulate sticks of dynamite in hoax bombs; radio-control devices ranging from model-airplane controllers to garage-door openers, which are commonly used to trigger remote-controlled explosives; and a long list of items carried by Radio Shack, which is known in the explosives community as the Bomber's Store because just about everything needed to make a bomb, besides the explosive, can be bought there. The oldest item in this collection is a blasting cap dating back to 1922.

Other file cabinets overflow with catalogues and manuals that allow investigators to determine exactly which company made the particular quarter-inch pipe used in a pipe bomb or where a certain part recovered from a car bombing belongs on a 1991 Chevy van. In addition to these hard files, in 1978 the unit initiated a computerized Bomb Reference File, which enables investigators to link bomb parts, bomb-design techniques, bombers' political affiliations, and the geographic locations of different cases. If, for example, a pipe bomb filled with Red Dot smokeless powder, detonated by an alarm clock and bearing a distinctive diamond-shaped toolmark, goes off against the side of a foreign airline office in Miami, these files can be searched for any other cases in which bombs with similar characteristics have been found.

Old bombs don't just blow away. Inert bombs, bombs that have been rendered safe, hoax bombs, and the recovered parts of detonated bombs are regularly submitted to the lab for examination. When that inspection is concluded the bomb is either added to the reference collection or returned to the submitting agency. Incredibly, even with all the safeguards built into the system, on occasion live bombs have inadvertently been sent to the lab. When a car was blown up in a southern state in 1987, for example, local police found several items at the scene that apparently had been dropped by the bomber in his haste to get away. Among those items was an ordinary flashlight. Because latent fingerprints are often found on batteries, police sent the flashlight to the lab, where Tom Thurman examined it. "When I looked at it," Thurman remembered with a trace of an embarrassed smile, "I found that the bottom end was sealed, so I tried to take off the top part, where the bulb is, to get to the batteries. It wouldn't move, and I assumed that the batteries had corroded and frozen up the parts. That happens. So I got out a hacksaw, put the flashlight in a vise and cut off the end. I was careful not to cut near the batteries because if there were any latent prints, I didn't want to ruin them.

"Thank goodness for that. When the end fell off, powder came pouring out. I knew what that meant as soon as I saw it—this was a live bomb. 'Oh boy,' I thought, 'oh boy.' Then I took a deep breath. Actually, I took several deep breaths. The flashlight contained two batteries and a pill container filled with smokeless powder. If someone had turned it on, the current would have caused it to detonate. But the bomb maker had used too much epoxy. He'd glued the switch closed. Of course, the bomb maker couldn't try it after he'd assembled it, so he never realized it wouldn't work.

"We found out later that the bomb maker had been abusing his wife and was trying to kill the doctor who'd advised her to leave him. It was the doctor's car he'd blown up. But he not only wanted to kill the doctor, he wanted to hurt anybody else who came along, so he built two bombs. We got the second one. I don't believe it would've killed me if it had gone off, but it would've taken off my hands or blinded me. We were very lucky on that one, very lucky."

Only once has a member of the unit been injured while examining a bomb. Dave Williams had his finger cut open when the fuse of an antique hand grenade that had been used in an Akron, Ohio, bank robbery turned out to be live. "Basically," Williams remembered, "the way a hand grenade works is that the striker hits the primer, which shoots a flame into the detonator, causing the grenade to blow up. When I X-rayed this device, I saw that the detonator had been removed, so the worst thing the grenade was capable of doing was shooting a flame out the end. I didn't even think that could happen. The grenade had been used as evidence at the robber's trial, and had been handled by a lot of people before we got it in here. A bomb technician in Ohio had inserted a paper clip as an added safety precaution.

"Just to be extra safe, though, I examined it in a stainless steel tank. I was cocking the striker back to put in a stronger safety clip when it slipped. The striker went through the paperclip, hit the primer, which flamed and for some reason the entire cowling blew apart. I knew immediately my hand was gone. I can't describe how good I felt when I pulled my hand out of the tank and saw that it was just laid open. I was real lucky. Without that tank I certainly would've been blinded, and I might have been killed."

Every bomb is designed to fulfill the specific objective of the bomb maker, and that may require the inclusion of timers and primers and safety fuses and an assortment of other devices. That's what makes bombs different. And every bomb, every single bomb, has to be put inside some sort of container or carrier so it can be delivered to the target. In cartoons bombs usually say "Bomb" on the side. In real life, for obvious reasons, they're always packaged and transported in something that will disguise their purpose. In many cases the bomb maker has been identified through clues developed from these materials rather than from the bombs themselves. That is precisely what happened when terrorists bombed the World Trade Center in New York City.

Dave Williams was planning to spend the afternoon of February 26, 1993, playing golf when his pager went off. There had been a large explosion in the parking garage beneath the World Trade Center. While authorities there believed a transformer had blown up, unit chief Chris Ronay wanted him to go to New York, just in case. Williams had joined the Explosives Unit in 1978 as a technician, with a degree in zoology, and after becoming a special agent in 1982 had spent almost five years working in the field before returning to the lab. Although he had a lot less than the average twenty years' experience held by other examiners in the unit, he had been around long enough to know from initial damage reports that this didn't sound like a transformer explosion.

The bomb had gone off just after noon on Friday. Williams walked into the crater for the first time Saturday morning. "It was surreal," he recalled.

"It was like walking into a bizarre cave. The explosion had ripped through five levels of the parking garage. Slabs of concrete as large as basketball courts, eighteen inches thick, were just hanging in midair, and they'd suddenly break loose and fall several stories and the whole building would begin to shake. Steel beams were broken and twisted. There had been sixteen hundred cars in the garage when the bomb went off, and their alarm systems had been activated. Wherever you looked headlights were flashing and lights were blinking and all you could hear were sirens and bells and whistles. Their electrical systems were sparking and starting pockets of fire, there was smoke everywhere, and some of the bravest people I've ever seen were risking their own lives to search through the rubble for victims. In two seconds one of the most modern buildings in the world had become a dark, dangerous cavern.

"The building was still moving. We put a spacer in a half-inch crack and walked a hundred feet, and by the time we got back the spacer was gone and the crack was six inches wide.

"I knew we had a bomb the moment I walked in. When I came down the ramp, I saw big pieces of debris that had been thrown more than seven hundred feet from the seat of the blast, and there just wasn't enough natural gas or methane in there to generate that kind of force. In the unit we have a policy of not attributing an explosion to a bomb until we have physical evidence of that bomb, but . . . When I was asked about it by [New York State] Governor [Mario] Cuomo I told him, 'If it looks like a duck and walks like a duck, it's a duck.' We found out soon enough that this was the largest improvised explosive device—meaning somebody made it, as opposed to a military bomb—that had ever functioned in the United States."

Within hours of the explosion, an extremely reliable informant in New York identified specific Serbian nationals as the bombers. On the basis of that information, the Bureau obtained court permission to set up extensive surveillance of these people. As it turned out, the informant was wrong; the Serbs had nothing to do with the bombing. They were actually diamond thieves, and the evidence developed in the bombing investigation enabled the Bureau to bust a major diamond-laundering operation.

"Although every bomb scene is different and every bombing is unique," Williams continued, "we try to follow some general guidelines. The first thing we do is get organized, get set up for the long haul. At this point there was still a tremendous amount of confusion. Headquarters in Washington thought New York had put me in charge of the bomb scene, while

New York thought Washington had put me in charge. In fact, when it came right down to it, in the middle of all the confusion I stood up on a chair and shouted, 'Listen up everybody. My name is Dave Williams and I'm in charge here. From this point on the FBI laboratory is coordinating this crime scene investigation. . . .' Everybody went to work and we never had another problem.

"People have asked me how I felt. Incredibly excited, obviously. And nervous. But I couldn't let anyone know I had some doubts. I'd been taught that if I looked or acted overwhelmed people would question my capabilities. So I maintained my composure.

"The first thing I needed to know was when I could get people in there to try to find the bomb, so I had the structural engineers do a damage assessment. The World Trade Center was not in imminent danger of collapsing from the bomb damage, but it was endangered for other reasons. The twin towers and the twenty-two-story Vista Hotel rest on twenty-four-inch steel columns spaced about twenty-five feet apart. These columns were held in place by the one-foot-thick reinforced-concrete floors on each of the five levels of the garage. Well, those concrete floors weren't there anymore. Now we had a one-hundred-fifty-foot-wide, seventy-foot-deep crater cutting through five stories of the building. And just to complicate matters, we had a snowstorm with high-velocity winds. Those columns were swaying back and forth freely. They were dancing, and their lateral movement was seriously weakening the massive concrete foundation, the wall that kept the groundwater from the nearby Hudson River out of the basement. By Tuesday morning that foundation was close to failing, and if it had we would have had the Hudson River in the basement. In my opinion, if that had happened Tower One would have been on the ground by Wednesday. The structural people prevented that from happening by installing wind-shear braces on the columns to hold them in place. It took about a day and a half before it was even relatively safe to get in there and start looking to see what we had.

"We began by looking for residues that would enable us to determine what type of explosive was used. We had people hanging from cranes taking swabbings off the walls, for example, because this can be very important. If we were looking at C4, a plastic explosive, for example, someone would have had to obtain a tremendous quantity of it to cause this amount of damage so we'd look for thefts of government supplies.

"The problem was that we didn't find any residues. What we did find was an unusually high percentage of nitric acid and urea. Eventually we found out that the explosive was a mixture called urea nitrate, a home-made explosive. In more than seventy thousand bombings or attempted bombings worldwide since 1971, the only other time we'd seen it used was in Rockville, Maryland, in 1988. Four college students were making a pipe bomb and it had exploded, killing all of them. What made it difficult is that the explosion breaks down urea nitrate into urea and nitric acid, both of which are very common in nature and could have come from anywhere. We didn't have any means of proving it had been used as the explosive.

"Looking at the way the damage was spread out, the force hadn't been directed right or left or up or down. That meant the explosive was probably just laid in some large container. When you have a homemade explosion like that and it's got some fluid on it, it's pretty sloppy, so we assumed it had been in a cardboard or wooden box or in some type of trash can. In fact, several trash cans would have been needed to carry that quantity of explosive.

"So now we were looking for a vehicle large enough to hold several trash cans. An attorney asked me how we could prove the bomb had been inside a specific vehicle. I told him that if you blow up a balloon until it bursts, the spit is going to be found on the inside. It's that simple."

Identifying the vehicle in which the explosive device has been carried had provided significant clues in many previous car bombings. When terrorists destroyed the Marine Corps barracks in Beirut, Lebanon, in 1983, killing 241 Marines and fourteen civilians, investigators traced the truck that had carried the bomb back to a small faction of Shiite Muslims.

"We were especially worried about pockets of gas those first few days," Williams continued, "so we had strict orders that everyone working in the crater must maintain visual contact with other people at all times. That way if somebody got into trouble we could get help to them. Early Monday morning, while chemists were taking swabbings to try to identify explosive residue, Joe Hanlin of the Bureau of Alcohol, Tobacco and Firearms, and Don Sadowy of the NYPD bomb squad found a large piece of a vehicle that either had been carrying the bomb or was very close to the blast. That was obvious from the particular type of damage. It was a big piece of the rear frame rail that probably weighed close to three hundred pounds. They put it on a gurney and carried it out. I was furious. When I saw them bringing it out, I started chewing their tail for leaving the chemists in the crater.

"It was the first piece that got us in contact with the bomb. I wasn't happy about the way they'd brought it out, but just by looking at it you could tell it had been very close to the explosion and was going to be very valuable to us. Finding that piece so quickly was the kind of luck that comes with experience, but without that kind of luck you're going nowhere."

Every vehicle has a VIN, a vehicle identification number, which the manufacturer stamps into the metal at the plant. The VIN numerically describes that particular vehicle. It's the vehicle's birth certificate. It's always in plain sight on the dashboard, but every vehicle also has a confidential VIN, or C-VIN. It's the same number, but it's stamped in three other places; for security purposes those places differ from vehicle to vehicle. The reason is that if you steal a car, you'd have to dismantle it to find those numbers. And just by luck, the piece that was carried out of the crater had a clearly visible C-VIN. An NYPD detective cleaned off the soot with a toothbrush and added some fingerprint powder, and the number came right up.

That number was immediately put into the National Criminal Intelligence Center computer—NCIC is the national clearinghouse for criminal information—and it popped right up. It was identified as a Ford Econoline van owned by the Ryder Rental Agency. It had been rented in Jersey City by a man named Mohammed Salameh and had been reported stolen the day before the bombing.

"I don't think anybody was surprised to discover that the van had been stolen," Williams explained, "but what did surprise us was the name of the person who'd rented it. Mohammed Salameh was known to the New York office of the FBI. He was someone they'd been interested in for a long time. So when his name came up on the computer, there was instant recognition. This wasn't a coincidence.

"Salameh had contacted Ryder to get his four-hundred-dollar deposit back. People have wondered why he'd risk coming back for only four hundred dollars. My personal opinion is that these people intended to knock down the tower. And, not knowing any better, they believed the van would be totally destroyed in the explosion. They certainly didn't know we could identify it. So we had agents waiting for Salameh when he showed up at the Ryder office. At first we were going to follow him, hoping he might contact the people he was working with, but reporters got wind of this and descended on the scene. Fearing that all this activity might scare Salameh away, the decision was made to grab him while we had the chance. I was conducting our nightly meeting at the bomb scene when I got a phone call and was told that an arrest had been made. I guess I was stunned. It was a tremendous feeling—but now we had to prove that he'd done it."

The most difficult aspect of any investigation is identifying a suspect. Once Salameh was arrested, the Bureau began applying all the other techniques used to connect an individual to a crime. Because it was Williams's responsibility to coordinate all evidence for the lab, he stayed involved throughout the entire investigation.

Salameh's personal records, phone bills and things like that, led agents to Nidal Ayyad and Mahmud Abouhalima, who'd helped him buy the chemicals and make the bomb. When the details of the arrest were made public, the owner of a Jersey City storage facility contacted the Newark FBI office and said that the day before the bombing he'd seen four men loading a Ryder van. He'd checked their storage space and discovered a whole lot of chemicals. At the site investigators found about three hundred pounds of urea, 250 pounds of sulfuric acid, about a dozen bottles of nitric acid, two fifty-foot lengths of hobby fuse, a pump, a light blue Rubbermaid thirty-two-gallon trash can, and six two-quart bottles of a substance that looked a little like onion soup, but turned out to be homemade nitroglycerin. Sitting in that storage area was everything needed to make another three-hundred-plus-pound bomb.

"What was incredible is that homemade nitroglycerin becomes unstable under seventy degrees Fahrenheit," Williams explained, "and this stuff had been stored in an unheated area all winter. Let's say that when we moved it out of there our pucker factor went way up.

"The hobby fuse told us we were looking at a nonelectric burning-type detonating system, meaning they just lit it and got out of there. I'd estimate it had been about a twenty-minute delay.

"Eventually we found pamphlets and a videotape describing exactly how to make urea nitrate and we were able to connect that material to a fourth suspect, Ahmad Ajaj. Urea nitrate is pretty stable. It passes the Coyote test, which is named after Wile E. Coyote from the Road Runner cartoons. You put stuff in a cardboard box and jump on it. If it doesn't blow you up, it passes the test.

"We located the lab where they'd mixed this thing. It was in an apartment in a wooden building in Jersey City. In one room we found acid burns on the rug and it looked like they'd had an acid reaction which had splattered on the ceiling. We also found some nitroglycerin on the floor. These people were definitely not experts. I'm firmly convinced that if these guys hadn't planted the bomb when they did, they would have ended up all over Jersey City in a lot of little pieces."

Records found in Ayyad's house showed he had purchased three tanks of hydrogen from AGL Welding Supply in Clifton, New Jersey. In an explosion, hydrogen acts as an accelerant. The remains of three hydrogen tanks with "AGL Welding" stamped on their sides were found in the debris. The Materials Analysis Unit showed that specks of blue plastic found on the remains of a rear post from the van were consistent with the blue trash can found in the storage area. The evidence was piling up.

"After the bombing, a letter was received at *The New York Times* from a group calling itself the Fifth Liberation Brigade, claiming responsibility for the destruction of the World Trade Center and threatening other attacks," Williams continued. "When we arrested Ayyad his computer was removed from his desk at the Allied-Signal Company. Our Computer Analysis Response Team was able to retrieve material from the computer's hard drive. In files that Ayyad had tried to delete, they found words from that letter verbatim, proving it had been written on that computer.

"The letter had been mailed in a gummed, stamped envelope. Our DNA Unit was able to develop a DNA profile from the saliva used to seal the envelope. I took saliva samples from the four suspects; you just swab the inside of their cheeks to get some cells. Their attorneys told them exactly what we were doing, and compared to the other suspects, when I touched Ayyad's mouth it was as dry as cotton, which is what happens when someone is extremely nervous. There was no question in my mind that the DNA test would confirm that Ayyad's saliva was on the envelope flap. That's what happened, proving he'd written and mailed the letter. The evidence against these four men was overwhelming. Each of them was sentenced to two hundred and forty years in prison.

"For me, it really was the case of a lifetime. Or at least until the next case of my lifetime comes up. In looking at the deaths and injuries and the damage, I won't say this was fun, but it was incredibly fascinating. It was exactly what I'd spent my career training to do. For weeks we were running on adrenaline, we were working twenty-three hours a day and the other hour I was too excited to sleep. And when we started making those arrests . . . oh, what a wondrous feeling that was."

A bomb is made to do one thing only: explode. It functions only once and it is successful only if it destroys itself. A bomb can never be tested so sometimes, fortunately, it malfunctions. In the entire world of sci-crime, a world completely dependent on the immutable laws of science, this is the one place where fate makes a difference. "We've seen all kinds of things in here that we can't explain," unit chief Ronay said, "so we just accept it thankfully and remember it. In the early 1980s, for example, a terrorist group called the United Freedom Front was responsible for bombing the Capitol building, as well as several buildings in New York City, among them the IBM building. We found one of their bombs consisting of five cartridges of dynamite in a briefcase in the Honeywell building in East Rutherford, New Jersey. It just hadn't gone off and there's no one who can tell you why. Maybe there was a bad contact on the timer, maybe a loose connection; when you look at it there's no reason it didn't explode. We don't do a lot of experimentation. We make a bomb safe by tearing it apart, and once that's been done it's almost impossible to figure out why it didn't work."

The history of the Explosives Unit is replete with stories of bombs that didn't go off. When President George Bush was visiting Tokyo, a small bomb was found on the grounds of the American embassy in a building overlooking the President's helicopter landing pad. This bomb used a windup clock as a timer—and the hands of the clock had stopped just a sixteenth of an inch from completing the circuit and detonating the bomb. There was no apparent reason for it to have stopped. Maybe it hadn't been wound enough, maybe it had been overwound, perhaps it was just fate, but it simply stopped, the width of an eyelash away from going off.

In the late 1970s and early 1980s, a series of powerful bombs were planted in Puerto Rico. Some of them went off, but others that seemed to be identical did not. These bombs used a pocket watch as a timer. Watches and clocks are easy to convert to timers. Two wires are attached to the clock, one to a moving hand, the other to a pin or screw stuck in the face at the precise instant the bomb maker wants his device to go off. One of these wires is connected to the power source, the other to the detonator. When the moving hand makes contact with the metal pin the circuit is completed, the current can go from the power source to the initiator, and the bomb goes off. In the Puerto Rican bombs that did not explode, the hour hand seemed to be making contact with a metal screw. As far as experts could determine, the only thing that prevented those bombs from detonating was a thin layer of black paint on the side of the hour hand, perhaps a thousandth of an inch thick, that had acted as an insulator. Apparently the battery wasn't powerful enough to overcome the resistance in the paint, and many lives were saved by that thousandth of an inch.

Sometimes a bomb maker's mistake prevents the device from detonating. One morning a Missouri state trooper working undercover in a narcotics investigation went out to his car and found a hose leading from his gas tank to a can. Believing someone had tried to siphon gas, he picked up the can to throw it away. As he did, the top of the can came off, exposing almost a thousand feet of detonating cord—a high explosive that looks something like clothesline—four batteries, four detonators, and four clothespins. When he had lifted the top of the can, the clothespins had snapped closed, which should have completed the circuit and caused the bomb to go off. But it didn't. The examiners discovered why. The bomb maker had incorrectly wired his device; it was in series rather than in parallel, and thus there simply wasn't a strong enough current to cause the detonator to explode.

In 1984 a cleaning attendant found an unclaimed bag on a Pan Am jumbo jet that had just landed in Rio. Inside the bag was a bomb, which was later proved to have been made by Abu Ibrahim of the terrorist May Fifteenth Organization. The plastic explosive PETN had been molded into strips thin enough to fit beneath a seat cushion. When a passenger sat down, a pressure-sensitive switch initiated a time delay, which should have eventually detonated the PETN. The best guess was that this one had been flying around the world on this airplane for at least a week, and had survived several hard landings without detonating. Other bombs made by Ibrahim had functioned perfectly. But whoever had planted this one had unknowingly broken off a small piece of plastic from the arming switch, which had gotten jammed inside the bomb and prevented the circuit from closing. Just a tiny piece of plastic, but it was lodged in the bomb and probably saved many lives.

In 1974 an extortionist who had toppled three power transmission towers and damaged eight others with bombs in the Pacific Northwest was threatening to black out a four-state area unless he was paid a million dollars. He planted his bombs in remote areas serviced only by helicopter and used a novel time-delay system, designed to give him plenty of time to backpack out of the region before his bombs went off. His homemade timer was a half-gallon can filled with water. His two wires, one connected to the power source and the other to the detonator, were jabbed through the bottom of the can, and a sheet of tinfoil floated on the water. He punched a tiny hole in the can, causing it to slowly drain. As the water leaked out, the foil descended until it made contact with both wires, becoming a bridge between them, completing the circuit and detonating the bomb. This time he had overlooked one thing: the weather in the Pacific Northwest. The water in the can froze, and the bomb sat for several weeks until it was discovered.

For investigators, getting a bomb intact is like finding the Holy Grail, only more valuable. The fact that bombs are so easy to make, and that there are an infinite number of ways to make them, means that each one is unique. As Dave Williams pointed out, "Fusing systems and explosive devices are limited by three things: the imagination of the bomber, his finances, and his skill." Even if given exactly the same components, two men—bomb makers are almost exclusively male—will not make the same bomb. Bomb makers develop their own style, their own technique. They like to use a certain explosive and a certain detonating system and a certain type of time delay or power source. For some bomb makers, making a bomb is an art form, and their productions, like those of great artists, bear their unmistakable handiwork. Their signature. No matter what subject van Gogh painted, his style was unique and identifiable. But the same was true of Mohammed Rashid, who made his bombs for a terrorist group, and Leroy Moody, who murdered two people with his letter bombs, and the killer known as Unabomber, whose deadly craftsmanship has plagued law enforcement for more than a decade.

"For most of my career I never used the word 'signature,'" Fred Smith remembered. "But as time moved on, I realized there truly are signatures in bomb making. If I learn one technique, that's all I know. I may make the most reliable bomb in the world, but I only know how to make it one way. Well, when a bomb has four or eight, whatever, points of construction that are the same as other bombs, it's appropriate to conclude that the same person made all those bombs or that they were made by someone following his instructions. To me, that's a signature."

The lab introduced the concept that bombs could be linked by a signature in the early 1980s, and after initial resistance the courts have accepted signatures as evidence. A signature can be the construction, the design of the circuitry, the materials used, including the explosive, even the method used to deliver the bomb. In an extremely controversial case, President Clinton ordered an air attack on Iraq after a bomb found during former President Bush's visit to Kuwait was identified by its signature as having been made in Iraq. It was a large bomb, eighty pounds of explosives, and it was hidden in the false bottom of a vehicle, between the gas tank and the floorboard. It was connected to three types of initiation systems; one was radio-controlled, so it could be detonated from a distance; the second was a time delay; and the third was a suicide switch. This was a serious attempt on the life of the former president. Intelligence agents learned about the bomb before it could be detonated, and even with that information the vehicle had to be searched three times before the device was finally discovered.

The signature was found in the modifications to the circuit board. The method used to add and remove wires, the locations and skill used to solder the controls, and the type of insulation were identical to other bombs that had been positively identified as having been made in Iraq. After the air attack on Iraqi targets, reporters questioned the evidence that had caused this bomb to be attributed to Iraq, but members of the Explosives Unit felt quite confident in their conclusion that it had been made by the same people who made other Iraqi bombs.

While in that case the signature enabled investigators to link two bombs to a common source, in some instances a signature can be used to specifically identify the bomb maker. In the VANPAC case, for example, it led authorities directly to Leroy Moody. In a 1992 case, the lab received reports about a bank-robbery team operating in seven states. After bypassing the alarm system, the robbers would flood the top of the vault with water, then put a small amount of nitroglycerin in a condom or balloon and blow open the safe. If the money started burning, the water would extinguish the fire. As Paul Schrecker, who joined the lab in 1972 as a clerk and later worked there nine years as a firearms examiner before transferring to Explosives in 1986, explained, "We looked at this description of the evidence and we knew we'd seen it before. It went back to a case we had in the late seventies. It's pretty unusual for two people working completely independently to come up with the concept of putting nitro in a condom and using water to prevent a fire. So we did some research and found out that several suspects had served time in prison with the people responsible for the earlier bombings. Obviously they'd shared the technology in prison. That certainly told us we had the right people, and helped us make the case."

Perhaps because bomb makers operate internationally, agents in the Explosives Unit maintain closer contact with their counterparts around the world than any other lab unit does. They worked particularly closely with

Northern Ireland's explosives experts on matters involving the Provisional Irish Republican Army, PIRA, an organization that regularly placed bombs in public places as part of its political strategy and received substantial financial and technical support from sympathizers in the United States. In one major case solved through international cooperation, the FBI learned through correspondence from a known IRA member that a Boston resident named Richard Clark Johnson, a brilliant electronics engineer with a top-secret security clearance, was making highly complicated proximity fuses and triggering mechanisms for IRA bombs. "He had quite an operation going," Ronay said. "He was building very sophisticated devices for their homemade surface-to-air missiles and bombs. We were able to connect him to bombs found in Northern Ireland through his signature. You could lay down one of the circuit boards we found in his lab on Cape Cod right next to an unexploded bomb recovered in Northern Ireland, and anyone could see that the handiwork was exactly the same. He might just as well have signed these things 'Richard Clark Johnson.'" On the basis of this signature, in addition to other evidence found in his lab, Johnson and several of his associates were convicted of making bombs for the IRA.

Sometimes the components of the bomb become a signature. A tiny piece of gold-plated wire found in the body of a Japanese boy killed on a Pan Am flight to Honolulu turned out to be the big, bold signature of Abu Ibrahim. "It was part of the leg wire of an E-cell battery timing device," Tom Thurman explained. "At first it didn't mean too much to us, but when we started seeing other devices with the same type of wire, it became important. We determined that the May Fifteenth Organization used this type of timer to the exclusion of any other group. Eventually we were able to compare the damage to the Japanese boy's body and to his seat and the airplane to several similar bombings, particularly the 1986 bombing of a TWA flight from Rome to Athens in which four American citizens were sucked out of the airplane. We were able to show that these bombs were made virtually the same way, that they were the same size and had been placed in precisely the same manner. More than twenty bombs were traced to this organization from the signature, and when we caught the individual who had planted them, Mohammed Rashid, we were able to successfully prosecute him."

The explosive substance can be the signature. There are thousands of substances that will explode when "hit" by the proper detonator, and any of them can be used in a bomb. "We have a program in which we'll analyze any foreign explosive sample submitted to us," Paul Schrecker said. "Different groups use different explosives. If it's a plastic explosive, for example, we'll analyze the nonexplosive component. What type of plasticizers are in there? What kind of oils? What kind of dyes? Semtex consists of eighty-six percent RDX and PETN, but the ratio of those two explosives has gone all over the map. Finding the same ratio of RDX to PETN in a Semtex sample enables us to determine if we've seen that particular explosive before. It's that much of a signature. We can say that a sample recovered in Germany matches a cache found in Northern Ireland and start working backwards. It's a big step toward identifying the source of the bomb."

Finally, the damage done by the bomb is a punctuation mark in the bomb maker's signature. The fact that explosive damage can be recreated is extremely useful. For example, when the body of a somewhat shady show-business entrepreneur named Roy Radin was found decaying in the Mojave Desert with his face blown off and eight holes in the back of his skull, a coroner ruled he had been shot in the back of the head with a shotgun. But an informer claimed that Radin had been shot with a smaller gun, and that an M-80, a small firecracker-like explosive, had been put in his mouth and detonated, causing the damage. To verify the informer's story the Explosives Unit constructed a twenty-five-pound head of clay and tried to duplicate the damage. The first M-80 was placed in what would have been the mouth cavity; it blew apart the entire clay head. The second charge was laid across the lip area—and it came very close to duplicating the damage done to Radin's head. It was enough to support the story told by the informer, which gave substantial weight to the rest of his testimony.

When a man named Michael Townley became a suspect in the bombing-murder of Orlando Letelier in Washington, D.C., he readily confessed that he had worked with Cuban operatives in making and placing the bomb under a contract with the Chilean government. Authorities believe he confessed to save his life, knowing he would have become a target if the people who had hired him knew he was under suspicion. Whatever his reasons, he provided authorities with strong evidence. His confession sounded almost too good to be true, so he had to prove he had made the bomb.

"We had to convince a jury that he was telling the truth," according to Ronay. "So we went out and got an identical car, except for the color, and had Townley build us a bomb. He assembled it and showed us where to put it on the car. We followed all his instructions and blew up the car. The results were incredible. The damage was exactly the same, exactly, something that even the best bomb maker in the world couldn't do on the first attempt unless he knew exactly how the bomb had been made and where it had been placed. This demonstration proved Townley's credibility to the jury. There just couldn't be any doubt about it, he'd built the bomb that had killed Letelier."

While explosives used responsibly can be a valuable tool, a bomb is simply a weapon, and is often used like any other weapon in the commission of a crime. Bombs are used in robberies and extortions and to commit murder. And sometimes the bomb maker is identified through traditional methods of crime solving.

"Our intent is to collect $1,000,000 or make you wish we had," wrote "J. Hawker," who was threatening to blow up the Portland, Oregon, power transmission system with his dripping-water-can bombs unless that ransom was paid. The bomb was the weapon, but the crime was extortion, and "Hawker" had to make arrangements to pick up his ransom payment. He created an elaborate communications scheme in which he issued instructions about the money drop over a citizens band radio frequency. He responded to questions by tooting on a birdcall: once for yes, twice for no. During his transmission FBI agents triangulated his location using direction-finding equipment—and found themselves driving behind a car being driven by a man with a radio in one hand and a duck call in his mouth. David Heesch was arrested, and in his refrigerator agents found copies of the threat letters. Asked by the judge during his trial about his intent, Heesch replied, bluntly, "To extort a million dollars." He was sentenced to twenty years in prison.

The threat of a bomb is every bit as effective as a real bomb during a robbery, and hoax bombs, devices built to look like real bombs, are often used in holdups. For investigative purposes these bombs, which can be very sophisticated, are treated exactly the same as real weapons, and can be traced through their signatures and components.

Bombs are used to kill for the same reasons any other weapon would be used: for vengeance, for passion, and for money. But a bomb offers the killer the advantage of being far from the scene when the murder is done. Jack Gilbert Graham coldly killed his mother and forty-three other people to collect her insurance policies and a sizable inheritance. Twelve years later, in 1967, and for the same reason, Earl Cooke put a bomb aboard an American Airlines flight on which his wife was a passenger. Although Cooke's bomb went off in the baggage compartment, it did only minimal damage. Cooke became a suspect when charred luggage tags were found to have come from the suitcase in which the bomb had been hidden. The bomb consisted of two sticks of dynamite to be detonated by four blasting caps. The timer was an alarm clock; when the alarm rang a metal hammer would hit a bell and complete the circuit, causing the bomb to go off. Toolmarks convicted Cooke. Agent-examiner Charles Killion was able to positively identify marks found on the alarm-clock bell as having been made by the jaws of a vise in Cooke's workshop. Added to other evidence, this led to Cooke's conviction and a sentence of two concurrent twenty-year terms.

A year later Sam Hammons, a NASA employee with a top-secret clearance, was killed by a package bomb sent to his Avon, Ohio, home. In Hammons's office FBI agents found letters written to him from a woman he had known in high school, and with whom he had recently became reacquainted. Agents were intrigued by this relationship when they discovered that the briefcase in which the bomb was mailed had been purchased not far from her home. Surprisingly, though, it hadn't been bought by this woman but by her boss, a man named Albert Ricci. The evidence against Ricci quickly piled up. He had been on vacation near Salt Lake City, Utah, the day the bomb was mailed from there. He had purchased parts of the bomb in a local hardware store and had persuaded a friend to get him eight sticks of dynamite. The motive was passion: Ricci was infatuated with his secretary, Hammons's high school friend, and his insane jealousy caused him to murder his supposed rival, an innocent man who didn't even know he existed. Before Ricci could be arrested, he drove his car into a deep pond and died.

In a bizarre 1993 San Francisco case, two male lovers tried to kill the third member of their love triangle, the estranged wife of one of the men, because she would get a sizable portion of the couple's $3 million estate in their divorce. The men sent her a lovely bouquet of flowers—with a pipe bomb planted in it. The woman and a co-worker were seriously injured, but survived. When police looked for a motive, they uncovered the love triangle, and the woman's husband and his lover became suspects. Doug Deedrick of the Hairs and Fiber Unit was able to match pieces of dried flower found on the floorboard of one of the men's cars with bits of the bouquet. A toolmarks exam proved that the nails used in the bomb had been fabricated on the same machine and within a few minutes as nails found in the apartment of one of the suspects. And smokeless powder that could be associated with the victim's husband was identical to the explosive used in the bomb. One of the men was convicted of delivering the bomb, but not making it. The victim's husband remained under investigation.

Perhaps the most complex bomb ever encountered by the Explosives Unit was the massive thousand-pound steel box used in an attempt to extort $3 million from Harvey's Wagon Wheel Resort Hotel in Lake Tahoe, Nevada. It was the kind of bomb usually seen in movies, a seemingly impregnable box made by a mad genius, ticking down the hours until a ransom was paid or it was detonated.

The device was wheeled into the casino in 1980, hidden under a cover with "IBM" stenciled on it to make it appear to be a business machine. Once it was in place on the second floor, the bomb was armed and an extortion note was left: "This bomb is so sensitive that the slightest movement either inside or outside will cause it to explode," read the note. "This bomb can never be dismantled or disarmed without causing an explosion. Not even by the creator."

"He was certainly right about that," admitted Chris Ronay, who supervised the case in the lab. "This was quite a bomb. It had twenty-eight toggle switches and it was designed so that if two specific switches were put in the correct position it could be moved. Supposedly when the ransom was paid, the bomb maker would tell us which two switches would make it safe, not that anyone would have dared move it, even with those instructions.

"It had eight different triggering mechanisms, each one designed to prevent us from using traditional methods to disarm the bomb. In the movies you see people disarming a bomb by cutting a wire or putting it in a bucket of water. You never cut wires. A lot of bombs have shunts so that if a wire is cut the bomb will go off; if anything, you might try to short-circuit it. And if you put a bomb in a bucket of water you're likely to be hit with sharp fragments of that bucket when the bomb goes off. To disarm a bomb you need to separate the power source from the detonator; if it doesn't have power it isn't going to go off. And that can be done in several different ways.

"In this case we started by X-raying the bomb. We thought we might be able to disrupt the wiring, but it was like spaghetti in there. The bomb maker had put in all kinds of relays and switches to confuse us, and it was impossible to trace the wires from the battery to the blasting cap. We couldn't move the bomb because he'd also put in a motion detector, a PVC tube lined with tinfoil that had a pendulum consisting of a piece of wire weighted with a nut and bolt. If we moved or shook or jolted the bomb in any way, the nut would hit the foil, completing the circuit. Sometimes you can disarm a bomb by filling it with liquid nitrogen foam, which freezes the parts and prevents them from moving. This bomb had a tinfoil membrane around the inside, so if you cut into it with a drill, the bit would make contact with the casing and the foil, completing the circuit and . . . He also had a toilet plunger in there, so if we filled the container with foam, the plunger would have been lifted, activating a switch that would detonate the bomb. And he had three different timers operated by the toggle switches.

"You can also render safe a bomb by shooting it with an explosive charge, a bullet, a high-impact water cannon, or anything that takes out the battery. That may cause the device to start functioning, but any initiator has to have a certain amount of current for a certain duration. If you're quick enough, it may start to get current, but you can disrupt it before it reaches full current. In this case the detonator was inside a smaller box sitting on top of the bomb. What we finally decided to try to do was disarm the bomb by taking out the detonator with a seven-pound shaped charge of C4. Pressure waves move off an explosive at right angles, so by shaping the charge you can actually aim the force of the explosion. We hoped we could rip off the top of the bomb faster than the current could get to the explosive. We knew it was a big gamble, but we really had no choice. There was no way of moving that thing."

Meanwhile, during the thirty hours that all this was going on, the other casinos in town were taking bets on what hour the bomb would explode. At the same time agents were trying to make arrangements to pay the ransom. The agents were told to fly over an area in a helicopter and land when they spotted a strobe light. They never saw the light. As it turned out, the extortionists had left the battery for the strobe light home and couldn't signal, so the drop was missed the first night. They stole a battery for the second night, but the helicopter flew over a different area. So the drop was never completed.

"In theory, the method we chose to disarm that bomb should have worked," Ronay said. "In reality, it toppled the bomb over and a thousand pounds of dynamite blew out the inside of Harvey's Casino. In this business, lives come first, then property. Disarming the bomb in place was the most reasonable approach toward risking the minimum number of people. The bomb blew a five-story cavity into the building, and I remember looking up and seeing bathtubs and TVs dangling in midair, but not one person was hurt. When the bomb went off, any plans we had to pay the ransom were abandoned, and the extortionists disappeared.

"We began our investigation by trying to trace pieces of the bomb. We found the manufacturer of the casters and tried to trace their customers. We looked for someone who'd recently sold twenty-eight or more toggle switches. The bomb was coated with four layers of paint; we looked for a common source. We went through the bomb piece by piece, looking for that one object that would put us on the track. And we didn't get anywhere.

"FBI agents and local police went to every motel within about a hundred miles, asking about guests who had been driving a vehicle large enough to transport the bomb. A reward was offered, and authorities finally got a tip from an individual who was friendly with the former girlfriend of a man named John Birges, Sr. According to this man, Birges's former girlfriend claimed he had been talking about the bombing. Police started looking for other evidence that might implicate Birges, and bits and pieces began coming together. One of Birges's two sons had gotten a speeding ticket in the Lake Tahoe area at the time of the bombing. Birges's girlfriend had been involved in a minor traffic accident and had been taken to the hospital. Finally, Birges's sons were subpoenaed by a grand jury and under oath denied having been near Harvey's when it was bombed. Confronted with evidence, they claimed they were scouting for fields in which to plant marijuana. When they were indicted for perjury and threatened with prison, they rolled over. They confessed and agreed to testify against their father in exchange for immunity from prosecution. John Birges, Jr., established his credibility as a witness when he correctly identified the two switches that would have disabled the motion detector.

"When I testified at the trial," Ronay recalled, "the senior Birges couldn't resist asking me if I wanted to know how the bomb could have been disarmed. Of course I did. He took out an automobile headlight with two alligator clips attached to it and told me how to hook it up to the full scale mock-up of the bomb we'd made for the trial. I did, the light went on, and he asked, 'If you leave it there for a long time, what'll happen?'

" 'Eventually it'll drain the battery and make it useless,' I said. 'Theoretically, that would disable the bomb.'

"I didn't want to get into a discussion with him, but even after the battery had lost power there were ways that bomb could've been detonated. For a man that intelligent, he was very simplistic in his approach to disarming it. But he had made some bomb. Birges was sentenced to two twenty-year terms without parole. And Harvey's? They rebuilt the whole place. It's bigger than it was before the bombing."

In most cases people make one bomb to achieve one purpose; they're amateurs and they make mistakes. But just as there are serial killers and serial rapists, there are serial bombers, individuals who make and place many bombs over a long period of time. They are professionals, they are very good at their work, and they are very difficult to catch. One bomb maker, known to the Bureau by his Major Case name, Unabomber, has killed two people and injured at least twenty-three with letter bombs since 1978.

In 1979 an explosive device aboard an American Airlines flight from Chicago to Washington went off and caused a small fire in the baggage compartment. Chris Ronay and the case agent, Tom Barrett, were intrigued by the unique improvised detonator and began showing it to other people in the explosives world. They found two similar devices that had been detonated within the past eighteen months that made it clear they were dealing with a serial bomber. Named Unabomber because the targets of his first bombs were university professors and airlines—more recently his letter bombs have also been sent to individuals associated with scientific and computer research as well as airline production—this bomber makes almost every component of his bombs. He makes his own boxes and hinges, his own endcaps and pipes and switches. He files down wire to make nails, and files away screws to eliminate toolmarks. He carves parts out of wood and uses old lamp cord for his wiring, and he has used several different types of powder in each bomb, possibly so he doesn't have to obtain his explosive from one source which might attract attention. In many of the bombs the initials "FC" have been stamped into a piece of metal. Officials believe "FC" stands for an obscene phrase used to belittle computers. This craftsmanship has become his signature. In December 1994, his most powerful device, about the size of a VCR cassette, killed advertising executive

Thomas Mosser when he opened it in the kitchen of his New Jersey home.

In many cases bomb makers claim credit for their work, or at least reveal a motive. With the exception of a single letter received by *The New York Times* that is believed to have been written by Unabomber, he has remained silent about his motive. In 1987 he was seen in Salt Lake City placing the bomb that resulted in his first killing, and law enforcement officals describe him as white male, about six feet tall, in his late thirties or early forties, with a medium build, ruddy complexion, and reddish-blond hair. The best clue was found with one of his bombs in June 1993; in indented writing, an impression made in paper by writing on a top sheet, the lab discovered a message reading, "Call Nathan R—Wed. 7 pm." Treasury Department investigators, admitting they are no closer to catching Unabomber than they were in 1978, have offered a million-dollar reward for information leading to the bomber. One additional intriguing bit of information: there were no bombings between 1987 and 1993. This leads investigators to suspect that Unabomber was in some sort of institution at the time, most probably a prison.

Not all bombers are as difficult to catch as Unabomber. Donald "Pee Wee" Gaskins, for example, who claimed to have killed as many as sixteen people, was on death row in South Carolina. The prisoner in the cell next to his, Rudolph Tyner, had killed several members of a South Carolina family, and friends of the victims were irate that he might live there indefinitely as his appeals moved through the legal system. Somehow they managed to smuggle bomb components, including high explosives, to Gaskins, who constructed a crude radio bomb. He strung a wire from his cell into the ventilation duct. The radio bomb was delivered to the killer in the next cell, who was told to open the vent, where he would find a wire, and hook it up to the radio, which would enable him to speak to Gaskins. He did just that, and when he put the radio to his ear, Gaskins blew him up.

The entire investigation was about three feet long, the distance between the two cells. Although previously sentenced to ten life sentences, for this murder Gaskins was executed by the state of South Carolina in 1991.

CHAPTER
– 4 –

Threads of Evidence:
The Hairs and Fiber Unit

U.S. ATTORNEY: *In addition to Mr. Camarena's blood and hair type, did you find at the crime scene any other hair that matches anyone else in this courtroom?*
FBI LABORATORY TECHNICIAN: *Yes, sir, we found hair that matches samples labeled as coming from Mr. Verona in the bathroom of the Lope de Vega house, from the rear bedroom where Mr. Camarena was held. . . . These were recovered from drains into the main sewer line.*

CBS-TV EMMY AWARD–WINNING MINI-SERIES,
Drug Wars: The Kiki Camarena Story

Look at the shirt or blouse or sweater you are wearing. Somewhere on this garment you are probably going to find some hairs—perhaps your own, perhaps someone else's—and some very small fibers. Grasp one of those hairs or fibers in your hand. It isn't very big; it weighs almost nothing. You didn't even know it was there. But in that hair or fiber there exists a world of information about you and about your life. Given samples for comparative purposes, it would be possible to determine through those few hairs and fibers how you have spent this day: where you have been, how you got there, whom you saw, what you did.

For some people, for some very unlucky people—DEA agent Kiki Camarena, who was tortured and murdered in a Mexican hacienda; five-year-old Melissa Brannen, who disappeared from a Christmas party and was never seen again; Nathaniel Cater, who was murdered by Atlanta child-

96

killer Wayne Williams—a few hairs and fibers, exactly like those you are holding, allowed detectives to determine how they spent the last moments of their lives, and led directly to their killers.

Sherlock Holmes would have searched a crime scene with his magnifying lens and perhaps a fine-toothed comb. Today he would probably use a handheld vacuum cleaner adapted to trap hairs and fibers in a special filter, or he would "sweep" the area with wide transparent tape. The tiny bits of debris he collected might allow him to connect the victim to a place, to other victims, or to the killer.

A hair is simply a filament growing out of the skin of a mammal, while a fiber is the smallest unit of textile material. Thousands of tiny fibers are twisted together to make thread or yarn, which in turn is woven into fabric.

Hairs have been used to link criminals with their crimes for more than 150 years. As early as 1838, French and British investigators were using hairs found at crime scenes to try to link a suspect to the crime. The first known use of hairs as evidence in an American courtroom took place in Massachusetts in 1869, when hairs found stuck to the dried blood on the end of a club helped convict a man of beating his wife to death. Fiber evidence was rarely valuable to investigators before the 1950s because there was little variation among natural fibers and colors available at that time. But the post–World War II explosion of synthetic fibers finally made it possible for investigators to make strong connections between fibers found at a crime scene and fibers that could be linked to a suspect.

The use of hairs and fibers as evidence is based on the work done by French criminologist Dr. Edmond Locard, whose theory of transfer states that when a person comes into contact with another person or place, some human hairs or fibers are going to be transferred to that person and that environment. It also states that they are easily shed, so the hairs and fibers found on an individual will reflect the most recent contact or environment.

When a person is involved in a crime, there is a significant chance that he will leave some of his hairs and fibers at the crime scene and he will take with him some hairs and fibers from that place. The objective of the Hairs and Fiber Unit in the FBI's sci-crime lab is to link hairs and fibers from an unknown source to hairs and fibers from a known source, thereby proving a connection, and once that connection has been made, figuring out how that exchange took place.

Sometimes a single hair can be sufficient to link a killer to his victim. In a Jackson, Tennessee, case, an escaped convict killed the priest who caught him burglarizing a church rectory. He was captured a short time later and denied both the burglary and the murder. The Tennessee Bureau of Investigation sent his clothes to the Hairs and Fiber Unit to be examined. Although the suspect was black, several brown Caucasian hairs were found on his jacket. Hairs known to have come from the priest—the "K," as items from known sources are referred to in lab reports, matched the hairs from an unknown source, the "Q," which were found on the suspect's clothing. This proved the two men had been in contact. The suspect was convicted of murdering the priest and was sentenced to death.

That's the way it's supposed to work. But rarely is it that easy. Often there are so many factors complicating a case that the value of hairs and fibers as evidence depends almost entirely on the ingenuity of the examiner. Making hair and fiber comparisons is a learned skill, but figuring out how to use them is an art.

On December 3, 1989, five-year-old Melissa Brannen disappeared from a Christmas party in Fairfax, Virginia. She just vanished, seemingly without a trace. Police learned that a man named Cal Hughes had abruptly left the party at the same time the child disappeared, although no one had seen them together. When police arrived at Hughes's home about one o'clock in the morning, he was busy washing and drying all the clothes he had been wearing that night, including his shoes and belt. It was an odd thing to be doing, especially at that hour, and Hughes became a prime suspect.

Hughes denied having any contact with the little girl and gave police permission to search his car. Detectives swarmed over the car, dusting it for fingerprints, searching for bloodstains, confiscating the floor mats for further testing and carefully running pieces of transparent tape over the seats to pick up the thousands of tiny hairs and fibers collected there, searching for any evidence that Melissa Brannen had once been in that car. All the evidence was sent to the FBI lab, as were the clothes Hughes had been wearing that night, strands of hair from both Melissa Brannen and her mother (taken from their brushes), and articles of clothing worn recently by the child.

There are no shortcuts in hair and fiber examinations. Even the most sophisticated computers can't help. An experienced examiner looks at hundreds, sometimes thousands, of hairs and fibers under a microscope, maybe makes some notes, and tries to remember as much as possible. Then he begins making comparisons, trying to find two or more hairs or fibers found in different places that came from the same source. Depending on the ability of the examiner to make those comparisons, lives will be changed forever.

The agent-examiner assigned the Melissa Brannen case was Doug Deedrick, who had joined the lab in 1972 as a clerk and tour guide, becoming an agent in 1976 and a lab technician a year later. With his neatly combed graying hair, his glasses, and his white lab coat, Deedrick looks more like a scholarly university professor than one of the most respected investigators in the sci-crime business.

In most cases submitted to the sci-crime lab, the Hairs and Fiber Unit gets the evidence first. Because the minuscule hairs and fibers can easily be shed and lost, the evidence is taken into a scraping room—a temperature-controlled, humidity-controlled, sealed environment—and hung on a rack. A clean sheet of white paper is laid under the evidence and a technician then scrapes it with a metal spatula. Clothes are scraped both inside and out. Hairs and fibers that might be of value are mounted on slides to be looked at under a microscope by an agent-examiner. Certain fibers—white cotton, for instance—are so common that they are worthless for comparative purposes, so they are never collected. But everything else goes to the examiner.

Deedrick began his investigation by trying to compare samples of hair recovered from Melissa Brannen's hairbrush and previously worn clothing to hairs found on the front seat of Hughes's car. Because children's hair changes drastically over short periods of time, he was unable to make any good matches. But when he examined the little girl's nightshirt he found several short black hairs stuck in the fabric. "That was the first break in the case," Deedrick explained matter-of-factly. "One of the things you have to have when working these cases is good recall. You have to log in your mind everything that you've seen as best you can. These particular hairs caught my attention because I knew I'd seen them among the submissions taken from the suspect's car. They were easily identifiable: they were black rabbit hairs. And they could be positively compared with hairs found in the car. I didn't know where they came from, but I knew I had a link between the little girl and the suspect's car.

"An agent spoke with Mrs. Brannen, who told us that she had worn a dyed black rabbit coat to the party, and that Melissa had previously played with that coat at home. We got the coat, and I compared the hairs found on Melissa's nightshirt, the hairs found in the suspect's car, and the hairs from the coat. They were the same hairs. It could have been a coincidence, we'd found only two or three of those hairs in the car, but I don't believe in coincidence that much. I felt we'd made a positive link to the suspect. But it wasn't nearly enough to make a case."

The few rabbit hairs found on the front seat of Hughes's car provided a tantalizing clue, but a defense attorney could argue that Hughes had picked up those hairs by accidentally brushing against the little girl or her mother at the party, then shed them as he drove home.

Deedrick also found one hair, one slender hair, on the passenger-side floor mat that exhibited all the characteristics of hair found in Melissa's brush. All his experience told him that Hughes had been with that little girl, but he still didn't have enough evidence to make a case. To prove that Melissa Brannen had been in that car, Deedrick had to find a way of linking the clothes she was wearing when she disappeared to the debris recovered from the front seat—a seemingly impossible task when you don't have those clothes. As Deedrick explained, "You look at the questioned debris and see if you can find fibers that might have come from the clothes the victim was wearing. It's kind of experienced guesswork and it's a real long shot. But we didn't have too much else. Melissa's mother told us she was wearing an outfit with a blue sweater. In the tapings from the car I'd seen a number of blue synthetic fibers. So I decided to try to recreate the clothes she was wearing."

The Hairs and Fiber Unit works almost 2,500 cases a year. Murder is just another faceless crime, another pair of pants to be examined. There are just too many cases, too much violence for people working in the unit to become emotionally involved in every case. But violent crimes involving children get the full attention of the lab. Many of the agents and technicians working there have their own kids. Doug Deedrick has three little girls, one of them born the same year as Melissa Brannen. And the disappearance of Melissa three weeks before Christmas got special attention.

The night Melissa disappeared she had been wearing a Sesame Street outfit consisting of red tights, a red plaid skirt, and a blue acrylic sweater with a picture of Big Bird on it. The outfit had been given to Melissa by her grandmother, who couldn't remember where she had bought it. Deedrick discussed this case with his wife, who by pure luck had saved an old J. C. Penney catalogue that featured children's clothing. And in that catalogue Deedrick found an outfit consisting of red tights, a red plaid skirt, and a blue acrylic sweater with Big Bird's picture on it. Melissa's mother identified it as the outfit her daughter had been wearing. As things later turned out, the outfit had been manufactured exclusively for Penney's, and this catalogue was the only place it had been advertised or sold. If Deedrick's wife hadn't kept her old catalogue, this case might never have been solved.

Meanwhile Deedrick painstakingly examined clothing Melissa had worn within the previous year. And on a pink coat he found one blue acrylic fiber, just one, that he could positively associate with the fibers found in Hughes's car.

Penney's obtained an outfit from a customer in another state. "It arrived in the lab about five-thirty," Deedrick recalled without any emotion in his voice, "and I'll never forget that night. The sweater was actually purplish-blue. As soon as I looked at the fibers under the microscope, I knew we had a match. Without question they were the same fibers that we'd found in the car. We'd found a total of fifty acrylic fibers on the passenger seat and one on the driver's seat. We'd also found ten red cotton fibers that I matched to the red cotton in the skirt. There was no longer any doubt that Melissa Brannen had been in that car, but we still had to prove it to a jury."

There are more than a thousand manmade fibers currently being manufactured, and more than 7,000 different dye formulations. Manufacturers do not duplicate each other's dyes; dye formulas are closely guarded trade secrets. So the chances that two dyed synthetic fibers from different sources would match are statistically almost nil. Said Deedrick, "We had three things we needed: the transfer of the fiber from the victim to the suspect; the persistence of the fiber, meaning we'd found a lot of them; and, finally, the uniqueness of the fiber. What we still had to demonstrate was that these fibers were so unusual that realistically they couldn't have come from an unrelated source. We had to show that it was much more than an amazing coincidence that they had been found in Hughes's car, that these fibers were proof he had abducted Melissa Brannen and taken her somewhere in that car."

Deedrick conceived a dramatic way to illustrate to a jury how unlikely it would be that these fibers had come from any other source but Melissa's sweater. He asked his co-workers in the lab to bring in any blue acrylic clothing they owned. Eventually he received 107 garments, from caps to socks, and identified 126 different blue acrylic fibers. He made 7,938 comparisons—and could not make a single match. No two of those blue acrylic fibers from different sources could be matched either visually or instrumentally.

"We proved that Melissa Brannen had been sitting in the front seat of that car," Deedrick said, a note of satisfaction in his voice. "The fact that Cal Hughes had denied speaking to her and had denied being with her were statements he just couldn't overcome. Although we were never able to discover what had happened to the little girl, Hughes was convicted of abduction with intent to defile and received a fifty-year sentence."

Making a hair or fiber match is a skill that can't be learned from a textbook. "There's really only one way to learn it," explained Agent-examiner Mike Malone, who spent almost two decades in Hairs and Fibers, "and that is to do it and do it and do it. You look at thousands of hairs and fibers and eventually you begin to see patterns, you learn what to look for."

An individual being trained to conduct hair and fiber examinations will spend at least a year in the unit assisting experienced examiners. The on-the-job training is supplemented with some classroom work, extensive reading, and several moot court sessions. "The object of our work is to be able to testify in front of a jury that a known and an unknown item came from the same source, to be able to convince a jury that the comparison we've made has real meaning," according to Agent-examiner Wayne Oakes. "And who better to teach this than the people who have testified collectively in more than a thousand cases?"

To assist in identifications, the unit maintains several large collections, among them a hair collection that includes samples from every part of the body from every race of people, as well as from almost every animal and rodent. The largest hair in that collection, and the toughest, is from an elephant, and it's so thick it can barely be mounted on a slide. That sample proved valuable when people charged with illegally bringing elephant-hair bracelets into the country falsely claimed that the material in their possession was a plastic facsimile.

Perhaps the most unusual request for an animal-hair identification came from the Spokane, Washington, sheriff's office. A local farmer reported seeing Bigfoot, the legendary beast whose existence has never been proven, running across his field. According to the farmer's story, Bigfoot escaped by leaping over a barbed wire fence. When the sheriff's office investigated they found a tuft of unusual black hairs caught in the wire and sent them to the lab for identification. Was this proof of Bigfoot's existence? Only if Bigfoot is actually a black horse, which was where the hairs came from.

The unit also maintains an extensive fiber collection, which includes most common and many unique fibers as well as doll-hair fibers and human wig-hair fibers, one of the largest feather collections in the world, a large wood collection, and a rope and cord collection.

Hair and fiber identification is not an exact science. This just isn't the kind of evidence that allows examiners to testify that two hairs or two fibers came from the same source to the exclusion of all other possibilities. "It's not fingerprints," Wayne Oakes said. "It's extremely rare that we see hairs from two different people that are so close we can't tell them apart, so this is the basis of a strong association. We can't testify that two hairs came from the same person. What we can say is that two hairs or two fibers are consistent in every measurable way and that it is highly likely they came from the same source."

Still a lot of information can be learned from a single hair: whether the donor was an animal or a human, Caucasoid, Negroid, or Mongoloid; what part of the body it came from; whether it fell out naturally or was forcibly removed; even whether the donor suffered from certain diseases or drank too much or used certain drugs. It's even possible to determine how long ago the hair had been dyed or bleached. Surprisingly, it isn't possible to determine if a hair came from a man or a woman unless the root is attached, or the age of the donor. Only head hairs, pubic hairs, and facial hairs are suitable for comparative purposes, as there just isn't enough difference between your body hair and someone else's to make a good basis for comparison.

Fibers are never unique. There are just too many of them. So in most cases it's not as important to trace a fiber to a single garment as it is to show that fibers found in different places came from the same source. There are four types of fibers: naturally occurring animal fibers, such as wool; vegetable fibers, such as cotton; minerals, such as asbestos; and manmade fibers. Manmade fibers are used in the production of about 75 percent of all textiles. There are twenty-one generic classifications of manmade fibers, among them the six most people are familiar with: acetate, rayon, nylon, acrylic, polyester, and olefin.

Although hairs and fibers exist in abundance, every hair and every fiber exhibits a combination of characteristics that makes it different from most others, and those are what examiners look at when making comparisons. A hair, for example, has external features such as length, color, degree of curliness or straightness, texture, thickness, diameter of the shaft, shape and condition of the root, appearance of the tip, and whether it has been dyed or chemically altered in any way. Numerous internal characteristics are also used for comparative purposes, including the width of the medulla (the hollow core running down the center of a hair), the type and condition of the scales that make up the cuticle, or outer layers, and the size, shape, and density of the pigment, which gives hair its color.

A lot of foreign material, from dirt to lice, is also found on hairs, and that material will often enable examiners to connect a suspect to a crime. Doug Deedrick had a murder case in which a woman was kidnapped and shot in the head at close range. When he looked at several strands of her hair, he found a bluish material he couldn't identify. Whatever it was, it was something he hadn't seen before, and unusual enough to make a good basis for comparison. When police arrested a suspect they discovered a loaded semiautomatic weapon under the front seat of his car. The first round in that gun was an unusual type of ammunition called a glaser round, a bullet with a Teflon shell that disintegrates upon impact and releases several small pellets. It's sort of a shotgun shell for handguns. Tests conducted by the Firearms Unit confirmed that the bluish material Deedrick had found on the victim's hair was Teflon that had fused to it on impact. That allowed Deedrick to make a strong association between the suspect and the victim.

In many cases it's important to prove that hair has been forcibly removed. If a hair has been torn out, its root will be stretched rather than bulbous, it may have skin tissue still attached to it, and it will probably contain some pigment because it's still in the growing stage. Hal Deadman, who worked in Hairs and Fibers for sixteen years before joining the DNA Analysis Unit, once received a pair of shoes worn by a suspect in an Indiana robbery-murder case. Several of the victim's hairs were found stuck to the dried blood on the tip of the suspect's shoe. The suspect claimed that the victim had been shocked when she found him in her house and had suffered a heart attack, striking her head when she collapsed. He testified that he had stepped in the blood from her head wound when he fled the house. But from the condition of the roots, Deadman was able to determine that the woman's hairs had been forcibly removed; this led to the inevitable conclusion that the suspect had stomped her to death. The suspect was convicted of murdering the woman.

The main characteristics of fibers used to make comparisons are the type and generic classification, the diameter and coarseness, the presence of additives used in production, machine marks made during processing, the cross-sectional shape—artificial fibers are made by forcing molten liquid through a spinneret, something like a shower head; the cross-sectional shape is determined by the shape of the holes in the spineret—and changes due to use, such as sun-bleaching or discoloration from repeated washings. Perhaps most important is color. In the sci-crime business, blue is never blue; it's a color produced by mixing various dyes. While to the naked eye two colors may appear to be identical, they have probably been made from different dyes, or different proportions of dyes. The presence and amount of different dyes can be determined by an instrument called a microspectrophotometer, which basically produces a "spectral" fingerprint of the color. Identical color fingerprints make a very strong basis for association between two fibers found in different places.

With the exception of the microspectrophotometer, almost all examinations in the Hairs and Fiber Unit are done visually. Most comparisons are done on the compound microscope, which magnifies a sample up to four hundred times, and the comparison microscope, which consists of two compound microscopes bridged together to allow an examiner to look at two specimens simultaneously.

What makes a match? Absolutely everything. There is no minimum number of characteristics that must match, no hard and fast rules of evidence that require a standard be met. Simply, everything that can be seen or tested must be the same for a match to be made. As soon as one difference in characteristics is seen, the examination is over: the two specimens are not the same.

Every examiner has his or her own standards. "If you can't find at least fifteen identifiable characteristics," Mike Malone said, "then it's not unique enough to be of value for comparisons. For me, I always looked for twenty characteristics to match, which is about as many as you're going to find if you don't include things like bleaching, dyeing, and damage."

"When I'm asked on the witness stand how many characteristics matched," Wayne Oakes explained, "my answer has to be, 'All of them.' People have tried to quantitate this for a long time, but no one has been able to figure out how to do it."

Although you never see Detective Columbo vacuuming a crime scene, every complete crime-scene search includes a collection of hairs and fibers.

"It's all there," Deedrick said. "It's always there. The pieces always fit if you look carefully enough. You find the body of a murder victim along the side of a road. What you want to establish is where she was when she died, who she was with, and how she got to this ditch. It's there, and with enough experience you can figure it out. You can determine the race of the person she was with, whether they had sex, whether they had a fight. Maybe she was on a carpeted surface; was she in a car or a residence? Was it an old carpet or a new one? Did she have pets, or did the suspect have pets? Was it a dog or a cat or something unusual? There's a tremendous amount of information right there, but only if you know how to look for it."

Hairs and fibers can be found anywhere and everywhere. They can be found on every type of clothing, but particularly on socks and stockings. Hairs and fibers are found inside pockets, in pants cuffs, under fingernails. In the controversial Tawana Brawley case, for example, charred cotton fibers found under the girl's fingernails matched the fibers in a washcloth that had been used to write racial slurs on her body, proving she had written them herself. In a Wilkes-Barre, Pennsylvania, case, Deedrick matched blue-jean fibers found underneath a murdered woman's fingernails to her husband's clothes, providing strong evidence that they had fought during the last few moments of her life.

When a victim is hit with a blunt instrument—a hammer or frying pan, for instance—head hairs can often be found stuck to the instrument's surface, proving this was the weapon used in the crime. The lab once received a five-hundred-pound rock with blood on it, sent air express. The victim had apparently been thrown against the rock during a fight, and the submitting agency wanted the unit to check the bloodstain for hairs and fibers. It took a forklift to get the rock in and out of the building.

Hairs and fibers are found on knives and screwdrivers and guns. When a gun is fired, a vacuum is created, and this "blowback" instantly draws anything close by into the muzzle. So when a weapon is used to commit suicide, hairs are often found in the muzzle.

Hairs and fibers can also be found in fecal material, and when a body decomposes they are found in deposits of body fats. Contrary to the popular myth, hair does not continue growing after death; rather, the scalp shrinks and often slips off the skull intact, forming what is known as a hair mask. The unit occasionally receives a hair mask with a request for as much information as possible about the donor. Because Hairs and Fibers serves as the liaison unit between the lab and experts in esoteric subjects at the Smithsonian Institution, at one time the Hairs and Fiber Unit received a lot of bones, particularly in the spring when winter snows melted and bodies were discovered. Since the Smithsonian would not accept skeletal remains with flesh still attached, someone had to remove that flesh. "I had a nice operation set up," Agent-examiner Chet Blythe remembered. "I'd have a leg boiling in sodium hydroxide or an arm in enzymes. I tried everything to remove the flesh. I even had a head once. But eventually people started sending us entire torsos, which we weren't equipped to handle, so we had to stop it."

In one serial murder case the unit received the entire contents of the suspect's apartment, shipped to Washington, D.C., in a twenty-seven-foot-long trailer, with a request that it examine all his furniture, even the tires from his car, to search for hairs or fibers that might be linked to one of his victims. In other cases the unit has received sections of walls, carpets, dirt, and just about every part of a car—including the entire car.

Smashed automobile windshields are sent to the unit because hairs and fibers found embedded in the broken glass can help determine who was driving the car. In rape cases, hairs and fibers have been found on dildos. In a North Carolina case, the wing of an Air National Guard F-4 jet sliced through a civilian aircraft. The civilian plane crashed into the sea, killing everyone aboard, while the F-4 managed to land safely. There was some question about how many people had died in the crash. Several human hairs were found on the leading edge of the F-4's damaged wing, enabling the unit to prove that at least three different people had been on the airplane that crashed.

Hairs can be linked to a specific person and can be used simply for purposes of identification. When the space shuttle *Challenger* exploded, Doug Deedrick examined hairs recovered from the wreckage to help identify the bodies, as well as to try to determine if there had been a fire in the cabin before it crashed into the ocean. He found no evidence in the hairs of a fire.

Because hairs can be linked to one person, their presence at a crime scene makes extremely good evidence. In the most common type of case, a North Carolina bank robber discarded a nylon stocking mask that had been worn during the robbery. Hairs were found inside that stocking and when a suspect was arrested, samples of her hair were sent to former unit chief Allyson Simons for comparison. Simons was able to make a positive association between the hairs found in the stocking mask and the suspect, thus proving that she had worn the mask while committing the robbery.

To prevent that kind of match from being made, suspects have been known to shave off all their hair or dye it or bleach it. But the courts have ruled that law enforcement agencies have the right to obtain hair samples, and suspects have actually been prohibited by court order from getting a haircut or changing hair color.

Connecting the victim to the crime scene can be just as important as proving the suspect was there. When newly married Patricia Giesick was killed by what appeared to be a hit-and-run driver while on her honeymoon in New Orleans in 1974, her new husband, Claude Giesick, Jr., stood to collect $350,000 on a double indemnity life insurance policy. But suspicious investigators discovered that Giesick had rented two cars the day before the accident, and they traced the second car to the rental agency. Although there was no visible damage to the car, two strands of hair were found stuck to the tie rod underneath the car. Two thin strands of hair. The Hairs and Fiber Unit found that those two hairs "were consistent in all microscopic characteristics to Patricia Giesick's hair." The car that had killed her had been rented by her groom. Her death had not been an accident. Tied firmly to the murder by those two hairs, Giesick confessed that he had pushed his wife in front of the car and testified against the driver. The driver was eventually sentenced to life in prison without parole, while Giesick received a twenty-one-year sentence for manslaughter.

The ability to connect victims to the crime scene through a few hairs and fibers proved invaluable in convicting the murderers of Drug Enforcement agent Kiki Camarena and pilot Alfredo Zavala. During unauthorized flights in Zavala's plane, Camarena had located several large marijuana plantations outside Guadalajara, Mexico, forcing the embarrassed Mexican government to destroy a marijuana crop with a street value of about three billion dollars. Soon after this, Camarena and Zavala were kidnapped. Witnesses saw Camarena being driven away in a large automobile. Two well-known Mexican drug traffickers, Rafael Caro-Quintero and Ernesto Fonseca, immediately became the primary suspects, but because they were paying huge bribes to government officials, it became impossible to develop any evidence against them.

Tremendous pressure was exerted on the Mexican government to cooperate in the search for Camarena and Zavala. The border between San Diego and Mexico was practically shut down. Every car was painstakingly searched, laborers couldn't get into this country, and the long, long lines caused fresh produce to start rotting in trucks. Finally the Mexican police, the MFJP, received information that Camarena and Zavala were being held at a ranch owned by the Bravo drug gang, a rival of Caro-Quintero and Fonseca. After misinforming the DEA about the time the raid would begin, the MFJP raided the Bravo ranch, killing all the members of that gang. Two days later the bodies of Camarena and Zavala were found on the ranch, wrapped in plastic bags lying near a road. A team of investigators from the sci-crime lab was sent to Mexico to examine them.

Both men had been tortured before they were killed. A metal rod had been driven into Camarena's skull. Zavala may have been buried alive. But from the dirt and other debris found on their bodies, agents from the Materials Analysis Unit determined that they had been buried elsewhere and then dug up and left at this site. The obvious intent was to shift responsibility for their murders from Caro-Quintero and Fonseca.

Agent Jack Dillon of the lab's Firearms Unit took hair samples and small cuttings from the clothing of each victim, as well as a piece of the rope and tape that had been used to bind and blindfold them. Mike Malone found a light-beige nylon carpet fiber in the cutting from Zavala's sweatshirt. "That was just about the first lead we got," Malone remembered. "It wasn't much, but it told us that the last thing Zavala had been in contact with was probably a light-beige rug. Early on we told the DEA that they would find a light-beige rug in the room in which Zavala had been killed."

A source informed DEA agents that one of Fonseca's most trusted assistants had parked a brand-new car in his garage and then bricked up the door. The brick wall was torn down and the car, a Mercury Marquis, was searched; Malone was able to match a single hair found on the rear floor mat with Camarena's. Kiki Camarena had been in that car.

In April 1985, two months after the kidnapping and murders, the MFJP claimed that it had located the villa where Camarena and Zavala had been held. It was a luxurious house hidden behind high walls at 881 Lope de Vega in downtown Guadalajara, a house owned by Rafael Caro-Quintero. "We wanted to get in there right away," Malone said, "but they wouldn't let us in. By the time we were finally allowed to search it the place had been scrubbed down, every wall had been repainted, and just about all the furniture had been replaced. A squad of Federales was living there, supposedly to protect the place. They were actually living in the crime scene. We weren't supposed to find anything. But just in case we did, armed Mexican soldiers watched us, ready to confiscate anything we might find."

The search team got one big break. New carpets had been installed just before the kidnappings, and they hadn't been replaced. Malone started his search in an unattached guest house that had unusually thick walls and a steel door with iron bars on it; the guest house was a perfect place to hide a prisoner so no one would know he was there. The first thing Malone saw when he walked into that house was a light beige rug. Malone divided the room into four quadrants, vacuuming each quadrant with a different filter. The fibers found in Zavala's sweatshirt matched the carpet fibers. But Malone also found tangled in that rug two head hairs, so small that even the most thorough cleaning hadn't dislodged them, two head hairs consistent in every way with head hairs taken from the corpse of Kiki Camarena. Both men had been held in that room.

A car parked next to the house was thoroughly searched. Two more of Camarena's hairs were found on the back floor, suggesting that he had been transported in both cars to or from the villa. But before the search could be concluded, Malone and Agent Ron Raywalt spotted a folded license plate at the bottom of a hole covered by a grate; it was the license plate witnesses had seen on the car driven by Camarena's kidnappers. This discovery caused anxious Mexican officials to end the crime-scene investigation, and only after months of negotiations was the FBI team permitted to return and complete their search.

The Mexicans had tried to erase all evidence from the crime scene, but hairs and fibers are so small it's almost impossible to get all of them. So in a bedroom inside the main house, a hair that had been forcibly removed from Camarena's head was found. The sheet in which Camarena had been buried was matched to linens in another bedroom. Pieces of the cord with which Camarena had been bound were matched to cord found on the property. Kiki Camarena and Alfredo Zavala had been held and probably killed at 881 Lope de Vega; they had been buried and exhumed, then left to be discovered in an attempt to satisfy the protests of the American government. "They never allowed us to take hair samples from Caro-Quintero or Fonseca," Malone said with obvious regret. "We've still got about five hundred hairs from those crime scenes that are unknowns. But I have no doubt that among them would be Caro-Quintero's and Fonseca's."

Additional evidence was developed linking those men and members of their drug gang to the crime scene. In several trials held in Los Angeles, during which hundreds of witnesses testified, six members of the Caro-Quintero organization were convicted of crimes connected to the kidnappings and murders and sentenced to life imprisonment. In trials held in Mexico all of the major members of the Caro-Quintero organization were tried and convicted and are currently in prison.

Hairs and fibers often connect the suspect directly to the victim. Among the most compelling evidence against serial killer Ted Bundy were ninety-eight cross-transfers of fibers between Bundy and a twelve-year-old victim named Kimberly Leach. Fibers from Bundy's coat and from the carpet of a van he had stolen were found on the young girl's clothing, while fibers from the girl's clothing were found on Bundy's. This convinced the jury that Bundy had been in close contact with Kimberly Leach, and helped convict him.

In a Wooster, Ohio, case two men were charged with the rape and murder of a little girl when orange carpet fibers found on her body appeared to be similar to orange fibers found in their environment. But when Agent-examiner Alan Robillard compared those fibers he discovered they were quite different. He eventually testified for the defense. "The DA attacked me pretty severely on the stand," he remembered, "because I was saying that these fibers were not the same. I didn't say the two suspects didn't do it, I just said no association could be made based on those fibers. But they were convicted anyway.

"Ironically, while these guys were in jail, another little girl was murdered, and the same orange carpet fibers that had been found on the first victim were found on her body."

Almost a year later a terrified woman was found running down a highway. The driver who picked her up thought she was wearing denim; in fact she was naked, but she had been beaten so severely her body was completely bruised. She had escaped from the home of a man named Eric Buell, and she was able to bring the police back to the house in which she had been held and tortured. In Buell's van, police found an orange carpet. Robillard said: "How many pieces of carpet like that exist in the world? We were able to show that the carpet had been made by J. P. Stevens, and because of the recession they'd made only four thousand yards. They had sold about a hundred and fifty yards to a store in Worcester, and that carpet was so ugly the store still had a hundred and twenty yards in stock. That allowed us to make a very strong association to Buell's van."

Robillard testified again, this time for the prosecution. Buell was convicted and sentenced to death.

The more unusual hairs and fibers are, the more valuable they are as evidence. When Green Beret Dr. Jeffrey MacDonald was accused of murdering his wife, Colette, and their two daughters—in the famed "Fatal Vision" case—he insisted that his family had been killed by a drug-crazed band of hippies led by a woman wearing dark clothes, a floppy black hat, and a long blond wig. After being convicted of the murders, MacDonald appealed several times on various issues. In 1992 his new attorney, Alan Dershowitz, claimed that blond wig hairs found in Colette MacDonald's hairbrush had never been produced at earlier trials and supported MacDonald's claim that a woman in a blond wig had been in his home that night.

At least five hairs found in the MacDonald home have never been identified, but the crime-scene search conducted by the military police was done quite carelessly. People were constantly going in and out of the house—someone even stole a wallet from the house during the search—so those hairs could have belonged to anyone. But the evidence against MacDonald was overwhelming. There was extensive blood-spatter evidence and a multitude of fiber evidence. MacDonald claimed that he had taken off his pajama top and used it to defend himself when the hippies tried to stab him, but a determined sci-crime lab technician named Shirley Green spent weeks working with that pajama top, folding it and refolding it, until she was able to align the numerous cuts in it to the twenty stab wounds in Colette MacDonald's chest, proving it had been laid over her while she was being stabbed.

Still, there were those unexplained blond wig hairs. Dershowitz's appeal for a new trial was based on his contention that these wig hairs, some hairs found on Colette's body, and some dark wool fibers constituted hard, scientific evidence to support MacDonald's story that intruders had been in his house. Mike Malone got the case.

"We ended up finding two different types of wig fibers," Malone said. "One of them we'd never seen before. Examiners in the Instrumental Analysis Unit did a spectrographic exam and identified it as a fiber called saran. We checked all our files, we checked our collection, we didn't know anything about it.

"So we did a lot of research and discovered that saran is a very unusual fiber, and it's never used in human wigs. It's used almost exclusively for doll and mannequin hair, dust mops, and patio screens. With two little girls we could assume there were some dolls in the house, but no one had kept them so we had no basis for a comparison. Eventually we found a woman who works for Mattel and has what might be the largest doll collection in the world. She's got thousands of dolls. We were able to find two different Barbie dolls with hair made of fibers similar to the fibers found in Colette's brush. We couldn't testify that they'd come from those dolls, but we could tell the court that they had not come from any known type of human wig. Those fibers were unique."

Malone was also able to match the questioned dark wig fibers to a fall owned by Colette MacDonald that had been kept by her father. One of the hairs found on Colette's body came from Jeffrey MacDonald; the other hairs were limb and body hairs and were therefore unsuitable for comparison. And finally, the dark wool fibers had probably been picked up by Colette when she collapsed onto a shag carpet and most likely came from her own clothing. On the basis of Malone's report, Dershowitz's appeal for a new trial was rejected.

In most cases hairs and fibers become significant only when they can connect a suspect to a place or person he denies having had any contact with. If the victim and suspect are known to have been in contact, or if there was a legitimate reason for them to have been at the crime scene, hair and fiber evidence has very little value. But there are exceptions, and this is where the agent-examiners become detectives. Generally it's extremely difficult to determine when the transfer of hairs and fibers took place. In the Camarena case the rugs in the villa had been installed just before the kidnapping. Therefore Camarena had to have been in those rooms after a certain date.

In 1987 Doug Deedrick had a triple murder case in Alaska in which he had to prove that a suspect had been in an apartment at a specific time through hair and fiber evidence. A woman and her seven-year-old daughter had been strangled, and her two-year-old daughter's throat had been slit. The woman's nephew, who had lived in the apartment for about a month, but had been thrown out ten days before the murders, immediately became the primary suspect. A substantial number of his hairs were found in the apartment, but because he had lived there they had very little value as evidence.

"The most compelling evidence was a rag that had been wadded up and left in the bathroom sink," Deedrick remembered. "I found a pubic hair with a partial egg case from pubic lice on it. I found the same egg cases on the nephew's pubic hairs, so we could pretty much conclude that the pubic hair found on that rag was the nephew's. My problem was establishing when he'd left that hair."

Just as Sherlock Holmes might have done in this case, Deedrick decided to find out how hairs moved through a house in a normal situation, then contrast those results to what had been found in that apartment. "I started by doing a pubic-hair study at home, just to see if pubic hairs were easily transferred out of one room and where they would most likely be found. I took a crime-scene vacuum home and for two weeks I vacuumed every room every night and preserved the material I found. Then I examined every hair and compared it to known samples from my wife and myself. I kept track of where I'd found hairs and how many I found. The results seemed to prove that there was a migration of hairs from room to room, mostly by getting stuck on clothing, particularly socks."

An important element in the case was the cleaning habits of the dead woman. Her friends testified that she had vacuumed the apartment often, and in fact had done so the day before she was murdered. Deedrick did a stratum search of the vacuum cleaner bag, estimating how much dirt might have been picked up each time the vacuum cleaner was used, then searching the dirt layer by layer, day by day, inch by inch. "I had to go down pretty far just to find hair that matched the suspect. The fact that I found none of his hairs in the top layers supported the contention that there weren't a lot of hairs left in the apartment from the time he was living there, and that most of the hairs we found had been left there while he was in the apartment committing the crimes."

Most, but not all. Obviously some of the hairs found there had been lying on the floor for weeks. Deedrick had to show a difference between those old hairs and newly deposited ones. "Hairs that have been in a particular environment for any length of time," he said, "especially hairs that have been on carpeting, tend to pick up residual dirt and debris. They get dirty. I looked at thousands of hairs found in that apartment and divided them by their condition. The pubic hairs we found on the children's bodies were clean; there was no dirt or soot or debris on them. The pubic hairs we found on the washrag in the sink were also extremely important because the washrag was still damp, and it wouldn't have been if it had been put there ten days earlier."

By tracking the movement of hairs and fibers in the apartment, Deedrick was able to determine how the crime might have happened. The suspect was wearing green wool gloves when he entered the apartment. He fought with the woman and grabbed her by the hair. This was proved by the forcibly removed hairs found on the gloves. Then he sexually assaulted her and strangled her with a towel. Fibers from that towel were also found on the green gloves. It was at that point he probably decided to clean himself, so he had to take off the gloves. In addition to finding pubic hairs on the washcloth, Deedrick also found green wool fibers from the gloves, fibers from the woman's nightgown, and fibers from her bed on the cloth.

After killing the woman he strangled her older daughter. This was shown by the fact that Deedrick found fibers from her mother's nightgown on the little girl's body, as well as several green wool fibers, probably remnants left on the suspect's hands after taking off the gloves. And finally the nephew killed the younger girl.

Deedrick had built a strong case against the suspect, who tried to flee, but was caught. Deedrick testified before the grand jury, then spent two days on the witness stand during the actual trial. The nephew was convicted of the three murders and received three one-hundred-year sentences.

Unlike hairs, which can be traced to a specific person, fibers are extremely difficult to trace back to a specific source—that blouse or those pants. But because fibers are transferred in such large numbers they are much more likely than hairs to be found at a crime scene. They are particularly valuable in allowing investigators to create links between victims, suspects and places.

In recent years fibers have often enabled police to link the victims of serial killers. Over an eight-month period beginning in May 1984, ten young women were raped and murdered in the Tampa Bay, Florida, area. The first victim had been strangled. She was found naked, her hands tied behind her back, her legs tied spread-eagled. A single bright-red fiber was found on her clothing. From the size and shape of the cross section, investigators determined that it was probably an automobile carpet fiber. On the basis of Locard's theory that fibers generally reflect the most recent contact, the Hairs and Fiber Unit informed Florida police that their suspect was probably driving a vehicle with red carpeting.

Two weeks later, the second victim was found. Her throat had been cut and she had been bludgeoned. She was naked from the waist down, her hands had been tied behind her back, and the same red fiber was found on her clothing. But this time there were additional clues. Several fibers from a second red vehicle carpet were also found on her clothing, suggesting that the killer was driving a vehicle with two different red floor mats. Some strands of medium-length brown Caucasian hair were found: the suspect was probably white and had medium-length brown hair. And finally, from tire impressions left at the scene, FBI lab examiners determined that the suspect's car had a Goodyear Viva tire with the whitewall facing inside on the right rear, and a somewhat unusual Vogue tire, which was made by a small manufacturer primarily for Cadillacs, on the left rear. The size of the tire indicated the suspect was driving a medium or full-sized car.

In June the decomposing body of a woman was found lying in an orange grove. Because she was fully dressed and her hands were not tied, she was not linked to the other victims. So the evidence was sent to a different examiner in the sci-crime lab, and to this examiner the red carpet fibers that were found meant nothing.

The murders seemed to stop for several months, but in early October the naked body of a young woman was found lying in a dirt field. She had been shot to death about five weeks earlier. Exposure to the elements had caused her scalp to slip off her skull, and this hair mask was found next to her decomposing body. Telltale red carpet fibers and a brown Caucasian pubic hair were recovered from her clothing. A week later the body of the fifth victim was found in a field. Two weeks later the sixth victim was found, just off a highway. The remains of the seventh victim were discovered several days later; her bones were scattered over a large area, but a single red carpet fiber was found tangled in her hair. Eventually ten murders were attributed to the serial killer, linked together by these red carpet fibers and strands of brown hair.

While the physical evidence was accumulating, there was nothing solid to lead police to the killer. They needed a break, and they got one. Very early on the morning of November 3, as a seventeen-year-old girl was riding her bicycle home from her job at a doughnut shop, a man leaped out of a car, knocked her off her bike, and kidnapped her. He covered her eyes with a blindfold and took her to an apartment, and for the next two days he sexually assaulted her. "This girl was very sharp," Mike Malone said admiringly. "She never lost her composure. She did exactly what he wanted her to do and, over time, he took a liking to her. On the second night he told her he was going to let her go. Once again she was blindfolded and he put her back in his car. She remembered two things: She could see under the blindfold and read the word "Magnum" on the dashboard; and before he let her out of the car, he had stopped at an automatic teller machine to get some cash.

"The Hillsborough County sheriff's office and the Tampa police department did a real good job on this case. Although this kidnapping didn't fit the killer's pattern, just to cover every possibility they sent her clothing to the lab. As always, my technician got the clothing and started to process it for hairs and fibers. A few minutes later she came running into my office, telling me that all kinds of red fibers were falling off the clothing. Most of our cases are routine, but every once in a while there's a moment of tremendous excitement. This was certainly one of them.

"I examined those fibers under a microscope; then, just to be sure, I analyzed the red dye. Bingo! I could make an exact match to the fibers found on the murder victims. There was no doubt about it. The same person who'd kidnapped this girl had committed those murders."

The only car manufactured that had the name "Magnum" on its dashboard was the 1978 Dodge Magnum. A team of detectives began compiling a list of every 1978 Dodge Magnum registered in the Tampa Bay area. At the same time, a second team of detectives began checking all the bank ATMs that had been used at approximately three o'clock in the morning of the day the girl had been released. Only one name appeared on both lists: Robert Joseph Long. Bobby Joe Long. The rape victim was shown a photograph of Long and positively identified him as the man who had kidnapped and assaulted her.

Long was put under around-the-clock surveillance. While he was in a movie theater an agent crawled underneath his car and examined the tires. On the left rear was a Vogue, on the right rear was a Viva. When Long came out of the theater he was arrested and charged with murder.

His car and apartment were thoroughly searched, and Malone flew to Florida to make the hair and fiber comparisons. The fibers taken from the two different red carpets in Long's car matched the fibers found on eight victims. Long's head hair and pubic hair matched the brown Caucasian hair found on several victims. Head hairs from six of the victims were found inside the Dodge Magnum.

When police confronted Long with the evidence he said, "I think I may need an attorney." Later, after accepting his situation, he admitted, "You got me."

For his crimes Bobby Joe Long received twenty-six life sentences—and the death penalty. "I guess the thing that was most surprising to me," Malone said, "is that when we finally got this guy, he wasn't some kind of monster. He was just an ordinary guy who liked to kill people."

While the fiber evidence provided the vital link between Long and his victims, detectives eventually compiled an abundance of hard evidence against him. Hairs and fibers have rarely been enough on which to base an entire prosecution, but in one of the most chilling cases in recent American history, the Atlanta child murders, it provided the only physical evidence needed to convict Wayne Williams, who was accused of killing at least twelve of the thirty victims.

During a twenty-two-month period beginning in July 1979, thirty black children and young men either disappeared or were murdered in the Atlanta, Georgia, area. The string of killings made headlines around the world, and a large task force, consisting of representatives from several different law enforcement agencies, was formed to investigate. The victims were murdered in different ways, causing investigators to believe that more than one person was responsible. But several of the victims could be connected to the same killer or place by the presence of greenish-yellow and violet acetate fibers found in their clothing and hair. The fibers indicated that each of these victims had been in the same environment either just prior to or after their death. Identifying the source of the fibers might lead police to the killer. Fibers can rarely be traced to a single source—it had never been done before—but there were absolutely no other clues.

By the time the FBI sci-crime lab became involved in the case, in 1981, most of the murders had already been committed. The greenish-yellow fibers had already been identified by Georgia investigators as carpet fibers. Because carpet fibers have to withstand continuous weight and pressure, they are usually thicker and larger than other fibers. But these fibers were different. "I'd been doing hairs and fibers work for a long time," remembered Agent-examiner Hal Deadman, who did the hair and fiber comparisons in this case, "and these fibers were unique. Every company makes its own fibers, but certain cross-sectional shapes and sizes are pretty common in the industry. These fibers had an unusual triangular cross section; they were unlike anything I'd ever seen before." The fact that the fibers didn't come from a common type of carpeting was good news to investigators, because the less common a fiber, the more valuable it is as evidence.

Agents eventually identified the manufacturer of the fiber as the Wellman Corporation, a Massachusetts company. Wellman had sold yarn made from this fiber, called 181B, to a Dalton, Georgia, carpet company, West Point Pepperell. West Point Pepperell had used 181B in the production of its Luxaire line for only one year, and among the colors it had produced was something called English Olive, a greenish-yellow identical to the color of the fibers found on some of the victims. A very small number of English Olive Luxaire carpets had been sold in the Atlanta area; theoretically, it might have been possible to track down everyone who had purchased them. If this had been done, eventually agents would have knocked on the door of twenty-three-year-old Wayne Williams.

But just before the FBI located the carpet manufacturer, an Atlanta newspaper reported that police had found unique fibers on the bodies of several victims. Until that story was published, the victims had been found fully clothed; after it appeared, the victims were stripped and dropped off bridges into the Chattahoochee River, presumably to allow the river to wash away any hairs and fibers. Because the killer's pattern had changed, the Atlanta task force began staking out bridges over the river. And one morning, at about two A.M., officers heard a loud splash. Minutes later they stopped the only car on the bridge at that time. The driver was a young black man, a music promoter named Wayne Williams. Police reported that Williams told them he had just dropped some garbage in the river; Williams denied telling them anything. But two days later the body of a man named Nathaniel Cater was pulled from the river near the bridge. And in his hair police found a greenish-yellow carpet fiber.

Williams's home, in which he lived with his parents, was searched for the first time. Eventually several searches would be made and hundreds of thousands of hairs and fibers would be collected and examined. But that first night Larry Peterson of the Georgia state police crime lab made the initial comparisons between the fibers found on the victims and fibers taken from the Luxaire carpet in Williams's home. "Peterson called me at about one-thirty in the morning," Hal Deadman recalled, "and told me very matter-of-factly, 'I've made some matches. You'd better come over here.' I went right over to the lab and looked at them. They looked fine. At that point both Larry and I were convinced that someone in the

Williamses' environment was involved in the murders. The chance of this being just a coincidence was essentially zero."

Williams vehemently denied any involvement in the murders, and police found no other physical evidence that would connect him to the victims. This pile of fibers, not even enough to withstand a strong breeze, was all prosecutors had. But the killings had stopped with Williams's arrest, and prosecutors were convinced he was guilty of at least some of them. Proving that was going to be very difficult. Hairs and fibers had never been used as the primary evidence in a murder trial, and no one knew if a jury would convict someone of murder, beyond a reasonable doubt, on the basis of hair and fiber comparisons.

Prosecutors decided to try Williams for only two murders, those of Nathaniel Cater and Jimmy Payne, but under Georgia law evidence from other murders that can be shown to be related to those crimes also can be introduced at trial. The carpet fibers proved the relationship between Cater and Payne and the other victims.

The hair and fiber evidence was initially used to link Williams and his victims. Twenty-eight different fibers, in addition to dog hairs, found on the bodies of one or more victims were matched to nineteen different objects found in Williams's home and his car. Connecting one fiber to an environment and a victim has very little significance, but the ability to make multiple associations is extremely important. "On some of the victims we found as many as ten fibers that could be directly related to Williams's home or a car he had in his possession at the time of that murder," Deadman said. "The chances that those ten fibers could have come from a place other than Williams's home or car are just about impossible."

That would be true even if all the fibers that could be associated with Williams were commonly found, but they weren't. Twenty-seven of those fibers could be classified as unusual or uncommon, meaning they formed the basis of a strong match. Prosecutors used statistical evidence to emphasize the importance of these fiber matches. To show how unlikely it was that the 181B fibers came from anywhere except the carpet in Williams's home, agents traced the entire production line of Luxaire carpets. Considering the number of yards manufactured and sold, and assuming that every carpet sold almost a decade earlier was still in use, there was still only a 1-in-7,792 chance of finding a similar carpet.

And those odds were multiplied by every different fiber found on the victims that could be linked to Williams. In addition to the carpet fibers, hairs that could be associated with Williams's dog, and violet acetate fibers that could be matched to a spread found in his bedroom were found on ten victims. Prosecutors used charts to show that it was virtually impossible that those three different fibers could all be found anywhere except Williams's home.

In addition to being used to link Williams to the victims, fibers were also used to establish a time frame. Nine victims were linked by automobile carpet fibers to three different cars used by Williams. When Williams was using a rented car, fibers that could be matched to carpeting from that car were found on victims. A noose comprises millions of fibers woven together to make an extremely strong rope. The hair and fiber evidence was forming a noose that was tightening around Williams's neck.

"There was no question that we tied his household and his automobiles to the victims," Deadman stated flatly, "no question about it at all. And while his mother and father also lived in that house, Wayne Williams was the only one who drove some of these cars. I testified for several days, trying to explain to the jury the significance of all these associations. But you never know if they really understand this evidence until the verdict comes in."

The knowledge that police had found a few fibers on his victims had forced Wayne Williams to change his killing patterns, and caused him to be caught on that bridge above the Chattahoochee River. And it was those small fibers, fibers no different from those you can pick off your clothing right now, that resulted in Williams's being convicted of murder and sentenced to spend the rest of his life in prison.

While it's not possible to claim that a fiber came from a specific source to the exclusion of all other sources, it is possible to make precisely that claim with pieces of fabric. Fabrics consist of millions of woven fibers, and examiners can show that pieces of torn fabric fit together by matching rough edges, tears and cuts, broken patterns, any kind of damage that allows an end-to-end comparison. "Fabric matches are part of our training," Wayne Oakes said. "Fabric matches make very compelling evidence. No matter how hard someone tried, they just couldn't reproduce the randomness of a cut or a tear or a ripped edge."

In a particularly brutal Port Orchard, Washington, case, three hitchhiking teenagers, two girls and a boy, were picked up by a man driving a van. After buying wine and beer, the man drove them out into the country. And there he pulled a gun on them and tied them up with strips torn from a sheet in the rear of his van. He sexually assaulted all three of them, then shot and killed one of the girls, killed the boy by slicing his throat and cutting out his tongue, then shot the other girl in the eye and ear, leaving her for dead. She survived, and when he went back to his van, she tried to escape through the woods. He tracked her down and slit her throat. Still she fought to live. And she was very, very lucky. She fell onto an upturned tree stump and the dirt and debris stemmed the flow of blood from her throat. Miraculously, she survived.

She was able to provide police with a good description of the killer and his van, and he was captured. Oakes testified that he was able to make a perfect match between the strips of cloth used to tie up the victims and the sheet found in the back of the suspect's van—important corrobative testimony to support the survivor's story. "Doing fabric matches is a lot like putting pieces of a jigsaw puzzle together," Oakes said, "but it's something a jury can see and understand. In this case it was such a strong match that it certainly helped convict him."

"Calling what we do just hairs and fibers examinations really isn't sufficient," Mike Malone pointed out, "because this is kind of a catch-all unit. While the majority of our work is done with hairs and fibers, we also do a little bit of everything else that might be considered trace evidence, things that are hard to see with the naked eye. If you have to use a microscope to look at something, we're probably going to get it. That might include plant material, glass chips, paint chips, even soil examinations."

And feathers. Those soft fluffy things that float on a breeze and are used to make people laugh. The body covering of birds. There's something pleasant and whimsical about feathers that may seem out of place at a crime scene, but feathers have unique characteristics that can be used to provide a strong link between a suspect and a crime.

Hairs and Fibers was once known as the Microscopy Unit because of the variety of exams conducted by the unit. And still, in addition to conducting hair and fiber examinations, most agent-examiners have at least one additional area in which they have qualified to testify in court as an expert. Doug Deedrick's is feathers. He is recognized as one of the leading feather experts in the sci-crime world. "I always wanted to get into something that's a little different," he admitted, "something that not everybody else was doing. I got interested in feathers and I nurtured that interest and eventually, without even realizing it, I'd accumulated all the information I needed. Then I built a substantial reference collection for the lab."

Feathers are often found at crime scenes. Down clothing is easily damaged in shootings and stabbings and beatings; bedding is damaged in sex crimes; Deedrick has even found feathers inside hoax bombs. He began learning about feathers in 1978 from the Smithsonian's feather expert, a remarkable woman named Roxy Laybourne. Now in her eighties, Laybourne has been working with the FBI for more than fifty years, and has worked with Deedrick in a variety of cases, from providing evidence against killers to helping discover the cause of airplane crashes.

Although it's possible to identify from a feather the family and body area of the bird from which it came, it isn't possible to prove that a specific feather came from a specific bird or, more important, a specific pillow or mattress or vest. But feathers still make strong evidence. In a Naples, Florida, case two people were shot to death at almost point-blank range. They were found sprawled on a bloody bathroom floor. A pillow with several bullet holes in it was lying nearby; it had been used to muffle the gunshots.

The vacuum that is created when a weapon is fired will suck all kinds of debris into the gun barrel. Sometimes the victim's blood or brain matter will be found, but in this case, when a suspect was arrested, several tiny feathers were found inside the barrel of his gun. Deedrick testified that the feathers found inside that gun exhibited the same microscopic characteristics as the feathers found inside the pillow, testimony that helped convict the suspect of murder.

Periodically, Deedrick receives feathers that have been ingested into airplane engines, particularly in cases of unexplained engine failure. When one of the Air Force's most sophisticated planes, a billion-dollar B-1 bomber, crashed, feathers found inside the engine were identified as coming from a brown pelican. Because of that finding, the Air Force changed the path of its test flights away from the migration route of the brown pelican.

The weapons used to commit crimes generally evolve with the times and technology, but criminals have been using ropes and cords throughout the annals of crime. While duct tape is now frequently used instead of rope, rope is still used quite often to tie up victims and on occasion can provide valuable evidence.

In the early 1980s two young newspaper boys in a small town just outside Omaha, Nebraska, were abducted and murdered while making their Sunday-morning deliveries. One of the boys was found bound with what appeared to be an ordinary white nylon rope, which is just too commonly used to make a good basis for comparison. But ropes are made by winding many different yarns around a center cord called a tracer, and when the unit's rope expert, Wayne Oakes, began unraveling this rope, he found it had been made from 106 different yarns and twenty-four different fiber types. It was mostly what is known as junk filler, yarns and fibers that have no real value, and it didn't affect the quality of the rope, but as a basis of comparison it was like discovering a vein of gold. "This was a unique rope," Oakes explained. "I'd never seen anything quite like it. I had photographs of it distributed to all the law enforcement people in the area, and emphasized that whenever they did a crime-scene search they should look for a white rope. If they found one, open it up; if it looks like the rope in the photograph, send it in. I knew if we found it we'd be able to make a very strong association between the killer and those kids."

The murders had caused a heightened sense of suspicion in the town. One morning, a worker at a day-care center noticed an unfamiliar car in the parking lot and wrote down its license-plate number. The driver spotted her and chased her, but she managed to get away. She immediately called the hot line that had been set up by the task force investigating the murders. The FBI agent who received the call traced the plate number to an automobile dealership. The car, he learned, had been loaned to a customer whose own car was being serviced. The agent immediately went to the dealership to investigate. He looked through the window; lying in plain sight was a short length of white nylon rope.

The suspect, an Air Force enlisted man, was questioned by both local police and the FBI. He gave authorities permission to search his quarters. Another length of rope was found there and sent to Oakes. The comparison was time-consuming, Oakes remembered, "We microscopically compared every one of those one hundred and six yarns and then we chemically tested them to make sure they'd been colored with the same dyes as the rope found on the boy's body. It was an identical match." Faced with this evidence, the suspect confessed. It was an old rope, he said, a rope he had had since his days as a Boy Scout volunteer. It was this rope that tied him tightly to the murder of two children. He was sentenced to be executed by lethal injection.

A few slender strands of hair, fibers almost invisible to the naked eye, the fluff of feathers, bits of cord, a torn piece of fabric: in terms of size and weight none of this adds up to very much, but as evidence it's strong enough to support the full weight of the law. It's the stuff that's always there but rarely seen, the stuff that proves, as the Chinese proverb warns, "Everything may depend on the difference between two hairs."

CHAPTER
- 5 -

The One and Only:
The Latent Fingerprint Section and
DNA Analysis Unit

Every human being carries with him from his cradle to his grave certain physical marks which do not change their character, and by which he can always be identified—and that without shade of doubt or question. These marks are his signature, his physiological autograph . . . and this autograph cannot be counterfeited, nor can he disguise it or hide it away, nor can it become illegible by the wear or mutations of time. . . .

This autograph consists of the delicate lines and corrugations with which Nature marks the insides of the hands and the soles of the feet. If you look at the balls of your fingers . . . you will observe that these dainty curving lines lie close together, like those that indicate the borders of oceans in maps, and that they form various clearly defined patterns, such as arches, circles, long curves, whorls, etc. and that these patterns differ on different fingers.

MARK TWAIN, *Pudd'nhead Wilson*

Just before midnight, on October 1, 1993, twelve-year-old Polly Klaas and two girlfriends were having a slumber party in her family's Petaluma, California, home. Suddenly, without warning, a man dressed in dark clothing and carrying a knife walked into the room and threatened to slit their throats if they screamed. The intruder ordered them to lie down on the floor; he tied their hands and pulled pillowcases over their heads. And then he kidnapped Polly Klaas.

"When I hung up the phone after being notified I just stared outside," remembered Captain Pat Parks of the Petaluma police department. "I realized it was a dark, cold night out there, and somewhere a terrified little girl was depending on us."

Within an hour Petaluma police were searching the Klaas home inch by inch, looking for the smallest clue. "We used all the traditional investigative techniques," explained Detective Michael Meese, "including the various fingerprint powders. But we came up with almost nothing."

An FBI evidence response team—crime-scene experts—got to the Klaas home about an hour after Petaluma police. After receiving permission from the local police, they began an intensive search. "When they got to her bedroom," Detective Meese continued, "they began by applying red fluorescent powder to precisely the same surfaces I'd just dusted for prints. I hadn't found a thing. But then they turned out the lights, put on tinted goggles that looked sort of like a chemist's safety glasses, and turned on a light that looked like sort of a wand."

This light was an alternate light source, ALS, as it is known. Viewed through filtered goggles, the light illuminates objects that cannot be seen with the naked eye. "Many different prints that we hadn't found were suddenly visible," Captain Parks said, "but there was only one that we could not account for. That was a partial palmprint found on the upper rail of Polly's bunk bed. We had a print, but initially it didn't do us much good. There isn't too much you can do with a palmprint until you have a bad guy to go with it."

Almost two months later some tattered children's clothing was found on a hillside. A computer search disclosed that on the night of the kidnapping two sheriff's deputies had reported that a car driven by a man named Richard Allen Davis had been stuck on a private road near this site. Further investigation revealed that Davis had served fifteen years in prison for burglary, assault, and kidnapping. Finally, here was a bad guy whose palmprints could be used as a comparison.

After Davis was arrested his palmprints were sent to fingerprint specialist Mike Smith at the sci-crime lab in Washington, D.C. It was a difficult comparison to make—the latent print found on the bunk bed wasn't very clear—but it was enough. Smith was able to make a positive comparison; he was able to say that the only person in the world who could have left that print in Polly Klaas's bedroom was Richard Allen Davis.

Eventually additional evidence against Davis was developed. The Materials Analysis Unit made a positive fracture match—it matched the torn edges of the strips of cloth found in Polly's bedroom and at the site where Davis's car broke down. Hairs and Fibers identified a single beard hair found in the bedroom as consistent with Richard Davis. But when Davis heard news reports that his palmprint had been positively identified, he asked to speak to Detective Meese. In that interview he admitted kidnapping and killing Polly Klaas. And then he led police to her body.

The most important piece of evidence was the partial palmprint. A square inch of wavy lines. And had this crime been committed only a few years ago, that print probably would not have been found.

Mark Twain was right. From the day you are born until the day you die the only physical aspect of your body that won't change is the shape of those funny lines in your skin. Prints—fingerprints, palmprints, footprints—are the only physical means of establishing your identity to the exclusion of everyone else who has ever lived. No two people—no two fingers—have ever been found that are identical. "And the day we find two prints that we can't tell apart," explained Danny Greathouse, the Latent Fingerprint Section chief, "that'll be the day we close the door and walk out of here forever because we'll be out of business."

Look at the undersides of your fingers. You'll see that they are covered with slightly raised areas of skin, called ridges. If you look a little more closely, you will see that these ridges aren't continuous; they stop, they start, they divide, and they make formations. It's the arrangement and relationship of these ridges that make your fingerprint unique and identifiable. And what makes that more than just a curiosity is the fact that almost everybody sweats. Sweat is secreted from the body through billions of microscopic pores in the skin. About 99 percent of perspiration is composed of water, with the remaining 1 percent composed of salt, amino acids, and other chemicals. That 1 percent makes all the difference. When someone touches an object, perspiration—or in some cases other substances that the person has touched, such as grease, oil, food products, dirt, even blood—is transferred from the ridges of the fingertips to that object, leaving an impression. Because no two prints are alike, this impression can be used to prove that a particular person was in a specific place or handled a specific object. If that impression is visible to the naked eye, as on a glass, it's a patent print, while an invisible print is a latent print. Depending on what material the print consists of, it can be made visible in a variety of ways. It's generally latent prints that put people in prison.

These strange lines in the skin have fascinated people for thousands of years. Ancient Indians in Nova Scotia etched pictures of hands with raised ridges into the side of a cliff. Clay tablets depict Babylonian officials taking fingerprints from criminals. And throughout history charlatans have thrived by predicting people's future on the basis of the lines on their hands.

Fingerprints as a means of identification can be traced back to eighth-century China, when they were used to seal business contracts. In fourteenth-century Persia, all official government documents were required to include fingerprint impressions. But it wasn't until 1858, when Sir William Herschel, the British administrator of a large district in Bengal, India, required Indians to seal contracts with their fingerprints as well as their signatures, that fingerprinting became an accepted means of identification in the modern world. Fingerprints were used for official purposes in the United States for the first time in 1882, when an officer of the U.S. Geological Survey engaged in mapping the continent used his own print to prevent forgery of his supply orders.

It was also around this time that fingerprints were first used in law enforcement. One of the basic problems faced by early law enforcement officials was how to register and identify criminals. Early civilizations branded criminals with tattoos or cut off a finger or a hand. In the early 1800s policemen with photographic memories would visit prisons and look at newly arrived convicts to see if they were familiar and to memorize their faces for the future. Newly invented photography was used for the first time in Belgian prisons in the 1840s, but since there was no means of reproducing photographs the work had very limited value. So, simply by taking an alias or slightly altering their appearance, repeat criminals most often went undetected.

In 1879 Frenchman Alphonse Bertillon invented a method of identifying people by measuring different parts of their bodies, ranging from the spread of their arms to the length of their left foot. As many as fourteen different measurements were taken; the odds against two people having the same Bertillon measurements were estimated at almost 300,000,000 to 1. The Bertillon Method became the primary means of criminal identification throughout Europe and America, and it might still be in use today if Will West hadn't been sentenced to serve time at Fort Leavenworth Prison in 1903.

When West arrived at Fort Leavenworth, his Bertillon measurements were taken—and when a clerk checked the files he found that a prisoner named Will West, who had essentially the same measurements, was already there serving a life sentence for murder. Improbable as it seemed, a second William West was indeed hard at work in one of the prison shops. Incredibly, although the two men did not know of each other's existence, they bore the same name, they looked like identical twins in prison photographs, and their Bertillon measurements were just about the same. In fact, the only thing about them that was remarkably different was their fingerprints. The next day the prison at Leavenworth abandoned the Bertillon system and began fingerprinting inmates.

A year later, a national fingerprint bureau, which included all federal prisoners, was established at Leavenworth. And in 1924 Congress established the Identification Division of the Bureau of Investigation as the national repository of all fingerprint records. For the first time, by comparing inked prints taken in association with various arrests of the same people, officials were able to connect crimes committed in different cities and states to the same criminals.

Fingerprinting caught the fancy of the American public during the gangster era, when it became the G-men's—as FBI agents were popularly known—first major scientific tool for tracking public enemies like Ma Barker, Jake Fleagle, and John Dillinger.

The Identification Division eventually became the largest operating unit within the FBI, employing more than 2,600 people. If your prints have ever been taken, they probably will be among the more than 200,000,000 prints representing more than 68,000,000 people on file in the bureau's Criminal Justice Information Services Division. About seventy percent of all people arrested already have their prints on file somewhere in the operations branch of this division.

But when Detective Columbo wants to know if a partial print found on a car radio button tuned to a rock-and-roll station belongs to a world-famous classical violinist, he submits it to the Latent Fingerprint Section, which officially was separated from the Ident Division and became part of the sci-crime lab in 1993. "Latents" works all criminal cases. The fact is that it's just about impossible to commit a crime without touching something at the crime scene. So the prints are there, but they're often invisible to the naked eye. To be of any investigative value, they have to be found and made visible, developed enough to be suitable for comparison, then compared to the known prints of a suspect. All that happens in the Latent Fingerprint Section.

Knowing where to look for prints and how to develop them is a fine art learned mostly through experience, and many of the nearly one hundred specialists in Latents have been on the job more than thirty years. "Often an entire case will hinge on the ability of the crime-scene investigator to find prints," explained Danny Greathouse, one of only five fingerprint specialists to become an agent. "The problem is that most of the time prints are invisible, so you have to know where to look for them.

"I always begin at the point of entry: Where did that unknown person come into the room? How did he get into the car? And the point of exit—how did he get out of there? Then I look around to see what's been disturbed, what's been moved. I look for footprints, which not only make good evidence, but they allow me to follow an individual's movements around an environment.

"There are always logical places to look. In motel rooms we often find prints on the wall next to the front window because someone has leaned on it while moving the curtain to peek outside. I remember one major drug case in which dealers hid out in an apartment and before they left they wiped down the whole place. The only print we found was on the bathroom mirror over the toilet; one of the men had leaned on it while going to the bathroom. In a bank robbery case the gang had carefully wiped down every inch of the apartment they'd lived in for weeks while planning the robbery, but when they left, someone forgot to turn on the dishwasher and we got all their prints off dirty dishes and glasses and silverware.

"When I was working in the field we had a case in which a young Wisconsin couple was kidnapped, the woman was murdered, and her husband was shot in the head but miraculously survived. While we were searching the area outside their apartment I picked up a cigarette butt and we were able to get a latent print off the filter. When the victims' car turned up at O'Hare Airport in Chicago, we found a different print on the inside of a window. I eventually developed two suspects and those prints enabled us to prove that one of them had been at the crime scene and the other one had been inside the car, evidence that certainly contributed to their convictions."

What makes fingerprints both unique and valuable is that they are usually invisible and can be found just about everywhere: Prints are found on paper in white-collar crimes, on ransom notes in kidnappings, and in blood at shootouts. In a car they are found on radio dials and seat levers and mirrors. Men's prints are often found on the underside of a toilet seat, made when they lifted it. In one murder case prints were found on the ear stem of a pair of glasses and proved the suspect had been in the victim's car. They have been found on a single match at a bank robbery. They have even been found on used toilet paper and used sanitary napkins and used condoms. They are found on all types of garbage, as well as on currency.

Sometimes the place prints are found is key to solving the case. In a Midwestern murder case, the prime suspect denied having access to the gun used in the killing—until his prints were found inside the gun, apparently left there when he cleaned it. Prints have been found inside bombs. In a New York City murder case the suspect's prints were found in a telephone book next to the listing of the victim's address. In a 1985 Mideast airplane hijacking in which five people were cold-bloodedly shot in the head by the hijackers and fifty-eight others died when commandos stormed the plane, one of the masked hijackers was identified and convicted from a print found in the charred remains of the cockpit. In a questioned suicide case the victim's own print was found on the plunger of the syringe used to inject the fatal overdose.

In a truly baffling Philadelphia robbery, an armored car picked up a locked sack filled with cash from the headquarters of a large bank, but when that bag was opened at a branch office, it was filled with rolls of toilet paper. Witnesses had seen the cash put in the bag, and the seal was still intact when the bag was delivered, but the cash had been replaced with toilet paper. The bag, the seal, and the rolls of paper were submitted to Latents. Everything was searched for prints, but the substitution remained a mystery until a specialist cut open the cardboard centers of the rolls and examined them. And on one of them he found a single fingerprint.

It belonged to a guard working on the armored car. Knowing the route the truck would follow, the guard had filled a money bag with toilet paper, sealed it, and stashed it in a trash can, and when the truck made a scheduled stop he had exchanged that bag for a cash bag. And except for that single print found on the inside of the toilet paper roll, he might have gotten away with it.

In one of the most unusual fingerprint cases, a print was found burned into a murder victim's pantyhose. When the body of a woman who had been tortured, raped, and then murdered was discovered floating in a creek, her clothing was sent to the lab for examination. Usually fingerprint specialists don't even look at fabrics because the weave obliterates ridge detail, and whatever oils might be present are rapidly absorbed. But in this case a specialist named Jerry Withers happened to notice an unusual pattern in the victim's pantyhose. When he looked at it a little more closely, he realized that a fingerprint had been burned into the nylon fibers. Rereading the details of the case, he learned that the victim had been tortured with a hot knife before she had been killed. The killer must have used the victim's pantyhose to protect his hand. The heated blade had melted the fabric; he had touched it while it was in a liquefied state, and when it cooled, his print was clearly and permanently impressed into the fabric—a print that led directly to a murder conviction.

Obviously, the more irregular the surface, the more difficult it will be to get the ridge detail needed for a comparison. It's difficult to get a print from a stucco wall or a cinderblock, for example. A lot of guns have rough or checked surfaces to make them easier to grip, especially when the shooter is sweating, and those surfaces pretty much eliminate the possibility that prints will be left on the weapon.

Once it was believed that it was just about impossible to develop prints on human skin, but under specific conditions it can be done. After a triple murder and rape in a Miami health club, for example, a local crime-scene technician decided to examine those areas that had to have been touched during the crime. One of the victims had been dragged across the floor by her feet and then raped, so the technician put fingerprint powder on her ankles and hips. Amazingly, he was able to develop several partial prints. In her terror, the victim had been sweating and had exuded various body oils. The killer had held her tightly, making clear prints in those oils. When she died her body had stopped absorbing the oils, leaving them on the surface of her smooth skin. The prints were eventually identified as those of a former club employee, who was convicted of the murders.

Prints can't be dated; there's no means of determining from a print how long it's been there. So other evidence has to be used to prove that a given print was made during the commission of a crime. In a Pennsylvania case, three men shot and killed the elderly owner of a grocery store during a holdup. When their prints were found on a glass counter, their defense attorney claimed the defendants had been in the store the day before. But the victim's wife testified that she had cleaned the counter the morning of the robbery, as she did every morning, so that the prints had to have been made after she had cleaned. The jury believed her and convicted the three holdup men of the murder.

The first rule of all latent-fingerprint examinations is that there are no rules. Where prints are involved, anything is possible. Nothing should be overlooked. For example, when labor leader Joseph Yablonski challenged the powerful leadership of the United Mine Workers union, he and his entire family were murdered. Pittsburgh police searching the area around his house found several discarded beverage cans. They had been lying in the rain and snow for at least a day, perhaps longer, and the freezing cold and wet weather certainly should have destroyed any latent prints. But this was a major case, so the cans were processed anyway—and to everyone's surprise several good prints were developed. It was later learned that the killers had waited patiently outside the Yablonski home, eating and drinking, until the family had gone to bed. Presumably grease or oil from the food had gotten on their hands and been transferred to the cans—substances that are particularly resistant to moisture. The prints enabled police to place the suspects at the Yablonski home at the time of the killings and contributed significantly to their conviction.

Making latent prints visible is really where fingerprinting becomes a science. Developing latent prints was once pretty simple. There were only four methods that worked. Dusting powder was used on nonporous surfaces, such as glass, plastic, or metal, while the chemicals iodine, ninhydrin, and silver nitrate were used on porous surfaces like paper, cardboard, and unfinished wood.

It was discovered almost a century ago that iodine fumes react with body fats and oils to make prints composed of those substances temporarily visible. In the 1950s scientists found that ninhydrin, the chemical most commonly used in fingerprint developing, reacts with amino acids or protein matter usually found in perspiration to make them visible. And silver nitrate combines with invisible body salts to form the very visible sodium chloride. These chemicals must be used in this order, or whatever latent prints might exist will be destroyed. And if these methods failed to produce prints on porous surfaces, it was generally accepted that they just weren't there.

That wasn't entirely true. The most historically significant exception took place on November 22, 1963, in Dallas, Texas, when President John F. Kennedy was assassinated by Lee Harvey Oswald. Less than two hours after Kennedy had been shot, Dallas police found a rifle lying next to a window in the Texas School Book Depository. A barricade of cardboard book cartons had been built around the window. Although Oswald's right palmprint was found on the rifle's stock, someone could have left the rifle there to implicate him. Following standard crime-scene procedure, detectives searched the area for latent prints. Oswald's fingerprints and palmprints were developed on three of the cardboard boxes and on a paper bag.

That proved nothing. If prints are to be connected to a crime, they have to be found in places they shouldn't be found. Oswald worked in the building, so it was not at all unusual that his prints would be found there. What the police had to prove was that these were fresh prints, that Oswald had been at that window within the last few hours. Since prints can't be dated, that was an almost impossible job. But not in this case, in which Dallas detectives had made one of the luckiest mistakes in sci-crime history.

Cardboard is a porous, or absorbent, surface. Detectives should have sprayed chemicals on the boxes, but they mistakenly used dusting powder—and they had developed several prints. The question was, why? The boxes were sent to the lab in Washington for a more complete examination. By experimenting with dusting powder on similar boxes, specialists discovered it would develop prints for up to three hours after they had been made, but then the body fluids would be absorbed into the cardboard, keeping prints from being developed. The fact that Oswald's prints had been developed with dusting powder proved he had been at that window within the time frame of the assassination.

The once-prosaic world of dusting powder and three chemicals began changing drastically in the 1970s as new chemicals and new techniques were discovered to make visible prints that once would have remained undetected. More than forty new methods of developing latent prints have been found, ranging from lasers to fumes from superglue—the same stuff you buy in the store and can't get off your fingers.

With so many different techniques available, the challenge in each case becomes picking the right process. Tim Trozzi, who joined the Bureau in 1979, said, "It's a combination of skill, experience, and intuition, and quite frankly, sometimes it's a bit of luck. You have to start by considering the nature of the object you're examining, how long the print might have been there, what type of atmospheric conditions it's been subjected to, and what else might have happened to it. If it's a car, for example, we'd want to know if it had been washed.

"Then we have to consider the properties of the different methods. I know, for example, that if I use iodine fumes first and that doesn't work, I can still go back and try superglue and fluorescent dyes. But if I use superglue first, I'll ruin it for iodine, and it might even inhibit me from using lasers. The problem is that every case is unique. What worked perfectly last time might not work at all this time."

In the past, making that decision was pretty simple: powders for non-porous materials, chemicals for porous ones. But now just about everything, porous or nonporous, is examined first under the laser. If prints cannot be seen under a laser, other methods are used.

Dry powders, which are available in a variety of colors to provide contrast against the surface, adhere to whatever moisture or chemicals remain on a nonporous surface.

If the evidence is fresh—if technicians are on the scene within hours of the crime's commission—the first thing they may try on a porous surface is iodine fuming. It used to be that prints developed with iodine fumes disappeared when the fumes dissipated, but now they can be fixed with a chemical spray and remain visible for as long as two days before fading. Liquid iodine has proved to be particularly effective in bringing up prints left on rubber gloves.

Ninhydrin is still used in a large percentage of cases. It works best in humid conditions, so many more prints are developed with it in the summer than in the winter, and it doesn't work very well at all in places with dry climates—Arizona, for instance. To produce humidity in the lab, after applying ninhydrin to a surface, specialists put the specimen in a "humidity cabinet" or apply heat and humidity with an ordinary steam iron.

Ninhydrin is especially good for developing prints on paper. In an Ohio murder case, the victim's body was found in his car, which had been pushed into the Ohio River. The only item found in the car that the victim's family couldn't identify was a map of the local area. The victim had grown up in that town; there was no reason he would need a map. So this map was put in a toaster oven and slowly dried. Once dry it was sprayed with ninhydrin and then steamed; several good prints immediately materialized. Those prints were linked to a suspect, who had apparently needed the map to find the river. The prints allowed the prosecutor to prove that the suspect had been in the victim's car, evidence that proved crucial in his conviction.

Silver nitrate is still used occasionally to develop prints on paper, but in many cases it's been replaced by a more effective multistep process called physical developer, in which the evidence is exposed to several different chemical solutions, much like developing a photograph.

Some chemicals will work only on very specific substances. Gentian vio-

let, for example, that old purple dye used for a variety of medicinal purposes, is very effective in developing prints left on adhesives, particularly on
the sticky side of tape. Multi-metal deposition develops prints left on photographs. Prints are often left in blood when a violent crime is committed,
but when the blood dries it loses its color and the prints disappear. Di-
aminobenzidine reacts with the enzymes remaining after the color is gone,
to produce visible prints.

Like many of these new techniques, the fact that common, ordinary superglue will cause prints to become visible was discovered by accident. In
1979, a British policeman used superglue, scientifically known as cyanoacry-
late, to repair a cracked film-processing tank in a darkroom. To his surprise,
he noticed that the glue illuminated fingerprints left on the side of the
tank. When he tried it on other surfaces he found that it produced distinct,
raised prints. Although it's now known that superglue adheres to the moisture found in latent prints, no one really knows why. It just does.

Superglue fuming quickly became one of the most efficient and produc-
tive means of developing latent prints. It works best when the glue is
heated in a dry, enclosed area—inside a sealed room or a car, for example.
Small evidence is fumed in a vacuum chamber, while a tent is built around
larger pieces of evidence. Colored dyes or powders may then be used to
make the prints stand out against the background.

In a San Mateo, California, case, a Taiwanese informant who was about
to reveal details of a major Taiwan government scandal to American reporters was murdered. His killers made their getaway on bicycles, which
were later abandoned. Traditional means of bringing up prints on nonporous surfaces failed, but when the bikes were superglued, a single print
became visible. The State Department then provided samples of the
prints of several high-ranking Taiwanese government officials, among
them some of the people who would have been implicated in the scandal.
And one of them was a perfect match. This official couldn't be linked
directly to the murder, but he was indicted for conspiracy. On the basis of
that single print, which only a few years earlier would not have been
found, he was convicted and sentenced to twenty-seven years to life in
prison.

The fact that lasers would make certain prints visible was accidentally
discovered in Canada in the mid-1970s. It seemed as if every time Cana-
dian researchers turned on their lasers, which are basically a high-energy
light source, the experiment was complicated by the presence of finger-

prints. Lasers were quickly adapted to law enforcement purposes. Lasers are nondestructive—unlike powders or chemicals, their use leaves no residue and won't damage the evidence. For that reason the first thing that happens when evidence arrives in the lab is that someone turns out the lights and turns on the laser.

No one knows why a laser will make some prints visible when other processes have failed to develop the same print. It's not known what the laser is reacting to in the print, but for some reason the method seems to work better on older evidence. For instance, in 1975 the U. S. Department of Justice initiated deportation proceedings against Valerian Trifa, a former archbishop of the Romanian Orthodox Church of America, claiming that when applying for naturalization he had concealed his World War II membership in the fascist Iron Guard, Romania's pro-Nazi party. Trifa denied these accusations and, after more than three decades, it was almost impossible to find any hard evidence against him.

But in 1982 the West German government produced a postcard Trifa sent to a high-ranking Nazi official in 1942; on it he pledged his loyalty. Trifa denied having written the postcard. The West Germans refused to allow the FBI lab to use any potentially destructive processes on this historic document, so powders, chemicals, and superglue couldn't be used. The laser was the only tool left. And under the intense laser beam, a left thumbprint, a print made forty years earlier, became visible. That print was identical to the inked print Trifa had voluntarily given when he became an American citizen. There was no question about it: the former archbishop was a Nazi war criminal. Technology had finally caught up with him, and he was deported in 1984.

In addition to the powerful lasers used in the lab, smaller portable lasers are used to search crime scenes. When a Vancouver, Washington, man was suspected in the abduction of several young children, authorities received permission to search his house. With the lights turned on brightly, investigators found nothing that could link the suspect to the missing children. But when the lab's Tommy Moorefield searched the house with the portable laser, he found a tiny footprint on a closet ceiling, a place no footprint should be found. That section of ceiling was cut out and sent to the lab for further processing with a more powerful laser; the footprint was identified as that of one of the missing children. It was later discovered that when the killer left his house, he would tie up his victims and leave them on the shelf at the top of this closet. One of those kids, struggling for his life, had left his footprint. The print was enough to link the suspect to the missing children.

Lasers are expensive; the laser used in the sci-crime lab cost $65,000, far beyond the budget of most law enforcement agencies. But among the new techniques now being used to develop latent prints is a combination of chemicals and alternate light sources. RAM, a fluorescent dye stain developed in the Latent Print Section, causes some prints to become visible under ultraviolet light, for example. So rather than needing a $65,000 laser, a police department can use a solution costing a few bucks and a hundred-dollar ultraviolet lamp.

Each process makes prints visible for a different length of time. Blowing on certain prints will make them visible as long as your breath lasts, for example. Prints made visible by a laser can be seen only as long as the laser is on, while superglued prints are almost permanent; they practically have to be chiseled off some evidence. Whatever method is used, a permanent copy of the print has to be made while it's visible. That means "lifting" it, or photographing it.

In the 1920s, when most prints were developed by powders, prints were lifted, or transferred from the evidence into a more permanent and transportable form, by using the sticky side of rubber patches made for automobile inner tubes. Those rubber patches have been replaced by rubber lifting tape.

But in almost every instance the preferred means of making a permanent record of a print is to photograph it. By placing various filters over the camera lens, it's possible to photograph prints that are invisible in ordinary light. For example, if a print left on a soda can is visible only when seen with filters under a laser, a photograph of that will show only the print—the can will disappear, because the camera simply doesn't "see" it at that wavelength.

Contrary to popular belief, finding a print at a crime scene or on other evidence is not enough to identify a suspect. The work really begins once the print is found and developed. Without the name or alias of a suspect, it's extremely difficult to find, among the more than two hundred million criminal prints on file, the part of one finger that matches.

Attempts to automate fingerprint searches so as to identify a suspect from a latent print began in the 1930s when the Bureau tried to create a database on punch cards, but that file was soon overwhelmed by the huge number of submissions. So until sci-crime entered the computer age, automated searches were rarely attempted and even more rarely successful. The art of fingerprint identification entered the computer age in 1968, when a rudimentary computer was used for the first time to assist in identifying the man who had assassinated Martin Luther King, Jr.

When Dr. King was murdered in Memphis, Tennessee, in 1968, detectives found latent prints on the rifle from which the fatal bullet was believed to have been fired, and on a pair of binoculars. When investigators find only a single print or a fragmentary print, it's very difficult to figure out which finger left that print. Sometimes that can be determined from the location of the print on the object. For example, people generally rip paper by holding it between their thumb and forefinger, so when a print is found on torn paper, it's generally assumed to be either a thumb or forefinger. In this case, because of the position as well as certain other characteristics, the prints were identified as that of the killer's left thumb. As Specialist Bobby Erwin explained, "We had a left thumbprint, we had the alias the killer had used when he checked into the hotel—'Eric S. Galt,' I believe it was—but we had nothing to match that print to. We needed a real name so we could find a card in our files.

"Memphis police and federal agents had developed a lot of suspects right off. But we just couldn't make a match. The police tracked this Galt to shoddy hotel rooms in several states, and we got a lot of paper items— newspapers and maps—and we developed more prints from those. We got one good print off a map found in a flophouse in Atlanta, identical to the prints found on the rifle and binoculars, that gave us a lot more detail."

Investigators checked the prints of known members of subversive groups like the KKK and the Minutemen, but were unable to make a match. With no other suspects, it was decided to compare that latent print to those of all current fugitives known to the Bureau. This turned out to be about 53,000 people. "But we had a physical description of the assassin and an identifiable thumbprint," Erwin pointed out, "so we asked our people, 'Can we narrow it down by physical description and a description of the type of print in the number six finger?' Using that information they conducted a computerized search and successfully narrowed it down to nineteen hundred individuals.

"Then we requested that the assembly section pull all those cards a hundred at a time and we were just going to sit there and go through them one by one. It was less than a needle in a haystack, because we didn't even know if the needle was there. So they brought the first hundred cards and I started going through them and I looked at the fifth card and there it was. The fifth card. I didn't have to compare it to our latent thumbprint. I'd looked at that print so often it was embedded in my mind. I saw this one and I almost fell out of my chair. The funny part of it was that the assistant supervisor, Dan Bailey, sat right across from me and at times during the search, just to shake things up, I'd say every once in a while, 'Hey, Dan, I got the guy.' He'd get excited and I'd confess I was kidding. This time though, I looked at him and said evenly, 'Dan, I got him.'

"He didn't believe me. 'I'm not kidding,' I said, 'I got him. It's him.' The fifth card. I handed the card to him and he just stared at it, then said softly, 'By God, it is him. Here goes the ball rolling.' That's how we finally identified James Earl Ray as the man who killed Dr. King."

Ray's prints were in the fugitive file because he had escaped from a Midwestern prison where he was serving time for robbery. He eventually pleaded guilty to Dr. King's murder and was sentenced to ninety-nine years in prison.

The procedure used to identify Ray has become far more sophisticated. Once it's determined which finger or fingers made a latent print, a computer search can be conducted. Prints are stored in the computer on the basis of the unique identifying characteristics found in a small portion of the center of the finger. The computer has a sort of digital map of that part of the finger. Obviously, the ability of the computer to identify an unknown individual by matching a latent print increases tremendously when additional information about the suspect is available, for instance his height or race, enabling investigators to be more specific in their search.

This system can be very effective. When an off-duty Harrisburg, Pennsylvania, policeman was murdered, his stolen van was spotted in Virginia. After a wild shootout on a highway, the killers escaped and abandoned the van in North Carolina. Several days later a van stolen from the North Carolina town in which the policeman's van had been recovered was found in Tallahassee, Florida. The same prints were found on both vans. Using a partial description of the killers, the Latent Print Section ran an automated search for those prints—and scored a hit. One of the killers, positively identified through his prints left on the vans, was subsequently convicted of the murder.

Every comparison between a latent print and a known print is done pretty much the same way, whether prints are being compared to try to find Martin Luther King's killer, or to identify putrefying remains from Jonestown, or simply to determine if an applicant for a civil service job has a criminal record. A specialist looks at one print and then another, back and forth, back and forth, comparing the shape and relative position of those thin lines.

The only thing that can be learned from a fingerprint is whether it matches another print. Prints aren't hereditary; there's absolutely no relationship between prints made by relatives, even identical twins. Neither race nor sex nor age can be determined from prints, although women generally have thinner ridges than men. It's impossible to determine health or occupation from a print, though some people who do manual labor tend to wear down the ridges of their fingers.

Prints either match or don't match, and that's all you can state positively about them. A print comparison is a subjective examination, it's a matter of expert opinion. One of the very first pieces of equipment adapted for sci-crime fingerprinting work, in the 1920s, was a linen counter, a handheld magnifying glass used in the textile industry to count threads. Many examiners still rely on a simple handheld magnifier, which enlarges prints three or four times, but they also have available a macroscope, which will magnify prints as much as $87\frac{1}{2}$ times as well as enhance the contrast; the comparison microscope, which enables them to look at two prints simultaneously; and the image enhancer, the first piece of equipment designed specifically for this work.

Prints that are just not clear enough to be used for comparative purposes can be further developed on the image-enhancer computer system, which converts the print into a digital image to make it suitable for a comparison.

A print comparison is based on ridges, the raised part of the skin, and their relationship to each other. Ridges start and stop, they change direction, they make circles and slopes, they make formations. A single ridge that branches off into two ridges is called a bifurcation. A ridge that stops suddenly is an ending ridge. A short ridge is, in fact, called a short ridge. A ridge that doesn't show direction is a dot.

For an examiner to decide that two prints have been made by the same person, every single characteristic of every identifiable ridge must be exactly the same. Most examiners begin by locating a similar point, a focal point, on each print. According to Greathouse, "We'll look at the thickness, the location of the pores, the breaks and changes in direction, everything. When we're confident we've found an identical point on each print we're comparing, then we'll look to see the relationship between that ridge and other formations. Maybe two ridges over and to the left there is a bifurcated ridge, and one ridge over and down from that there's an island formation, and three ridges over and to the right there might be another ending formation. Points begin to fall into place. Once two points of identity are located, the next step is to count the number of intervening ridges between them; if you've found two similar ridges, for two prints to be the same there must be the same number of intervening ridges between them, whether it's two or four or ten."

Most comparisons are based on the portion of the finger above the first joint. In that small area there are as many as three hundred identifiable points, known as minutiae, that can be used as the basis for comparison. There is no minimum number of points that must be identical for a match to be made; when a specialist decides that two or more prints are the same, for all legal purposes they are the same. British law mandates that at least sixteen points must be matched before a suspect can be indicted or an expert can testify in court. The sci-crime lab has matched prints with as few as seven points. But there only needs to be a single unexplainable dissimilarity between prints for them to be considered different.

For as long as law enforcement agencies have been using fingerprints to link suspects to crimes, criminals have been trying to find ways to destroy, disfigure, or disguise their prints. They have often tried to obliterate their prints with sandpaper, dental sanders, even acid, but ridges are several layers of skin deep and are not easily destroyed. Perhaps the most-publicized attempt to destroy prints was made by Public Enemy Number One, John Dillinger, who in the early 1930s paid a surgeon $5,000, plus $25 a day room and board at the doctor's house, to cut off his fingerprints and perform some minor facial surgery. The operation succeeded in creating scars that obscured the ridges in the center of each finger above the first joint, but the ridges outside that small center section were left intact, and that was more than enough to make a match. Legend has it that the man shot and killed by G-men outside Chicago's Biograph Theater was not Dillinger, but rather an unknown man who had been set up by the arch-criminal. But Special Agent Gerry Engert, one of the first agents assigned to the lab—and the man who took the prints from the dead body—said flatly that it wasn't true. "I know that was Dillinger's body," he said, "because I had the prints in my hand and I made the comparison to his known prints myself. There was absolutely no question about it."

In 1941, a criminal named Roscoe James Pitts gained a painful place in sci-crime history by having the skin surgically removed from his fingertips, which were then sewn onto his chest until they healed. That actually worked. Pitt's fingertips had no ridge pattern; he had successfully destroyed his fingerprints. But unfortunately for him, both his original print card, as well as the prints taken when he was arrested, included portions of the ridges just below the first joint, allowing him to be positively identified by a comparison of the ridges in the middle of his fingers.

No criminal has ever escaped prosecution by obliterating his fingerprints, although they continue to try. In 1990 Miami police arrested a suspect in a drug case whose prints were severely scarred. Latent-print experts soon discovered that the suspect had actually sliced his fingerprints into small pieces and transplanted those pieces onto other fingers. His fingertips had healed, leaving him with new prints in which broken ridges ran in all different directions, making it impossible to link him to previous crimes by comparing his prints.

Or so he thought. Latent-print specialist Tommy Moorefield was intrigued by the problem. He cut photographs of these prints into small pieces and began trying to fit these ridge patterns together; it was literally a human jigsaw puzzle. Nights and weekends, working at home and in his spare time in the office, Moorefield painstakingly restored small sections of several prints to their original pattern, until specialists in the Technical Section were able to match them to those of a fugitive convicted in another major drug case. That comparison led directly to the man's conviction.

Fingerprints are also a primary means of identifying a dead body. After 913 men, women, and children were murdered or committed suicide in Jonestown, Guyana, each one of their decomposing bodies had to be identified. When the shriveled body believed to be another victim of Atlanta child-killer Wayne Williams was pulled from a river, he had to be identified before police could trace his relationship to Williams.

Identifying a body is often a routine task. A local police department finds a body in the woods and needs to confirm its identity. So a set of fingerprints is taken from the body and submitted to the lab for comparison with prints on file in the Technical Section. But at times the job can be extraordinarily gruesome. Terrible things happen to bodies, things that make them unrecognizable as human beings, and those thin lines on their fingers may be among the very few physical clues to their identity.

In addition to the psychological problems caused by dealing with charred or mutilated or decaying bodies, it can be very difficult to obtain a print suitable for comparison. Very often the hands of people who die in accidents are found clenched into tight fists, and while that might be beneficial to specialists because the fingerprints are somewhat protected, first the hands have to be pried open. This can be done forcefully, it can be done by making small cuts in the base of the fingers, or it can be done by severing the hand from the body and heating it in a microwave oven for several minutes.

To return shriveled or badly wrinkled skin to a natural, rounded shape so as to obtain a print, investigators can soak it in water, heat it for a short time in a microwave, or inject it with a chemical substance called tissue builder. Conversely, if the finger is swollen, as it might be if the corpse was a "floater"—a body that has been in the water for a long time—sidelighting will create shadows in the fingerprint valleys, which can then be photographed. If the top layer of skin, the epidermis, has been destroyed or damaged or charred in a fire, it can be cut off, and usable prints can be obtained from the second layer of skin, the dermis. If it's intact but too soft or flabby to be printed, it can be sliced off, and after being briefly bathed in alcohol, slipped over the specialist's own finger, and printed as if it were part of that finger. Sometimes the ridge detail on the outer part of the skin has been mutilated but is still visible on the inner side. In that case the skin can be cut off and turned inside out and printed, but the valleys will show up as dark lines and the ridges will be the blank areas between them.

Very few law enforcement people are qualified to do this kind of work. So when a body is found, the necessary legal permissions are obtained, and the entire hand or the fingers are severed from the body and submitted to the lab. There they are processed in a neat, quietly respectful place called the Dead Room, officially known as the Deceased and Special Processing Room, room number 10986. There is nothing unique or special about the Dead Room to set it apart from the other offices in the lab. It's neat and clean and very quiet and has an antiseptic look about it. There are several long work counters, the microwave, and a large refrigerator in which the body parts are stored. Body parts are supposed to be submitted to the lab in a protective container; perhaps the most unusual submission came from a Texas sheriff, who sent a hand in a Kentucky Fried Chicken bucket.

The agents and examiners and specialists and technicians who work in the sci-crime lab have become accustomed to dealing with the horrors human beings can inflict upon each other. But of all the jobs in the lab, perhaps the most difficult assignment is working on the FBI's Disaster Squad. This is the front line of horror. In August 1940, a Pennsylvania Central airliner carrying twenty-five passengers, among them an FBI agent and an FBI stenographer, crashed into a Virginia cornfield. Most of the bodies were burned beyond recognition, so local FBI agents, wanting to give these victims their names back, volunteered to fingerprint the corpses and submit them to the Bureau for identification. That crash marked the birth of the little-known Disaster Squad. Since that time more than one hundred print specialists have worked almost two hundred disasters. They were in Puerto Rico to try to get prints from the charred bodies of the ninety-seven people who died in an arson fire at the DuPont Plaza Hotel; in Lockerbie, Scotland, to identify the victims of Pan Am Flight 103. They printed the Jonestown victims, the marines who died in the bombing of their Beirut, Lebanon, barracks, soldiers killed in Operation Desert Shield and Desert Storm, and Americans who have died in floods, fires, volcanic eruptions, and airplane crashes around the world. They even identified the remains of the astronauts who died in the explosion of the space shuttle *Challenger*.

As Carl Collins, a member of the Disaster Squad for more than two decades, explained, "The most important thing is not to think of a hand or body as being a person. It's a job to do."

"You just learn to cope with it," said Ron Hurt, who has been doing fingerprint work for more than three decades. "We know what to expect before we go in, and with the exception of the odor—you never get used to the odor, and once you've smelled it you never forget it—you find a way of dealing with it."

Just as in criminal cases, after a victim's print has been obtained it has to be compared with a known print for a positive identification to be made. If a victim's known print isn't on file, law enforcement personnel will go to the victim's home or office and lift prints off objects that person was known to have used: a telephone, a cosmetics case, a glass-top desk. Almost 60 percent of all remains examined by the Disaster Squad have been positively identified.

While fingerprinting remains the primary means of positively identifying an individual, it isn't the only way. In many cases, blood will tell. And, in fact, so will every other body fluid: semen, vaginal fluid, saliva, perspiration, and urine. There are grand tales written in blood, tales of passion and horror and murder, tales accessible only to those with the knowledge to read them. It's the job of the lab's DNA Analysis Unit to decipher these tales told by body fluids.

"We deal in violent crime," unit chief Dave Bigbee said; "that's all we have time to do. We're the people who get bloody clothing with bullet holes and knife tears in them, rocks covered with blood and hair and brains, a cinder block that's been dropped on somebody's skull. That evidence can give us a lot of information about what happened."

In violent crimes—murders and rapes, assaults, child molestations—body fluids are recovered more often than any other type of evidence, including fingerprints. Serial killer Ted Bundy was conclusively linked to one of his victims through saliva found in a bite mark on her body.

As the discoveries of science are applied to law enforcement, different areas of sci-crime take on a new significance. Until recently only a limited amount of information could be learned from body fluids. But now these fluids are the focus of the most significant advances since the amazing discovery more than a century ago that people could be positively identified by the lines on their skin.

Throughout history blood had often been found at the scene of violent crimes and on suspects, but it wasn't until 1901 that it even could be proved that blood had come from a human being rather than an animal. A few years later it was discovered that all human blood could be typed into four groups, A, B, AB, and O. Blood-group typing allowed police to associate suspects with a crime, but since so many people shared the same blood group, it was still not possible to identify a specific person from blood found at a crime scene.

While most often blood typing served to eliminate suspects, in very specific cases it could be valuable. In a 1955 case, a dishonorably discharged marine driving a stolen car was stopped by California highway patrolmen, who found both the marine's clothes and the car's interior covered with blood. A few hours later the body of the car's owner was found in the Nevada desert. Tests confirmed that the blood found on the suspect marine and in the car was type A, the same as the victim's, while the suspect himself was type O. The blood couldn't have been his. Additional evidence was found and the suspect pleaded guilty to murder.

Other body fluids—semen, saliva, perspiration, and vaginal fluids—had almost no value to law enforcement until researchers discovered in the 1950s that about eighty percent of all Americans secreted certain chemicals into those fluids, chemicals from which their blood group could be determined. These people are known as secretors, while the remaining twenty percent are known as nonsecretors. When an elderly woman was raped and murdered in Baltimore, for example, seminal stains found on her slip showed that she had been raped by a type B secretor. Eight suspects were identified—but only one of them was a type B secretor. Although the suspect had been linked to the crime by other evidence, it was when he was confronted by those test results that he confessed.

But this was still "class evidence," limiting the number of potential suspects to a small group rather than to a single person. It remained the dream of sci-crime researchers to find a method other than fingerprints by which a specific individual could be linked to a crime. That method was finally developed in the mid-1970s; surprisingly, it wasn't DNA.

Blood is partially composed of enzymes and proteins, which are collectively known as genetic markers. While they function exactly the same way in all human beings, they don't have the same chemical makeup. For example, the enzyme phosphoglucomutase, known as PGM, is found in everybody's blood, but thus far ten different types of PGM have been identified. Two people may share the same blood type, but statistically it is much less likely they would share a blood type *and* a PGM marker. Thus far scientists have identified twelve different genetic markers, each of them containing between three and ten types. Although all twelve are rarely identified in a blood sample, finding even three or four makes it possible to prove that a sample had come from one person in a million—in some cases, one in a hundred million.

In the small Tennessee town of Maynardville, a young married woman was abducted and beaten to death. A friend of her husband was suspected but there was little physical evidence to link him to the murder. Because he was often in their house, the fact that his hairs and fibers and fingerprints were found there had no value. Police searched his house, and in a clothes hamper they found the new Levi's jeans he'd been wearing earlier that day.

The jeans were sent to Dave Bigbee for examination. "Usually it's very difficult to do anything with blood found on Levi's jeans because the blue dye interferes with testing," Bigbee said. "But in this case we got lucky. One of the first things we routinely do is turn clothes inside out and cut them open at the seams. Sure enough, we found a dime-sized bloodstain in one of the pockets. The pockets are made of white cotton, and white cotton is a terrific material for typing. The suspect claimed that he'd been in a fistfight and had skinned his knuckles.

"We ran tests for all twelve enzyme systems, but we were able to get results in only five or six of them. Three of the enzymes could not possibly have come from the suspect, but were consistent with the victim's blood. The assumption was that he'd skinned his knuckles when he punched her and, probably without even thinking about it, had put his hands in his pockets. Statistically, chances were extraordinarily high that this was the victim's blood, and that's exactly the way I testified in court. This was the evidence that ultimately led to the suspect's conviction."

Genetic markers make very strong evidence. While serial killer Wayne Williams was convicted of two murders, authorities believe he may have been responsible for as many as thirty deaths in the Atlanta area. For example, some very small bloodstains were found underneath the seat of his car. The genetic markers developed from those stains were consistent with the markers found in the blood of two victims who had been stabbed to death. Had Williams been tried in those cases, this would have provided almost insurmountable evidence against him.

Chances that two people would have twelve identical markers are estimated at about 1 in 1,300,000,000. But the problem with genetic markers has turned out to be that they are not very stable; once blood is outside the body, the enzymes immediately begin deteriorating. By the time a bloodstain dries, several of the markers will have disappeared completely. And since most blood samples are submitted to the lab for analysis in the form of dried bloodstains on a piece of cloth or on other evidence—liquid blood is rarely received in the lab—from which small pieces can be removed for examination, many of the genetic markers have been lost by the time the samples arrive in the lab.

Enter DNA—deoxyribonucleic acid, the human genetic blueprint, the stuff that makes each of us each of us. DNA is extraordinarily valuable to scientists all over the world in investigating the secrets of life and death, but in sci-crime labs DNA is the long-sought connection between body fluids and the specific person from whom they came. DNA is the biological equivalent of fingerprints.

Basically—very basically—DNA is an extremely complex chemical consisting of four sub-units, called bases, that combine in various proportions to form molecules called nucleotides. There are three billion nucleotides in the nucleus of every one of your cells, linked in a chainlike sequence in an almost infinite variety of arrangements. Except for identical twins, each arrangement is unique; no one else in the world will have the same arrangement as you. And in every one of your cells, cells in your blood or your skin or your hair roots or your sperm, that arrangement will be exactly the same.

Different segments of that chain are responsible for different things—your eye color, whether you go bald or not—but for law enforcement purposes none of that is important. What matters is that a small segment of the chain can be isolated and printed on a sheet of photographic film. The result, called an autorad, looks just a bit like an out-of-focus bar code. But, unlike the countless cans of tomato soup that all bear the same bar code, no two people—again, except for identical twins—will have the same genetic code. So by developing an autorad from materials connected to a crime and comparing it to DNA taken from a suspect, investigators can link that suspect to that crime, or clear him of suspicion.

Like fingerprints, DNA can be used to make a positive identification. When an arm and hand were found in a shark's belly, the lab was able to identify the victim from a fingerprint. But fingerprints were of absolutely no value when part of a leg was found floating in a Florida river a few days after a woman college student had disappeared. However, because DNA from any part of the body is identical to DNA from any other part of the body, the lab was able to determine that this was not the missing student's leg. Even if a DNA specimen from the student hadn't been available, the examination could have been conducted by comparing DNA taken from the leg to DNA taken from a blood relative. Unlike prints, DNA is inherited, so a small segment of the DNA chain will be identical in all blood relations. Incredibly, in 1993 British DNA experts were able to confirm that a skeleton was indeed that of Czar Nicholas II of Russia, who had been slain in 1918 by Bolsheviks, by comparing DNA taken from those bones to a

DNA sample volunteered by England's Prince Philip, a distant blood relative of the czar.

One of the many advantages offered by DNA is that it's found everywhere white blood cells are found. Obviously, it's found in blood; it's found in semen in rape cases; it's in the skin found beneath a victim's fingernails after a struggle; it's in hair root follicles; it can even be found in saliva cells left on the mouthpiece of a telephone after a conversation.

But contrary to what has often been written, it isn't actually part of the composition of saliva or perspiration or urine or tears. DNA is found in only one place, the nucleus of cells. It is these cells that are often carried by body fluids, floating like weeds in a river. So while the best place to obtain a DNA sample might be from blood, it's much more easily obtained from the inside of the cheek. The epitherial cells on the inside of the cheek are among the loosest in the body; when you speak or cough or chew gum or smoke cigarettes or spit or dribble, some of these cells are expelled in your saliva, and a DNA profile can be developed from them. After the bombing of the World Trade Center, the FBI received a letter claiming responsibility for the explosion and threatening further attacks. A DNA profile was developed from cells found in the saliva used to seal the envelope flap. When a suspect in the bombing was identified, that profile was successfully matched to his known sample.

In another case, when Exxon executive Sidney Reso was kidnapped from his New Jersey home in April 1992, detectives traced ransom calls to the public phones from which they had been made. They not only dusted these phones for fingerprints, they also wiped them with cotton swabs to try to find DNA samples on the mouthpieces. Their hope was that when they found a suspect they would be able to use this evidence to prove he or she had used these phones. Unfortunately, matters never got that far. Reso died from a bullet wound suffered during his kidnapping, and his killers were captured when they tried to collect the ransom.

The use of DNA for sci-crime purposes was pioneered in the early 1980s in England by Dr. Alec Jeffreys at the University of Leicester. Britain's national sci-crime lab, a branch of the Home Office, began working cases in 1986. The FBI lab officially began accepting requests for DNA comparisons in December 1988, and its value so quickly became obvious that the lab ceased testing for genetic markers and changed the name of the unit from the Serology Unit to DNA Analysis.

Historically rape cases have been the most difficult of all violent crimes to solve. Only half of all reported rapes ended in arrests, and less than half of the people arrested were convicted; this is by far the lowest conviction rate for any violent crime. Part of the reason is that there was no way to connect the most important evidence in a rape case—the semen—to the suspect. DNA changed all that. In Tacoma, Washington, for example, a suspect confronted with DNA evidence pleaded guilty to the rape of an elderly woman suffering from Alzheimer's disease, even though the victim had no memory of the crime. In Cheyenne, Wyoming, a five-year-old girl was abducted and raped, and her body was found floating in a river. Three suspects were identified, among them her natural father. Her father's contribution to her DNA showed up clearly on the autorad, but his DNA did not match the semen found on her body. He was innocent. But the profile of his best friend's DNA did match. Confronted with this evidence, the suspect admitted that he had kidnapped and raped the little girl while he was drunk, but claimed she had died when she ran away from him and fell from a bridge into the river. He was sentenced to life in prison.

Conversely, in many cases DNA has provided defense attorneys with proof of their client's innocence. In fact, one of the early cases worked in the DNA Analysis Unit was eerily similar to the 1903 Will West case that established fingerprints as the accepted means of positive identification. It began one night in a dark bedroom when an intruder raped and beat a Parkville, Maryland, woman. Although in the dark she never got a good look at her attacker, she positively identified him as the man with whom she had recently ended a stormy four-year relationship. She had lived with this man and she said he had done it, and that was about as close to an open and shut case as possible. The man was arrested and charged with assault and rape.

The accused man had dark, curly hair and a dark, bushy beard. While in prison awaiting trial, he encountered the former boyfriend of the victim's roommate. This man, who had lived in the same neighborhood, also had dark, curly hair and a dark, bushy beard—in fact, he bore an uncanny resemblance to the suspect. In a dark room, in the terror of an attack, these two men easily could have been mistaken for each other. The suspect pleaded with detectives to investigate the second man.

Four months after the victim's boyfriend had been arrested, DNA tests conducted by the FBI lab proved he was not the rapist. The victim's positive identification had been wrong. Prosecutors then obtained a court order allowing them to take a blood sample from the second man. This time the DNA profiles matched; the second man was the rapist. Just as fingerprints had been the only means of telling the two William Wests apart, DNA was the only means of keeping an innocent man out of prison, and of putting the man who could have passed for his twin brother in prison for assault and rape.

In a similarly bizarre case, after five female college students were brutally murdered in Gainesville, Florida, in 1990, an eighteen-year old suspect diagnosed as a manic-depressive confessed to the killings, claiming they had been committed by his evil alter ego. But three of the victims had been raped, and DNA comparisons proved the confessed killer could not have committed the crimes. A week after the last murders a man named Danny Rolling was arrested on burglary charges in Ocala, Florida. Rolling was wanted in Shreveport, Louisiana, for attempted murder, and authorities there informed Gainesville police that several unsolved killings in that city were similiar to the Florida murders. A DNA comparison proved that Rolling had raped the victims. He was subsequently tried and convicted of murder and sentenced to death.

Another advantage offered by DNA is that, unlike genetic markers in blood, it's remarkably durable. Although DNA will deteriorate if exposed to radiation—sunlight, for instance—under proper conditions it can remain viable for thousands of years. Researchers have extracted DNA from body lice found on Egyptian mummies and from American Indian hair follicles hundreds of years old. This property allows examiners to reopen particularly heinous cases that occurred before DNA typing was available.

In 1972, an Oklahoma man named Gene Leroy Hart was charged with sexually assaulting and killing three Girl Scouts. The girls were on a camping trip when their killer cut his way into their tent, raped them, and murdered them. Hart had been tried for the crimes, but acquitted. Oklahoma authorities firmly believed he was the killer, but they hadn't been able to prove it. The triple murder had officially remained unsolved. It was possible the killer was still on the loose.

Hart was later convicted in another rape case and died of a heart attack while in prison. The Oklahoma state crime lab, anxious to finally close this case, sent the DNA Unit a sample of Hart's blood and the pillowcase with which the killer had wiped himself after raping the girls. Amazingly, specialists were able to develop a DNA profile from the twelve-year-old semen on the pillowcase. It was identical to the profile from Hart's blood. There was no longer any doubt about it: Gene Hart was the killer. The case was finally closed.

Often the only source of DNA is a drop of perspiration found on the sweat band of a cap or the saliva used to lick a stamp or left on a cigarette butt. Rapists have even attempted to destroy DNA in semen by pouring bleach or vinegar on their victims. But while a dime-sized blood sample is needed to detect some genetic markers, scientists can now develop a DNA profile from just a few human cells.

Researchers at Quantico have been working with a technique called polymerase chain reaction that allows them to amplify, or make copies of, that portion of the DNA chain needed to produce a profile. With this technique they can take one small cell found on the back of a stamp and, as if they were using a biological copying machine, reproduce it until they have the quantity needed to create a profile. This is about as close as law enforcement has ever gotten to being able to identify a criminal from the air he breathed.

In criminal cases DNA can be used only to either include or exclude a suspect. Presently there is absolutely no way of using it to develop a suspect. But several states are participating in the establishment of a national database in which the DNA profiles of convicted felons, especially sex offenders, will be stored. In addition to allowing police to identify repeat offenders from DNA left at a crime scene, the database will enable them to associate rapes committed in different places to the same man, and to coordinate investigations. In Indiana, for example, seven rapes were committed in the same area within a brief period of time. Authorities believed the crimes had been committed by a single serial rapist, but DNA typing proved that while five of the rapes had indeed been committed by one man, another man was responsible for two of them.

The embryonic database proved to be of extraordinary value when a twenty-four-year old Ritchie, Illinois, man was murdered and his twenty-one-year old wife was raped, shot in the head at point-blank range, and left for dead on a cold November morning in 1991. A year and a half later police still had no solid leads in the case. But in June 1993, Illinois sci-crime specialists entered the DNA profile developed from the killer's semen in their data bank. The Illinois state program was so new that it contained only six hundred DNA profiles developed from the blood of convicted sex offenders. Incredibly, the computer identified the DNA from the murder scene as that of an individual who had previously served time for sexually molesting a seventeen-year-old girl. Further testing confirmed the match. The individual was arrested and charged with the crime. A year later he was still awaiting trial.

The only information included in the planned national database will be the short chain used for comparisons. The FBI lab doesn't even develop the more complex profile needed to determine the race or sex of individuals, other physical attributes, or their medical history. They simply create an autorad, the bar code, and it either matches another submission or it doesn't.

There is a misconception that DNA eventually will replace just about every other sci-crime technology, particularly fingerprinting. This isn't true. DNA provides evidence that has never before been available in violent crimes, but it's complementary to prints. DNA is rarely found on paper, for example, but prints found on paper provide valuable evidence in a variety of crimes from money laundering to bank robberies to kidnapping.

It isn't only what's in blood that tells a tale. There's much to be learned from the patterns made by blood, the bloodstains and blood spatter. Sherlock Holmes once determined a man's height by measuring a bloodstain found on a wall, and perhaps that was the beginning of the study of blood spatter. Blood spatter is based on the fact that blood is a fluid and will act according to the laws of physics, like any other fluid. It will act the same way under the same circumstances every time.

According to Agent-examiner Bob Spaulding, one of the sci-crime world's most respected blood-spatter experts, "By observing the spot size, quantity, shape, distribution, location, angle of impact, and the target surface of a bloodstain, a lot of valuable information can be learned about what took place." Certain things will be true in every case. If an individual has blood spatter on himself, he was at the scene when a bloody object was being struck in some way. The more force with which someone is hit, the smaller the size of the resulting spatter. So a low-velocity impact, a punch in the nose causing blood to drip straight down to the floor, will leave larger spots, while a medium-velocity impact, perhaps from a stabbing or beating, will result in smaller spots. Bloodstains caused by the high-velocity impact of a bullet will be mistlike in appearance, with droplets about 1/25 of an inch in diameter. This mist will travel only a very short distance from the point of impact and will be dispersed in a conelike shape.

A path of elongated droplets several feet apart indicates that the victim was running; rounder droplets closer together mean he or she was walking. Some bloodstains will show directionality, and by drawing a line from the center of several stains, it's possible to determine where the assailant was located when he struck or shot the victim. A large stain on a surface—clothing, in many cases—is called a contact stain and means the surface was in touch with a bloody object.

A large bloodstain with an area void of blood means that something blocked the spray of blood, and therefore that it will be on some person or object. Several relatively straight lines of elongated bloodstains are called cast-off or in-line staining, and are caused by blood being thrown from a moving object, a knife or a club, as it changed direction. Castoff is often found on a ceiling in particularly brutal assaults, when each time the attacker drew back his weapon he threw off another line of blood. Castoff allows investigators to determine how many times the victim was struck—the total of blows is always at least one more than the number of stains, because at the first blow the weapon has no blood on it—and the direction from which the attack came, because blood is almost always cast off during the backswing.

The value of blood-spatter evidence was probably best exemplified in the case of Green Beret Dr. Jeffrey MacDonald, who claimed that drug-crazed hippies had broken into his home at the Fort Bragg Army Base in North Carolina, and murdered his pregnant wife and his two young daughters. MacDonald told a chilling story of what had happened that night, explaining that he had been stabbed and knocked unconscious, and on awakening found that his family had been slaughtered. All three victims had been stabbed repeatedly, and MacDonald's two daughters had also been beaten with a blunt instrument. He was the only survivor.

But the blood told a very different story. Although there was a great deal of hard evidence that contradicted MacDonald's version of the murders, Agent-examiner Paul Stombaugh, then chief of the Chemistry/Toxicology Unit, was able to use bloodstain and blood-spatter evidence to reconstruct the crime. What made this case so unusual was the fact that each of the people involved—MacDonald; his wife, Colette; and their two daughters, Kristen and Kimberly—had a different ABO blood type. By identifying the blood type found in each room and on the knives, ice pick, and clubs, Stombaugh was able to show where each person was struck and with what weapon.

Stombaugh's riveting testimony at a grand jury hearing in 1975 formed the key part of the prosecutor's case. Point by point he refuted MacDonald's story. "This is Kristen's room . . . ," he said matter-of-factly as the grand jurors were shown a color slide of the bloodied room. "This is the top sheet on that bed and it has a huge bloodstain on it. Yet there was no bloodstain underneath, on the bottom sheet. In reading the reports, it was reflected that the huge bloodstain on the top sheet in Kristen's room was type A blood—Colette's blood type. Kristen had type O blood, and the rest of the blood in that room, the bulk of it, was type O. . . .

"The only way you can get staining such as this is from a steady flow right down onto it. . . . At one time this had a very heavy flow of blood from a type A person directly onto it. . . . Now, if this bedspread had been placed down on the floor of Kristen's room, and Colette's body were lifted off the bed where she was bleeding, she would have bled directly on the spread. Then her body could have been covered with this sheet. . . . The spread, you see, is very heavy and blood does not soak through it. It acts like a bit of a well in there, and holds it. . . ."

The bedspread also had blood on it, but this was type AB, Kimberly's blood type—and the same type found on the club that was used to beat her to death. "This stain is not the result of direct bleeding," Stombaugh continued. "It's been a transfer of blood. In other words, a very bloody object having AB blood on it was placed there. It could have occurred by resting the club, in a bloody condition, on the bedspread."

Later in his testimony, Stombaugh told the jurors, "I think he picked Kim up, carried her into her bed and, due to the AB blood spatters on the wall, I believe he hit her again with the club and killed her."

Asked if he had any response to Stombaugh's testimony, MacDonald replied, "No, except that by my being unable to explain blood spots you make me guilty of the homicide of my family." Exactly what bloodstain and blood-spatter evidence is supposed to do.

MacDonald was indicted by the grand jury for the murder of his wife and children. Prosecutor James L. Blackburn told jurors during his summation, "I can only tell you from the physical evidence in this case that things do not lie. But I suggest that people can, and do. . . ."

And later Blackburn concluded, "[MacDonald's attorney] said earlier that the physical evidence doesn't mean anything—it doesn't speak. It is only the attorneys speaking. I say to you that physical evidence simply cries out an explanation."

The evidence spoke forcefully. MacDonald was convicted of the second-degree murder of Colette and Kimberly, and the first-degree murder of Kristen. He was sentenced to three consecutive life sentences, the most severe penalty the law could impose.

Reading blood spatter is an inexact science; there are a lot of variables involved, and rarely is blood-spatter evidence as significant as it was in the MacDonald case. But bloodstains and spatter can be particularly valuable in determining whether a death was a suicide or homicide. To the uneducated observer, it can also be very misleading. During a Texas heat wave, the body of a man was found hanging in his home; the walls and ceiling of the room were covered with tiny drops of blood. It looked as if he had been brutally beaten, then hanged. But only to the untrained eye.

"He'd been hanging there three or four days before they'd found him," Agent-examiner Linda Harrison said, "and during a Texas heat wave, that's a long, long time. His body had begun decomposing. When I first took a look at the photographs of the walls and ceiling, it did look like it might be blood spatter. But as I looked a little more carefully I could see that it wasn't. What it was all over those walls was fly excrement.

"Flies had been feeding on the body, then landing on the walls and ceiling with blood on their legs and excreting the blood they'd digested. One of the things that had made that obvious was a photograph showing a light bulb that had been left on. There wasn't a spot on it. The flies hadn't gone near it because it was too hot for them. If we had been dealing with blood spatter, we certainly would have found some there. We couldn't tell them for sure that this was a suicide, but we could tell them that the scene was not the result of a beating."

Once again, the blood had told the story.

CHAPTER
- 6 -

The Match Game:

The Materials Analysis and Elemental Analysis Units

Elementary.

SHERLOCK HOLMES,
in Sir Arthur Conan Doyle's "The Crooked Man"

"Evidence is sacred," Fred Whitehurst, an agent-examiner in the Materials Analysis Unit, said frankly, "because it can lead to me taking away your life and your liberty. So if society is going to use it to take away your most basic privileges, it better be damn good."

In a quiet, well-groomed suburban neighborhood just outside Tucson, Arizona, an eight-year-old girl rode her bike around the corner and was never seen again. In El Salvador, three American nuns and a lay worker arriving on a peace mission were murdered by government troops, who claimed that they had driven through a blockade. In Michigan, the bones of a fifteen-year-old girl were uncovered ten years after her murder, and the two men who had watched her die each swore the other had killed her. In Texas, the naked body of a young woman was found in a ditch at the edge of a highway, her hands and legs bound with tape; she was the victim of a serial killer.

Dead men do tell tales; evidence speaks for them. And anything, absolutely anything, can become evidence. Pause for a moment and look at your surroundings. If a crime were to occur right here, which of the things you see would you expect to become important evidence?

Evidence is anything that can be used to connect someone with a crime, a crime scene, or a victim, and you have probably overlooked the most ob-

159

vious things. What you saw when you looked around is the world of the FBI's Materials Analysis Unit and the Elemental Analysis Unit. "In most other crime labs we'd be referred to as the trace evidence unit," explained Jim Corby, the trim, soft-spoken chief of Materials Analysis. "We work with paints, glass, plastics and polymers, tapes and adhesives, soil and building materials, explosive residue, gemstones, cosmetics, lubricants, and just about anything else that doesn't seem to readily fit into another unit's expertise.

"We use them to try to put a suspect back at the crime scene by associating him with something he left there or something he took away with him. And we do that with some pretty good science. We compare samples microscopically, microchemically, and instrumentally. Everything we identify has to be confirmed by two different scientific methods following established protocols before we'll go into court with it. If we conclude that two samples came from the same place, you can be certain they did. And if we can't make an identification, we try to provide some information about a sample that might be of probative value to investigators. We try to tell them what it is and where it might have come from. To do that we've established sample collections in several different areas, ranging from our first collection, the National Automotive Paint File, which was started in 1932, to our newest collection, which consists of eighty-five different types of petroleum jellies."

Objects that the Materials Unit doesn't analyze, Elemental Analysis does. Elemental Analysis looks at the nuts and bolts of crime. Literally.

The unit was formed in the mid-1970s to take advantage of neutron activation, a sophisticated technology that allows examiners to determine the elemental composition of a substance in parts per billion—to get down to its basic chemical makeup. While the unit originally specialized in identifying gunshot residue—proving that someone had recently been very close to a fired gun—it has expanded to include the identification, comparison, and behavior of metals.

The substances frequently submitted to crime labs for identification and analysis are paints, glass, and soil. Paint may well be the most commonly encountered manmade substance in the world. We have covered our world in color. Pause again and think of a color, any color, then look around for objects that color. All sorts of things will jump out at you. And even though so much of the world is painted, the paint from a specific place may be unique. White paint is not just white paint. It's composed of organic and inorganic pigments to give it color, the solvent that carries the pigment, a binder to hold it to a surface, and additives that make it waterproof or shinier or longer-lasting. It may have been put on with a brush or a roller or a spray gun. And it has been exposed to environmental conditions ranging from bright sunlight to a kid with a crayon. Every one of these characteristics can make a given sample of white paint different from all other white paints, and also make it possible to establish that a sample came from a specific place or object and to connect that place or object with a suspect or victim.

While to most people the only important characteristic of paint is its color, the fact that paint is durable, chips or breaks easily, can be unique, and is transferred from one object to another makes it terrific evidence. In September 1984, in the small town of Flowing Wells, Arizona, eight-year-old Vicki Hoskinson went for a ride on her pink bicycle and disappeared. The bicycle was found hours later lying in the street, its frame slightly damaged, but the little girl seemed to have vanished. Seven months later some of her remains along with her crushed skull were found in the desert, the rest of her skeletal remains having been carried away by animals. There were no clues, no suspects.

The first break in the case came when a jailhouse informer claimed that a prisoner named Frank Jarvis Atwood had told him that he had bumped a little girl off her bicycle, then taken her into the desert, where he had sexually molested and strangled her, leaving her for dead. According to this story, Atwood had left the scene, but had dropped his car keys during the assault and had returned to find them. To his surprise the little girl was still alive, so he beat her to death with a rock.

It was an incriminating story, but without corroborating evidence it had little value. A good defense attorney would rip the informant's story apart, claiming that he had invented it to get his own sentence shortened. But proving that Atwood's car, which was in police custody, had hit the little girl's bike would put Atwood at the scene. Both the bicycle and the car's bumper were submitted to the sci-crime lab. On the bumper, Agent-examiner Tim Carlson found specks of pink paint, no larger than the dot over an "i." Carlson compared those specks with the paint on the bicycle. They were identical in every measurable way. And it was enough evidence to indict Frank Atwood for kidnapping and murder.

"It really wasn't more than a trace," Jim Corby remembered, "but it was enough to make a comparison. It had required extraordinary detective work by the local law enforcement to come up with this evidence. We work with

161

minute amounts of evidence and if we handle it carelessly or touch it the wrong way it might literally jump across the room. A breeze from an air vent can blow away the most important evidence in a case. At one time or another probably every person in this unit has been down on his knees searching the floor for a chip of paint."

Tim Carlson died of cancer before the trial began. In order to have an expert witness testify about the significance of the evidence, it was resubmitted to the lab and examined by Corby. Much of the prosecution's case rested on this trace of pink paint. Atwood's attorney tried to stop the tests, claiming, "The State will readily admit that they have absolutely no connection between Vicki Lynn Hoskinson . . . and Frank Jarvis Atwood, except insofar as the State alleges that the paint on the bumper of Frank Jarvis Atwood's vehicle originated from the bicycle of Vicki Lynn Hoskinson or another similar source."

The court permitted Corby to proceed with his examination, and he began by using a microscope to compare the pink paint from Atwood's bumper to a paint sample from the child's bicycle. The samples were the same color and had the same general physical appearance, that of an enamel paint. If anything about them had been different, Corby would have reported that they had not come from the same source. As in almost all other types of comparisons, there is no minimum number of characteristics that must match. Everything that can be measured or observed must match.

If Corby had been conducting this examination as he would have when he first joined the lab in 1965, he then would have applied various solvents to the two samples to see if they reacted the same way, and he would have reported that they had the same general class characteristics. But modern science has made it possible to go much further, to look at substances on a molecular level. Corby took a tiny piece of the speck and put it in the pyrolysis gas chromatograph mass spectrometer, which burned it at 760°C. The mass spec separates and charts the gases released by a substance as its organic components are vaporized, providing a detailed analysis of the chemical makeup of a sample. The chemical makeup of the pink paint from Atwood's car and the paint from the bike were alike.

Finally, Corby took the sample to Dennis Ward in Elemental Analysis, who examined both substances under a scanning electron microscope, which enabled him to identify the metallic elements present in the paint. As Corby testified at Atwood's trial, these tests could not prove that the pink paint on the bumper and the pink paint on the bicycle had come from the same source to the exclusion of all other possibilities. It simply meant they could have come from the same source.

But Ward suggested that if there had been a transfer of paint from the bicycle to the bumper, there also might have been a transfer of the bumper's nickel coating to the bicycle. Although to the naked eye there was no nickel present, in three different places on the bicycle the scanning electron microscope detected traces of nickel similiar to the nickel plating on the bumper of Atwood's car. The very unusual two-way transfer of paint and nickel enabled Corby to tell the jury, "In my opinion the pink paint on the bumper came from that bicycle or another source that had to be painted exactly like that bicycle." Legally, that was the strongest statement he could make. It was strong enough. Atwood's attorney called it "the most damning testimony in the case." The jury found Atwood guilty of the murder of Vicki Lynn Hoskinson, and he was sentenced to death.

A few chips of paint don't seem like very much, but in hit-and-run cases they are often the only evidence found at the scene. Compared to more highly publicized crimes, hit-and-run accidents have become so common it's easy to forget how brutal they can be. But the people who investigate them never forget. "We've gotten the clothes of hit-and-run victims in here that are like soup," Corby said. "They're just drenched with blood and body fluids. Sometimes a victim's body will be thrown more than a hundred feet from the point of impact, and when a body is hit with that kind of force it just explodes." Paint chips have been found embedded in victims' clothes, on their eyeglasses or belt buckles, in their shoes, under their fingernails, even on their false teeth. Almost no chip is too small to be useful; the basic rule of the unit is that if you can see it, you can work with it.

The National Automotive Paint File, which consists of more than 40,000 original paint finish samples, enables examiners to identify the year, make, and model of a car by comparing the physical characteristics and chemical composition of paint found at the crime scene with that of known specimens. For example, when a ten-year-old Los Angeles boy was killed by a hit-and-run driver, his clothing was sent to the lab. It was processed in an airtight scraping room and carefully scraped with a metal spatula. Several tiny sparkling paint chips fell from his pants, perhaps having been held there by the boy's dried blood. Using the paint file, these chips were identified as a gold metallic acrylic paint used on three car models by the same manufacturer. The lab reported to Los Angeles police department that the killer would be driving one of these models.

It didn't take the LAPD long to discover that one of the boy's neighbors drove a gold sports car. The suspect claimed he had recently replaced the hood of his car because it had been damaged in a traffic accident. When the hood was recovered and submitted to the lab, examiners were not only able to match the paint chips found in the victim's clothes to the car, they also found fibers caught in the metal that could be matched to the boy's jacket. Faced with this evidence, the owner of the car confessed to the crime.

The paint file includes only factory-applied paint. Obviously it isn't possible to use a sample from that collection to identify the make of a car that has been repainted. But once a suspect is identified, repainting does make it easier to prove that paint came from a specific vehicle. Each layer of paint makes a car just a little more unusual. The more layers of paint, the more remote the possibility that a paint sample came from any other source. In a Wisconsin hit-and-run case, the lab's ability to identify the eight layers of paint from a chip found at the scene allowed police to make an extremely strong association to the suspect's car. The chances of finding two cars that had been painted the same eight colors in the same sequence were considered very remote.

Ironically, as the ability of the lab to match evidence to samples has improved, car manufacturers have begun changing their paint systems to combat environmental hazards like acid rain, with the result that less paint is being found at crime scenes. As for Jim Corby, who probably knows as much about automotive paint systems as any sci-crime examiner in the world, he still relies on the old method of protecting the paint on his gray car: "I let a thick coat of dirt protect my paint. Washing it too often wears down that protective coating."

Paint can provide key information in any crime in which a car is involved. As a San Diego bank robbery team made their getaway from a parking lot, for example, they accidentally bumped into a parked car. The paint smudge left on that car enabled lab examiners to identify the make and model of the car the robbers were driving. The motor vehicle bureau provided a list of everyone in the area who owned that model, and that enabled police to identify the suspects. The foreign paint found on the car in the parking lot led directly to the apprehension of the bank robbers.

While a significant percentage of paint exams involve automotive paint, the Materials Analysis Unit also provides assistance in cases in which information can be learned from any kind of paint. For example, the lab's understanding of how paint is transferred when two objects collide provided valuable evidence for investigators trying to determine exactly what had caused an Air Florida jet to crash into Washington, D.C.'s, Fourteenth Street Bridge. Particles of automotive paint and glass found embedded in the fuselage of the plane were matched to the cars that had been on the bridge at the time of the crash. By comparing the places on the fuselage where paint and glass were found to the areas of the cars from which they had come, investigators were able to determine the angle of the plane as it skimmed over the bridge. That angle was an important clue to the cause of the crash.

While most paint examinations involve the comparison of two submissions, the expertise of the unit's examiners has been applied to several unusual and difficult cases. When a Navy helicopter crashed, for instance, investigators wanted to verify the craft's maintenance logs, which reported that several key parts from the rotor assembly had been stripped of paint, examined for cracks and metal fatigue, and then repainted. Some of these parts were sent to the lab and were examined by Jim Corby. "The question was how could we determine if the examinations recorded in the log had actually been conducted," Corby remembered. "Well, we know how certain paint formulations migrate, and we knew that if the cracks had been present when the parts were repainted we'd find a trace of that paint inside those cracks. And that's what we found. In at least some instances, the stress fractures, the tiny cracks, had been present when the parts were repainted, meaning that if the proper maintenance examinations had been done, those cracks should have been detected and the critical parts replaced or repaired."

Like any substance in use for centuries, the paints we apply today have evolved slowly and can often be dated by their components. If a paint contains a certain chemical compound, it must have been manufactured after that compound was in production. That can be very useful information. One of the great mysteries of this century is the fate of aviator Amelia Earhart, who vanished while on a flight around the world in 1937. So when parts of an airplane were discovered on a remote Pacific island in 1991, the FBI lab was asked to determine whether the paint on those parts could have come from Earhart's plane. The difficulty in conducting this type of examination is that there is no paint sample known to have come from the plane to use as a basis for comparison. The Materials Analysis Unit confirmed that the paint contained pigments and resin consistent with those known to have been used in paints in 1937. The parts could have come from her airplane, but without having other parts painted at the same time in the same place, it wasn't possible to conclude that they in fact had come from that airplane.

By finding chemicals in the paint that were not in use in 1937, the lab could have proved that the parts hadn't come from Earhart's plane. This is precisely what happened when the lab was asked to authenticate a painting purportedly by Renoir. Had it been a Renoir, it would have been worth a fortune. Using X-ray diffractometry, a process in which compounds are identified by the way X rays react as they pass through a substance, it was discovered that the pigment contained titanium dioxide and barium sulfate. Renoir had lived and painted long before titanium dioxide was used in pigment, so its presence in the sample proved that this painting was a forgery.

After paint, glass may well be the most ubiquitous manmade substance in our world, and glass fragments are found at a surprisingly large number of crime scenes. While people think of glass as fragile, in fact it is one of the hardest substances in the world, harder than steel—on geologists' scales, that is, in which substances are rated by their ability to scratch other materials. But glass breaks easily. And because it reacts in a highly predictable manner, detectives who understand the properties of glass can learn a great deal about what happened at a crime scene.

While a piece of glass may shatter into countless fragments of all sizes, every one of those fragments, the largest and the smallest, will have identical properties. The color will be the same and the density, dispersion, and refractive index will all be the same, allowing investigators to prove the tiniest sliver came from a specific picture window.

Among the many properties of glass that make it so valuable to detectives is that it adheres to almost any surface without people being aware of it, and it stays there for a long time. If you break a pane of glass, for example, tiny shards from that glass may get caught in your clothing, your hair, even the soles of your shoes, and may still be there after showering or laundering. In a classic example of the importance of glass as evidence, Chris Fiedler was assigned a case that involved what appeared to be a pretty ordinary examination of glass found on a suspect after an attempted rape in Baltimore. "Several elderly women in the area had been raped, and everybody in the neighborhood was very scared," he recalled. "One night a man broke into the home of an older woman and was confronted by her son, who had been staying there to protect her. The rapist panicked, dove through a window, then ran several blocks before he was captured. Baltimore police submitted samples from the window he'd dived through, as well as numerous slivers of glass that had been found on his body, in his clothing, and on a pair of leather gloves he was wearing when they caught him.

"I was able to associate some of the glass found on the suspect and the glass from the broken window, but what surprised me was that some of the glass found on the suspect hadn't come from that window. Who knew how long he'd been carrying it around? The police went back to several other houses where the rapist had gained entry by smashing a window. The broken glass had been replaced, but by wiping down the windowsills with a damp cloth and searching the floor inside and the ground outside they were able to come up with fragments from the broken windows. No matter how hard you try to clean up broken glass, there are usually going to be a few slivers left behind. By measuring the refractive index, the dispersion, and the density of the glass, and then by looking at it instrumentally to determine the elemental composition—how much of which elements made up the glass—I was able to connect the suspect to three other rapes. This significantly contributed to his conviction and he was sentenced to a long prison term."

Few people realize how hard and durable glass is. Because it is stronger than most other substances, glass is often found embedded in hammers, crowbars, and other tools used to smash into a home or building. Even if the suspect knows that the chips are there, it's just about impossible to remove them all. That fact turned out to be the key to the solution of a mass murder in Georgia. An entire family, six people, were shot and killed by an intruder. Local police had no clues, no suspects, no apparent motive—no place to start their investigation. But several weeks after the murders, a young boy fishing in a pond snagged a .22 Magnum, the same caliber as the missing murder weapon.

Police were able to trace the gun back to its owner, who admitted knowing the murdered family but provided a reasonable alibi for the night of the slaughter. The gun and the bullets recovered from the victims' bodies were sent to the Firearms Unit. The bullets had been too badly damaged for a match to be made, but a Firearms examiner noticed several long scratches on the gun barrel. There was nothing really special about them, but he was curious. So he brought the gun over to Chris Fiedler to see if those scratches might be significant.

Fiedler found tiny bits of glass and powder in the scratches. There wasn't even enough glass to cause a small cut on your finger, but it was still more than enough to use as a basis for comparison. To gain entry into the victims' home, the killer had smashed a small pane of glass with an unknown object. A gun, maybe? Even though the gun had lain at the bottom of a pond for weeks, the glass was still firmly embedded in the barrel. Fiedler was able to make a match between those slivers and the broken glass from the victims' back door. The gun had been used in the killings. To escape the death penalty, the suspect pled guilty to murder and was sentenced to life in prison.

In many violent crimes, bullets are fired through glass, and an examination of that glass can reveal certain details about the crime. In an ideal situation, three things about a shooting can be determined from a sheet of glass: which side the shooter was standing on; the angle from which the bullet was fired; and, if more than one shot was fired, the sequence in which they were fired.

It's logical to assume that when someone shoots through glass the fragments will be found on the opposite side of that glass. Logical, but wrong. Glass is elastic, and when a projectile of any kind hits it or goes through it, glass will bend like a tree in the wind, then snap back violently. This phenomenon is called blowback. Glass will blow back as far as eighteen feet in the direction from which the projectile came. In many cases police have been able to place a suspect within twelve to eighteen feet from a piece of glass through the particles found on his clothing or body.

In addition to knowing how far from the glass the shooter was standing, it's possible to approximate his location by determining the angle at which the bullet struck the glass. If the bullet hole in the glass is symmetrical, perfectly round, the bullet was fired at a right angle to the glass; the shooter was standing directly in front of it. As the angle of the shooter to the glass increases the hole will become elongated; the greater the angle the more elongated the hole will be.

It's also possible to determine from a sheet of glass the order in which shots were fired through it. This has proved to be particularly important in cases in which suspects claim that a law enforcement officer had fired first, and they returned fire in self-defense. In just about every TV shootout, a single bullet causes a window to burst into countless pieces. Most of the time that isn't what happens. Tempered glass or glass that is held securely in a frame will usually crack but not shatter. In fact, you can shoot several bullets through a pane of glass before it falls apart, and under certain circumstances it's possible to examine that glass and determine the sequence in which the shots were fired.

When a wounded suspect was charged with attempted murder for shooting at a California highway patrolman, he claimed he had fired in self-defense, after the officer had fired at him. It was the suspect's word against the officer's, with the suspect's freedom and the officer's career at stake.

Several shots had been fired through the windshield of the suspect's car. It looked a bit like a crazed spider's web, and long thin cracks emanated from each bullet hole, turning the windshield into a glass maze. Figuring out the sequence in which the shots had been fired meant finding a path through that maze. Cracks will radiate from anything that pierces a sheet of glass, but they will stop when they meet another crack. So the first shot will cause many uninterrupted cracks. The cracks created by the second shot will terminate wherever they cross paths with cracks from the first shot; cracks created by the third shot will stop when they meet cracks from either of the first two shots; and so on. The cracks must make contact; there is no way to determine when an isolated shot was fired. But once two or more bullet holes are put in sequence, the size of the hole, the angle of the shot, and the residue found around the point of entry together enable investigators to determine which gun fired what bullet. In the California case it was proved that the suspect had fired first, and had been hit when the patrolman returned his fire.

Proving that pieces of glass have the same composition makes for a strong association, but showing that they once fit together makes for a positive match. In hit-and-run cases, in particular, the fitting of a shard of headlight glass found at the scene to the broken headlight on a car means that this car, to the exclusion of every other car in the world, was involved in the crime. But glass fracture matches can be made in other types of cases, too. In Butte, Montana, the badly burned body of a murder victim was found smoldering in the woods. From the lack of blood at the scene and the fact that there were no signs of a struggle, it was obvious that he had been killed elsewhere, then dumped in the woods and set afire. His clothing had been destroyed, but police found several pieces of glass that had not been damaged by the fire.

A suspect was identified and in his garbage pail investigators found several pieces of glass from a broken window. Agent-examiner Bruce Hall was asked to try to link the fragments. "The first thing we usually do when we get large fragments of glass in here is try to fit the pieces together," he said. "That's about the most meaningful evidence there is. In this case we got lucky. The pieces found on the body fitted perfectly to pieces found in the suspect's trash. It was like putting a jigsaw puzzle together. Apparently a window in the suspect's trailer had been smashed during a fight and the suspect never realized that some fragments of glass had struck his victim. We got a guilty plea in that case."

Because bits of glass are small and just about impossible to trace, glass is often used to contaminate consumer products. In many instances consumers claiming to find bits of glass in a product have demanded payment from the manufacturer. In these cases, the fault might lie with the manufacturer, the glass might have been put into the product by someone tampering with it in the store, or the consumer might be committing fraud, hoping for a quick payoff.

One of the most publicized product-tampering cases occurred in 1988, when mothers around the country began complaining that they were finding tiny pieces of glass in jars of Gerber's baby food. That kind of publicity can ruin a company, even if it's not responsible, by destroying consumers' confidence in the safety of a product. Dozens of jars of baby food in which glass particles supposedly had been found were submitted to the lab from all over the country. Chris Fiedler got the case. The fact that supposedly contaminated jars had been found in so many different places made it very unlikely that this was a true product-tampering case—unless somebody was doing a lot of traveling just to put glass in baby food—so the presence of the glass was either the fault of the manufacturer or consumer fraud. "We spent a tremendous amount of time looking at those jars," Fiedler said. "We knew that if the contamination had occurred at the plant level, we would find the same type of glass in different jars. Well, we didn't. Instead we found many different types of glass—mirror glass, headlight glass, lightbulb glass—but we didn't find the same glass in two different jars. The glass in every single jar was unique. We have had cases in which a bulb broke over a packaging line and bits of glass got in several boxes or cans, but this wasn't one of them. In my opinion, the fact that different glass was found in the jars meant it had been put in there by different consumers, presumably because they thought the company would pay them."

Because glass is so common, people often forget that it can be extremely valuable, valuable enough to be counterfeited. One of the largest product-counterfeiting cases in recent history involved high-quality crystal. The manufacturer estimated that over a five-year period more than $40 million in counterfeit crystal was sold to consumers. To the consumer the products, including the packaging, looked exactly alike, but tests performed in the lab showed that the counterfeit crystal had a lower lead content than the authentic crystal. That didn't mean the glass was weaker, but rather that it wasn't as clear. Nor was it worth what consumers had paid for it. In this examination it was relatively simple for the examiners to see right through the fraud.

Sometimes dirt can make the facts of a case as clear as glass. In March 1975, a fifteen-year-old Michigan girl about to give information to authorities about two men with whom she was involved in a bad-check scam disappeared and was never seen again. In April one of the two men was sent to prison for an unrelated crime. A decade later, the other man involved in the check-passing scam claimed that his former partner had strangled the girl in his car, shot her in the head, then buried her. He didn't know exactly where she had been buried, he explained, because when his partner took her body into the woods, he had fled. On the basis of this testimony, the first man was tried and convicted of the murder, even though the girl's body was never found.

After being sentenced to prison for the murder, the first man appealed, invoking the classic "The other guy did it" defense. According to his story, in August 1975, while he was behind bars, the second man had thrown the girl off a railroad trestle onto the rocks below, then buried her in the area. Thus two men each claimed that the other one had committed the murder. There were no other witnesses. How do you determine which man was telling the truth? How do you know either man is telling the truth?

Among the discrepancies in the conflicting stories was the claim that the girl had been shot in the head. If she hadn't been, the second man's testimony, the testimony that had sent his partner to prison, would be discredited. In order to prove that she hadn't been shot, the man convicted of the murder finally told authorities where her body had been buried. Her skeletal remains were found precisely where he said they would be, and there was no bullet wound in her skull. She had not been shot. Which man was telling the truth: the man convicted of the crime, who had supposedly shot her in March, or his accuser, who had supposedly killed her in August? If she had been killed in August, the convicted killer could not have committed the crime because he had been in jail.

The victim's decayed clothing and several pounds of dirt found at the grave site were submitted to the lab. The case was assigned to Chris Fiedler, who enlisted the help of Wayne Lord, the Bureau's entomologist, the bug expert, who was working in the Research and Training Unit in Quantico, Virginia. Fiedler and Lord visited the grave site in late spring. As Fiedler remembered that trip, "She'd been buried in a swampy area and when we were there, there was a tremendous amount of insect activity. The mosquitoes were just awful; we were getting bit all over.

"Back in the lab the first thing we did was send her clothes over to Hairs and Fibers to determine what they were made of. We only had some scraps, but we knew that if she had been wearing winter clothing—wool socks, a jacket—we were probably talking about March rather than August. Then Wayne Lord started examining the soil for evidence of insect activity. Soil is very predictable; we knew what we should find. The soil in the area was very sandy. It was soft when we were there, meaning insects would have been able to get into the ground pretty easily—unless, of course, it had been frozen when she was buried.

"There were no insects in the soil. And she had been wearing heavy clothing. The combination of the Hairs and Fibers exams and the fact that Wayne Lord found no insect activity in the soil led us to conclude that she'd been killed and buried in March. We never found out why there was a discrepancy about the gunshot wound to the head. Maybe the guy took a shot at her and missed, but it didn't make any difference. His appeal was denied and he's still in prison for her murder."

Specifically, in the sci-crime business, "soil" or "dirt" means any type of natural ground cover that has accumulated over a period of time, whether it comes from a fertilized field in the country, a park in the city, or a sandy beach. The fact that soil has predictable properties—it freezes, it migrates, it absorbs fluids—makes it valuable in cases like the Michigan murder. But its primary value is that it allows investigators to associate a person or an object with a specific place because, while one soil sample may look like any other, soil is unique to a specific location. And as every mother with a once-clean floor will attest, it's very easily transported.

Soil is naturally composed of four parts: minerals, organic matter—anything once part of a living organism—air, and water. It's also subject to changes wrought by the environment or by humans: bird or animal droppings, floods, the presence of fertilizer, building materials, or even particles from roof shingles. And all of these things combine to make soil from a specific place unique and identifiable.

The first step in a soil comparison is to compare the color of the soils under different light sources. If two samples are different in color, they came from different places. Why they're different isn't important for law enforcement purposes; the fact that they look different under the same conditions means they are different. A nationally used color chart allows soil comparisons to be made by telephone so investigators will know if they are, literally, on the right track.

Next, the texture of the soil samples and the presence of any peculiarities—things like plants, seeds or droppings, building materials—are compared. If they match, the soil is then washed in an ultrasonic cleaner. Washing dirt with high-frequency sound waves enables examiners to isolate the minerals or extraneous matter like glass or bricks that might be there. The washed samples are then dropped into a heavy liquid called bromoform, a chemical with a high specific gravity; the lighter minerals, like quartz, float on the surface, while the heavier minerals sink to the bottom. If two samples came from the same place, they will contain essentially the same type and density of minerals in addition to all the other matter.

If soil samples from two things found in different places match, they prove that the items were once in the same place. And that can cover a lot of ground. A month after Adolph Coors of the Coors Brewing Company was kidnapped in Colorado in 1960, a car belonging to the prime suspect was found burned in an Atlantic City, New Jersey, dump. The fire had destroyed just about everything that might have provided clues to Coors's whereabouts. But four different types of soil were found under the front fender. One of the soils came from the dump, but the other three were consistent with soil from the Rocky Mountain area. When Coors's buried body finally was found several months later, one of those soil samples from the car could be matched to an area not far from the grave site. It was enough to show that the suspect had been in that area, and it became one of the key pieces of evidence at the trial. The suspect was convicted and sentenced to life imprisonment.

Much more recently, when DEA agent Kiki Camarena disappeared along with the pilot who helped him discover large marijuana plantations near Guadalajara, Mexico, the primary suspects in the kidnappings were the owners of the plantations, who were known to be paying large bribes to

173

Mexican government officials. But two days after a government raid on a smaller plantation, in which all the members of that drug gang were killed, the bodies of Camarena and his pilot were found wrapped in sheets lying in a ditch. Agents from the FBI lab were given a few minutes to examine the bodies, which were covered with dark soil. The agents were surprised that the bodies had suffered no animal or insect damage. An exposed body normally will be attacked by animals and insects very quickly. These bodies showed no signs of such activity.

The reason for that became obvious the next day, when the agents were permitted to visit the spot where the bodies had been found and where they had allegedly been lying for several weeks. Even a casual look at the site made two things clear. No body fluids had seeped into the soil, and the dirt was light-gray in color. The lack of body fluids proved that the bodies had not been buried there for any length of time, and the fact that the dirt found on the bodies was not light gray indicated that they had been buried elsewhere first and then brought to the ditch to be discovered. The Mexican government's attempt to blame the murders on the smaller drug ring had failed.

Contrary to the TV-created myth, it's just about impossible to trace soil back to its source without a lot of additional information. Finding soil on a shovel doesn't do detectives much good if they don't know where the grave is. When a dirt-encrusted packet of the ransom money paid to skyjacker D. B. Cooper turned up near the mouth of the Columbia River, investigators studied the layers of hardened dirt in an effort to pinpoint the area in which the money had landed; the hope was to find some evidence of Cooper's fate. Certain clues can be obtained from a soil sample, among them whether it was close to a road or near a structure of some kind, how close it was to fresh water or salt water, what type of plant and animal life might be found nearby, whether the area was urban or rural, whether it had been fertilized or planted, and while some information was elicited from the Cooper sample, no additional money or evidence of Cooper's fate has yet been found.

Sometimes it's the manmade materials found in a soil sample that enable detectives to link a suspect to a crime. A realistic pipe bomb used in a Miami extortion case turned out to be filled with soil, to give it the necessary weight, rather than gunpowder. Among the extraneous materials found in the soil were bits of solder and tiny green chips from roof shingles. When a suspect was identified, his attorney pointed out that the soil found in the bomb could have come from anywhere on the suspect's block. That was true, but the only house on the block with green shingles belonged to the suspect. Every other house had red shingles. Additionally, the suspect had recently installed an outdoor faucet and the solder used in that job was consistent with the solder found in the soil. The combination of the type of soil, the green chips, and the solder allowed prosecutors to show, within a few feet, the source of the soil found in the dummy bomb.

While detectives often speak of tying a suspect to a crime, they are much more likely to be able to tape him to it. One of the most common denominators of violent crimes is the use of duct tape. In fact, criminals use it so often that it's commonly referred to as crime tape. Duct tape is used to bind victims' hands and feet; it's used to cover their mouths or blindfold them; it's used to hold bombs together; it's used in burglaries—in the Watergate burglary, for instance—to keep doors open; and, while it usually isn't the murder weapon, it often plays a significant role in killings. In an Indiana case the victim was taped to railroad tracks. He was killed by the train, but he was held in place by the tape. The killer was tied, or taped, to the crime when the tape used in the murder was proved to have come from a roll of tape found in his pickup truck.

Because tape is so often found at crime scenes, the Materials Analysis Unit has set up a tape collection, which currently consists of approximately one thousand samples from around the world. According to chemist Roger Keagy: "When we get an unknown tape in here, we want to be able to tell the contributors what they should be looking for. Generally we can tell them who manufactured the tape, what color filler yarns it'll have, whether it was made for consumer or industrial use, and in some cases, if it's a specialized tape, even the type of industry. We can at least provide some leads."

When a piece of tape used in a crime, and tape from a known source that might be linked to that piece, arrive in the lab, the examiner first tries to match their ends. That's the strongest of possible matches. In the mid-1980s a serial killer was raping and murdering women in several Southwestern states. Each of his victims was found nude, her hands and feet bound together with duct tape. Police estimated that he had murdered as many as ten women. Soon after a body was found just off an interstate highway in Amarillo, Texas, a truck driver named Herbert Benjamin Boyle became the prime suspect. In the cab of Boyle's rig, police found a strip of duct tape that he had used to make a temporary repair. Jim Corby examined the evidence. "We got the tape in from the body of his last victim and the sample from his truck. And we were lucky. I was able to fit the torn end of the tape found on the victim to the piece found in his truck. It was an absolutely positive association.

"But then I was able to go further than that. As his other victims were found, we were able to prove, either by an end match or by the chemical composition of the tape, that the suspect had used the same tape on several of his victims. When I testified, I had about fifteen segments of tape, and I demonstrated to the jury how they all fit together—and how every one of them could be matched to the tape found in Boyle's truck. It was as if the string of murder victims was being held together by this tape. Boyle was sentenced to death."

Linking segments of tape together is valuable only if the tape can be associated with a suspect. Otherwise all you have is a torn roll of tape. After the examiner attempts to make an end match, the crime tape will be sent to Hairs and Fiber, where they look for bits of hair or material in the adhesive, and to the Latent Fingerprint Section, where examiners try to find fingerprints. It's pretty difficult to use tape without touching the adhesive, so prints are often found on tapes. In the Boyle case, for example, his thumbprint, found on a segment of tape used to bind one of his victims, provided very strong evidence that he had used the tape in his killing spree.

If an end match isn't possible, then investigators compare the tape's physical characteristics—color, width, thickness, number of work yarns (the threads that run the length of the tape) and fill yarns (the threads that run across its width)—and, finally, the chemical composition of the tape backing and the adhesive. A primary difference between various brands and grades of duct tape is the type and amount of the adhesive. While not as conclusive as an end match, a characteristic and compositional match is still significant evidence. In a Garrison, Texas, case that received national attention because the police officer involved videotaped his own murder, three men were stopped by Constable Darrell Lunsford on a lonely highway. While a camera mounted in Lunsford's police cruiser recorded the scene, the officer searched the suspects' car for drugs. Suddenly one of the men grabbed the officer's gun and, off-camera, shot and killed him.

The videotape was sent to the Materials Analysis Unit, and after it had been enhanced by the lab's Video Support Unit, it was probably enough to ensure the conviction of the suspects, who had been captured. But it was still important to tie the suspects to drugs, because that would provide their motive for shooting the police officer and would make a life-or-death difference in their sentences.

While no drugs had been found in the suspects' car, several bags of marijuana were found in a nearby field. The bags were sealed with tape, and a roll of similar tape was found in the suspects' car. Proving that the tape on the bags had come from the roll in the car would link the suspects to the drugs. The ends of the tape didn't match, and no fingerprints or fibers were found, so a compositional exam was done.

The adhesive was analyzed on a pyrolysis gas chromatograph. This instrument separates the different chemicals that make up an organic substance. As each of the components of a substance turns into a gas, it registers a peak on a printed graph. By comparing the time at which a given sample's peaks occur with the known reactions, it's possible to characterize the sample's chemical makeup. The tapes found on the marijuana bags registered three more peaks, or components, than the tape found in the car. There was no match. This could have been invaluable to the defense.

Agent-examiner Richard Buechele, a chemist who prior to joining the lab had worked in private industry researching explosive residues and developing a method for extracting toxins from body tissue, then worked three and a half years as a street agent in New York City, did the analysis. "Using other techniques I was able to identify the additional chemicals," he said. "I just didn't know what they were doing there. And as long as I couldn't figure that out, I couldn't testify that these tapes were the same. I couldn't link the drugs to the suspects. The detective who had found the bags told me they'd been wrapped in the sweet-smelling paper sheets used in washing machines to eliminate static cling, which are used by drug smugglers to help prevent dogs from smelling the drugs. I tested several different brands of those sheets, but they weren't producing the extra peaks. I thought: Maybe it's just a fragrance. So I contacted fragrance manufacturers. A chemist at Custom Essence in New Jersey finally suggested that my unknown chemicals could be the volatile organic compounds found in marijuana. Suddenly it became very clear. The scent of the marijuana had been absorbed by the adhesive and was being detected and recorded by the gas chromatograph. Eliminating those peaks not only allowed me to make a match between the tapes, it also allowed me to demonstrate that the tape had been used in the transportation of drugs. All three men were convicted, and I know the work we did here contributed to those convictions."

Sometimes it just seems as if the world is made of plastic. Once again, wherever you are, look around and see how many things right in front of you are made out of plastic. So much of our world is plastic, from rigid automobile panels to flexible wire coating, that plastics have become a substantial part of the Materials Analysis Unit's workload. But even though so many things are made of plastic, a given plastic can be unique. Some plastics, or polymers as they are known scientifically, are produced for only one specific product or application. Nothing else in the world is made of that polymer; this fact allows examiners to prove that a piece of plastic came from that item.

The best way to associate two pieces of plastic is to show that they fit together. For example, a woman in Chicago was severely injured when she was bashed over the head with a large radio. A chip found at the scene fit perfectly into a radio found in the suspect's home, providing the critical physical evidence needed to convict him of assault.

As plastics replace metal in automobile panels, it's becoming common to find small pieces of plastic rather than paint chips and fragments of metal in crimes committed with cars. In a case eerily similar to the Vicki Hoskinson murder, an eleven-year-old girl in Louisiana disappeared while riding her bicycle. When a suspect was identified, investigators found a small colorful chip, which they believed to be paint, on the trunk latch of his car. The little girl's bike was eventually recovered from the bottom of a lake, but it was not the same color as the chip found on the trunk latch. Finally, lab examiners realized that the chip wasn't paint, but rather a thin plastic material that appeared to be part of a label. Examiners matched it by color, texture, and chemical composition to a plastic label on the seat post of the bicycle. That turned out to be the only hard evidence to link the suspect to the little girl, but it was proof that her bike had been in the trunk of his car, and was enough to contribute to his conviction.

When pieces of plastic don't fit together, a compositional match is attempted using something called differential thermal analysis. Often the best way to show that two substances are either alike or different is to determine their basic chemical makeup; different substances will be made of

178

different chemicals. That method doesn't always work for plastics. Sometimes two plastics will have the same chemical makeup, and the only difference between them will be that they were molded under different pressures, depending on how much flexibility was desired. So the best way to chemically compare two pieces of plastic is to reverse the manufacturing process—to unmake them.

When a plastic object is made, certain chemical changes take place at specific temperatures. When the process is reversed, when plastic is heated rather than cooled, those transitions will be reversed. If two pieces of plastic have the same source, those transitions will take place at precisely the same temperatures. If they are different, even though they may look the same, feel the same, and even consist of the same polymers, the transitions will occur at different temperatures. While this process allows examiners to show that two pieces of plastic have the same characteristics, it doesn't prove they came from the same specific item.

But sometimes similar characteristics can be enough. In an Indiana murder case a young woman was shot in the head at point-blank range during a robbery. When Doug Deedrick of Hairs and Fibers examined her clothing, he found some unusual blue dots, which he sent over to Materials Analysis to find out what they were made of. They turned out to be a pretty common plastic, polyvinyl chloride (PVC), which is used in numerous products from garden hoses to household items.

Those blue dots formed a trail. When a suspect was developed, the same blue dots were found on the floor of his car, in his gym bag, which had been tossed into a Dumpster, and, finally, on the plastic-coated palms of a pair of old work gloves found in his possession. The gloves had dried out; when they brushed against something, little blue dots fell off the coating.

Jim Corby first tried to fit some of the dots back onto the gloves to prove they had come from those specific gloves. Although he wasn't able to do that, by analyzing the PVC he was able to show that the plastic dots found on the victim's pantyhose, scarf, and clothing, and the dots found in the suspect's car and in his gymbag, were identical in composition to the textured blue plastic dots on his gloves. Those little plastic dots let police follow the suspect's trail from the murder scene to his own home, a path that led directly to a guilty verdict and a death sentence.

Among the most common plastic items regularly used are plastic garbage bags. And while they all may look alike, in some small way every garbage bag is different. Because garbage bags are heat-sealed (in this process, an impression is made in heated plastic) most cases in which plastic garbage bags are evidence are sent to the Document Section. Perhaps the best-known case in which a plastic garbage bag comparison proved significant was the brutal murder of a baby in Illinois. Four days after a woman named Paula Simms reported that her baby had been kidnapped, the baby's nude body was found in a garbage bag that had been tossed into a trash container not far from Simms's home. An examination showed that the baby's body had been frozen before being discarded. This was Paula Simms's second child to be murdered, so she immediately became the prime suspect. There were many inconsistencies in her story, but the only physical evidence was the garbage bag in which the body had been found. Somehow that garbage bag had to be linked to Simms.

Police found two rolls of garbage bags in Simms's house. One was still sealed. Forty-four bags remained on the second roll, while three other bags were in the house. Jim Gerhardt did the examination. "It's hard when you look at evidence like this not to think about the baby," he said softly, "but all we can really do is examine the evidence and bring out what's there. The first thing I tried to do was match the ragged edges on the hem and mouth ends of the bag in which the baby was found to other bags in the house through what we refer to as fish eyes, the dark dye lines that run from one bag to the next in an irregular pattern. They can be very strong evidence. For example, if we can link three plastic bags filled with drugs found in different locations, we can prove they came from a common source. In one case I was able to put four hundred plastic meat-packing bags back in the right order to prove they'd all come from the same roll. But I wasn't able to do that in the Simms case. Either this was the first bag on the roll or the bags on either side of it were missing. So we had to find a different way to do it."

One of the many things that make the FBI's sci-crime lab unique is the freedom given examiners to thoroughly research unusual subjects, to make themselves experts in very narrow disciplines. In this case Gerhardt learned all he could about plastic garbage bags by visiting manufacturers. "I learned how these bags are made and I found out what the unique aspects of the manufacturing process were. It turned out to be the method used to close the bag on the hem end, the seals. As the bags go down the line, a heated bar presses down on the plastic and melts it into a seal. It's sort of like typewriter keys making an impression on paper. I could see that there were imperfections in the sealing process, that when the bar hit the plastic it left tiny impurities, burrs and creases and pinholes. What made them valuable to me was that they were transient: they would appear for a number of bags, then disappear. These impurities would change drastically every minute, which meant that only a limited number of bags were going to have similar imperfections. If we could match those imperfections found on the bags in Simms's home to those on the bag in which the body had been found, we could positively link Paula Simms to the murder.

"Once we knew what to look for, it was a pretty straightforward examination. There were several transient imperfections present on the bags found in her home and in the bag used in the murder. During the trial we used enlarged photographs to show the jury just how the bags matched. In fact, we were able to show that the bag in which the body had been found was made within ten seconds of the last bag left on the roll. So either this bag had come from that roll, or the killer had come into the Simms house, kidnapped the baby and put it in the garbage bag, then left it in the park. The jury didn't believe that had happened. They convicted Paula Simms of the murder of her baby."

Originally Materials Analysis and Elemental Analysis were combined as the Instrumental Analysis Unit; while they are now independent, they often collaborate. In many cases, after Materials has determined the physical characteristics and organic composition of a substance, it is sent over to Elemental, where people like chemist Charlie Peters are able to measure how much of each chemical element is present down to parts per billion, and Dennis Ward puts it in the lab's scanning electron microscope to look at the distribution of the elements. By the time these units have finished analyzing a submission, they have developed a complete chemical profile— and a positive comparison made on these levels is very strong evidence that two samples have a common source.

In addition to assisting other units in their examinations—for example, doing gunshot-residue tests for the Firearms Unit and bomb-residue tests for the Explosives Unit, Elemental Analysis has responsibility for all metals exams. And while gunshot-residue cases make up a significant part of the workload, it also includes any case in which questions about metals or stress systems have to be answered. How long has this gun been in the water? Did a gunshot cause this helicopter to crash? Has this foil pack been opened and then resealed? As Agent Bill Tobin, the lab's metallurgist, said, "We just never know what kind of case is going to come through the door. I might work a plane crash today, a product-tampering case tomorrow, a serial killing the next day. When I first came into the lab, I intended to put in the required time, then get back on the street as an agent. But after I was here a little while, I realized that this was where I wanted to be."

Most crime labs rely on chemists to perform their metals examinations, and that can make a big difference in the results, according to Tobin. "A chemist might get a bullet that has been taken out of a body and find iron and titanium on it. But a metallurgist will look at that same bullet and realize there isn't just iron on it; there are iron, manganese, carbon, and some sulfur. And he'll know that titanium is an important component of many paints, so there's a strong possibility this bullet ricocheted off a painted surface before it struck the victim. Unless, of course, the victim had an artificial limb or medical implant in his body that might have contained the same elements."

For sci-crime purposes the most important properties of metals are that their behavior is predictable—metals react the same way to external forces all the time—and that they "remember," retaining a shape or chemical change for a very long time. These properties proved to be particularly important in one of Tobin's most unusual cases, the well-publicized murder case in which a trauma caused a woman to suddenly remember that more than two decades earlier she had witnessed her father killing her playmate by bludgeoning her with a rock.

How do you begin to substantiate a twenty-year-old murder that might never have happened? There was almost no physical evidence to support the woman's story, so it came down to her memory against her father's denial. But among the very few pieces of potential evidence was the victim's ring. Tobin discovered that it had been struck with enough force by an object with an irregular surface to cause substantial damage to the metal band. The marks left by the blow were not uniform, as they would have been had it been hit by something with a smooth surface, a hammer, for example, or an automobile fender.

"That ring told me several things," Tobin explained. "I could see it had been subjected to forced contact with an aggregate surface. I could see that the damage was not typical of normal service abuse—it didn't just happen in day-to-day wear. And I could see that the damage was very typical of what we expect to see when metal has been in forced contact with an object having an irregular surface profile. Based on all that, the best inference I could make was that it had been hit by a rock. To me, it looked like the person wearing the ring was probably raising her hand to ward off the blow.

"I see a lot of this type of damage. When people are being hit, they'll raise their hands to protect themselves, and whatever objects they're wearing—rings, bracelets, watches—get smashed in the attack. The damage to this ring was consistent with that sort of assault."

While Tobin's finding could not prove conclusively that the woman's memory was true, it provided physical evidence to support it, and may well have been a key factor in the eventual conviction of the father for the murder of the little girl.

Commonly encountered items like screws, drapery hooks, paper clips, staples—just about every type of metal fastening device—may not seem very important or exciting; in fact, they are often used in crimes and can be the evidence that links a suspect to a crime scene. One of the most important cases in which the lab helped nail the suspect was known as the Boston hitchhiker murders.

In the late 1970s several young women last seen hitchhiking in the area of Boston University were found brutally murdered. As Bill Tobin described the case, "Among the most remarkable things about these murders was that the crime scenes were almost pristine. We never found hairs or fibers, any serological evidence, no fingerprints. These were almost perfect crimes."

Boston police eventually charged a man named Anthony Jackson with the killings. Jackson was a genius, a Ted Bundy type. In half of his trials he handled his own defense. Although officially he was a suspect in ten murders, unofficially police believed he might be responsible for twice that number. By the time Tobin got involved in the case, Jackson had been tried for four murders and had been found guilty of two of them, for which he had received two separate life terms. What made this fifth trial so important was that in Massachusetts a felon serving a life sentence was eligible for parole after six and a half years, but under a recidivist statute an individual convicted of three felonies was considered a career criminal and lost all rights to parole. So it was three strikes and out, forever.

"I don't usually speak to a suspect when I'm testifying," Tobin remembered, "but during one recess, a Boston detective and I approached him and asked, 'Off the record, Jackson, how many women are you responsible for in the Boston area?'

" 'Just in Boston?' he answered. 'I left my mark in Detroit, too. They're not gonna forget me up there for a while.' He paused, then admitted, 'All together, twenty-seven.' " Only one man, John Wayne Gacy, had admitted killing more people.

Tobin had been brought into the Jackson case because one victim's body was found stuffed into a closet that had been nailed shut. In Jackson's garage police had found a collection of nails, screws, and drapery hooks, the jumble that anyone who makes minor home repairs might have. They had sent the lab this collection and the nails removed from the closet door, to see if an association could be made. What made the hardware collection more important was that it had been accumulated over time rather than purchased all in one store and all at the same time, so it was unlike any other collection in the world.

In a universe of billions of nails, how do you prove that two of them came from the same collection? "Nails are not high-spec items," Tobin explained. "There's no big deal if there's a tenth-of-an-inch difference. So I began by separating them by size. That really narrowed down the community. Then I examined the composition of the plating with an X-ray fluorescence spectrometer. Every element on the periodic chart responds differently to X-ray bombardment; it gives off a certain amount of energy. The X-ray fluorescence spectrometer measures that energy, allowing me to interpret which elements are present. Two nails manufactured at the same time are going to have the same plating. So that further narrowed the community.

"Finally I looked at fabrication characteristics. Metal is formed into a final shape by either forced contact with another metal or by casting the molten metal. The manufacturing process is going to leave a 'fingerprint' on the workpiece, the nail, that is unique to that piece of equipment. Even better, it's transient because the die that is making the nail is wearing down with every nail it makes. So whether it's a nail or a spoon or a screw or a paper clip, if I get the right samples I can show that two items were made by the same manufacturer with the same specific equipment at just about the same time.

"In this case I was able to show that three different and unrelated nails found in the door, and three different and unrelated nails taken from Jackson's garage, were made by the same manufacturers on the same equipment at about the same time. Those nails had come from Jackson's garage or another collection of nails exhibiting similar characteristics. The latter possibility was concluded to be extremely remote."

Attempting to diminish the importance of Tobin's testimony, the defense bought nails in fifteen different hardware stores—but failed to find even two series of nails that matched each other. With Tobin's testimony playing an important part, Jackson was convicted and will spend the rest of his life in prison.

Metals bend and break, they deform, and they corrode, but in a predictable manner. Things happen to metal for a reason that can be learned by examining it. When a government helicopter on a top-secret mission in Europe mysteriously crashed into the ocean, for example, a computer analysis of the damage to the rotor blade indicated that it had been struck by a bullet. The helicopter had been shot down. And that might mean that terrorists operating in the area had escalated their attacks on American military targets. If so, some sort of forceful response would be required. The blade was delivered to the lab for an exhaustive examination. No residues of bullet constituents were found, so the rotor might not have been hit by a bullet. And rather than the unpredictable and continually changing marks caused by a bullet striking metal, there was an elongated groove in the blade with unchanging marks. Finally, the absence of rust in the groove indicated that the damage had taken place after the chopper crashed. So, rather than confirming the report, the lab suggested that the damage to the rotor blade had occurred after the crash, probably during recovery operations. Further investigation proved that this was precisely so. The helicopter had crashed because of an engine malfunction, and the blade had been damaged when a grappling hook slipped while lifting the craft out of the sea.

The first clue a detective looks for, and one of the most important, is what time the crime took place. Knowing that allows detectives to begin piecing together events. Sometimes it's an easy thing to determine: watches are broken during assaults; clocks are knocked over in a struggle. In a Florida case a man sneaked away from a party for the sheriff's department to kill his wife, his in-laws, and his business partner—but his party alibi fell apart because a stray bullet smashed through a wall into a clock in the next room, stopping it at the precise moment of the murders. While the suspect could prove he had been at the party slightly before and just after the killings—several of the guests remembered his being very specific about the time—no one recalled seeing him at the time pinpointed by the clock. So it became important to prove that the clock had been working until the moment of the murders.

Although the bullet had missed the clock's mechanism, it had struck the case with enough force to knock the workings out of alignment. Since there was no real damage, the prosecution had to show that the bullet had stopped it. In the trial's most dramatic moment, Bill Tobin explained to the jury why the clock had stopped—then proved it had been in perfect working order by putting a gear wheel back on its track, then stepping back as the clock started ticking. The suspect was convicted of murder.

It's also possible to tell time by understanding nature. A metallurgist can make important determinations from the presence of rust. While at best it's only an approximation, measured in weeks and months rather than minutes and hours, the amount of corrosion enables the examiner to figure out how long a metal object has been exposed to the elements. Evidence like this is rarely conclusive, but it can help police corroborate testimony or piece together the details of a crime.

In one of the most complicated and potentially explosive cases in Boston history, a white man named Charles Stuart claimed that he and his wife had been robbed and shot by a black man while they were stopped at a traffic light. Mrs. Stuart had been killed, and her husband had suffered a superficial gunshot wound. A black suspect was arrested, but as the city of Boston tensed for a racial confrontation, Stuart's story started falling apart. Just as it became obvious that he had invented the tale, he committed suicide by jumping off a bridge.

According to Stuart's brother, Matthew, the crime had been planned as an insurance scam, a fake robbery. Matthew claimed he had taken the gun from his brother, not knowing his sister-in-law had been murdered, and had thrown it into the Charles River. Boston Police scuba divers recovered the rusty gun and submitted it to the lab. Obviously the case wasn't going to turn on this evidence. It was just another small piece in a very complex case. But it was important to determine if the gun had been in the river as long as Matthew Stuart claimed, or if he had tossed it in the river more recently to back up his story.

All rust is not created equal; objects rust quite differently when subjected to different conditions. So corrosion is a useful tool for determining how long anything metal, from a gun to an airplane, has been underwater.

Tobin began by examining the environment in which the gun had been found, to make sure it was consistent with the type of rust he had found on the gun. In addition to looking at hydrological—water-analysis—data, he studied a videotape, made by the divers, of the place where the gun had been recovered. As he explained, "Probably the most important thing I need to know is whether this is an aerobic environment, meaning oxygen is plentiful, or anaerobic, which means little oxygen is present. I can usually figure that out by looking at the biological activity, the plants and the fish. Then I look at the condition of other submerged objects, the things we generally find in urban rivers, like box springs, cars, and wheelchairs. If they have a light whitish coating, I know the environment probably contains calcium carbonate, magnesium, and some silicate. If they have a darker coating, I'd expect to find sulfur compounds there.

"Everything matters, everything that contributes to corrosion behavior, and if the corrosion I find on a submerged object isn't compatible with the environment, then I know we've got a problem. I know it probably hasn't been in that environment or hasn't been there for the period of time in question. But if everything is consistent, then the extent of the corrosion will give me a good idea how long it's been in the water.

"In the Stuart case I found that the amount and type of rust was consistent with the testimony."

In product-tampering cases, if a metal object is found in a package, or if the question is whether a foil seal has been opened after leaving the factory, the evidence goes to the Elemental Analysis Unit. Perhaps the first major product-tampering scare in America took place in the 1970s, when consumers around the country began reporting that they had found various metal objects in boxes of Girl Scout cookies. Hundreds of boxes of cookies were submitted to the lab; almost without exception they contained either a needle, a straight pin, or a razor blade—and almost without exception the object had been put there by the consumer after the product had left the factory.

Usually it was obvious. There was a cookie with a bite taken out of it and a pin bisecting the missing portion, like a bridge, something that couldn't occur naturally. In some instances, the needle was longer than the cookie; in others, two or three bites had been taken out of the cookie, leaving only a narrow sliver with the object in it. And in almost every case the consumer had expected a "settlement" payment from the manufacturer or was seeking publicity.

Not every submission was fraudulent, however. Accidents—and sometimes crimes—take place at the factory level. A few of the cookies contained bits of tungsten carbide and tool steel, alloys commonly used on production lines and rarely found in the home. Thus it was likely that damaged machinery had contaminated those cookies.

The primary means of separating true product-tampering cases from manufacturing problems is to inspect the packaging. People will often go to great lengths to conceal the fact that a package has been opened then resealed, but it's impossible to reseal a package perfectly. When poison was discovered inside a bottle of Tylenol, it was vital to determine whether it had been put into the container at the factory—perhaps by a disgruntled employee—or whether someone had taken the bottle off the shelf, opened it, added the poison, then resealed it.

Using a scanning electron microscope, an instrument capable of magnifying an image sixty thousand times, chemist Dennis Ward examined dozens of factory-sealed bottles to familiarize himself with the structure of a properly sealed bottle. When Tylenol is bottled, a foil seal is heat-welded to the polyethylene bottle; the bottle cannot be opened at the top without breaking that seal. Whoever had put the poison in the bottle had tried very hard to conceal his work. After slitting open the foil and adding the poison, he had used heat to reseal it, perhaps an iron. To the naked eye the bottle looked normal, but under the scanning electron microscope, it was very easy to see that some of the polyethylene had been melted and had flowed down the side of the bottle. Although the poisoner was never found, the lab proved that this case was one of true product tampering rather than the manufacturer's fault.

In a Lakeland, Florida, murder case, a man named George Trepal, angry at his neighbor, put the odorless, tasteless poison thallium into eight bottles of Coke and managed to get those bottles into his neighbor's home. Peggy Carr died; five members of her family were also poisoned, but recovered. A Florida state lab examined more than four hundred different items taken from that home, from food to wall scrapings, before discovering traces of the poison in three empty Coke bottles. Four other bottles appeared to have been unopened. Once again the question became whether the poison had been put into the bottles before or after leaving the factory. So while the

U.S. Centers for Disease Control, in Atlanta, began to consider ordering the recall of millions of bottles of Coke, executives and scientists from the company worked with examiners in the sci-crime lab to answer that question.

It was decided that the best way to determine if the bottles had been opened after being shipped was to measure the pressure inside the four bottles that appeared to be intact and compare it to other sealed bottles. After a frantic search, Coke located several bottles that had been sealed in the same plant at about the same time as the questioned bottles. The caps of all four sealed bottles were punctured, the soda was shaken up, and the pressure was measured. Each of the bottles found at the Carr home showed a reduction in pressure. Once the caps had been pierced, the Toolmarks Unit discovered striation marks on the inside of the caps, confirming that they had been pried open and then crimped back into place.

And George Trepal? After he moved out of his house, FBI agents moved in and found a small vial of thallium. He was convicted of murder, attempted murder, and product tampering.

Although it might seem unusual for the Elemental Analysis Unit to be involved in poison cases, heavy metals like arsenic, thallium, mercury, and lead make excellent poisons because they are odorless and colorless and are just as fatal when ingested in small doses over a long period of time as they are when taken in a single massive dose. The disadvantage of using heavy-metal poisons is that while almost every other poison deteriorates over time, elemental poisons remain in the body forever. In a chronic-poisoning case—one in which the poison has been administered over a period of time—traces of heavy-metal poison can be found in tissues and bones, even in hair and nails.

In most cases the submitting law enforcement agency suspects that a specific poison has been used and simply wants to confirm its presence, but on occasion an unknown sample needs to be identified. Chemist Charlie Peters, who joined the lab in 1975, remembered one case like that very well. "We had a man in the hospital dying and no one knew why. It was later learned that drug killers believed the victim was a narcotics agent and tried to kill him by giving him a white substance he believed to be cocaine. He collapsed, and when we got the substance he was in a coma. We were able to look at the particles under the electron microscope and tell them pretty quickly that it was thallium. That enabled them to save his life."

Often questions of physics need to be answered by the lab. Basically anything to do with stress or strain is assigned to the metallurgist. When a prisoner in a New Jersey jail hanged himself with his shoelace, the question was whether a shoelace could really have supported his weight.

Using a tensile tester, an instrument that measures force, it's possible to answer that question. The shoelace was more than capable of supporting that prisoner's weight. In a Southwestern murder case a man wrapped a sphygmomanometer, a blood-pressure cuff, around his sleeping wife's neck and then inflated it, strangling her while leaving almost no marks on her neck. The question local investigating police wanted answered was whether the cuff could generate enough force to choke someone to death. "That's not as simple an examination as it sounds," said Bill Tobin, who did the testing. "It's a tricky physics question to isolate the forces constricting the neck. I did some research and found out that it takes six point seven pounds of force to occlude the carotid artery in the neck and cause unconsciousness. I asked a somewhat frail female technician to pump up the cuff with her weak hand, her left hand. I put the cuff around a simulated "neck" designed with electronic force-measuring capability. I found out it's pretty easy to generate three hundred and fifty pounds of force, more than enough to kill someone."

Escaping prison by sliding down tied-together bedsheets is an old, if not particularly honorable tradition. While it's occasionally successful, more often the sheets rip or knots come undone and prisoners are injured or killed in the fall. In one New York City attempt, a prisoner was killed when the sheets came apart and a second prisoner fell on him. So when an Illinois prisoner weighing 390 pounds escaped by sliding down a length of sheet, a very suspicious warden wondered if the sheets were meant to divert attention from a friendly guard who had simply opened the door. The sheets were submitted to the lab with a request to determine if they could have supported the prisoner's weight. Tensile-strength tests were stopped at 2,238 pounds; the sheets probably could have supported more than two tons, so the prisoner could have lowered a Volkswagen down the sheets without difficulty.

The most elementary of all structural examinations done in the sci-crime lab are conducted by chemist Dennis Ward on the scanning electron microscope. While other analytical instruments provide numerical, quantitative analysis of composition, the SEM, as it is known, can provide the examiner with a picture of the distribution of elements in a material. This is a very effective tool for comparing materials with a complex internal structure such as multiple-layer paint chips. Using the SEM, Ward was able to visualize the nickel from Frank Atwood's bumper on the fender of Vicki Hoskinson's bicycle. "We perform practical, nuts-and-bolts electron microscopy," he said. "We adapt the procedures to fit the needs, because every problem that comes through the door is different and requires a different approach."

Electron microscopes, which can cost as much as $250,000, were first adapted to sci-crime use in the 1960s. Very simply, they work by scanning an electron beam over an object, then imaging the signals that the sample produces. Everything examined under an electron microscope has to be electrically conductive so usually a conductive layer, carbon or gold, is added to the object. "We're actually imaging at the gold," Ward explained, "but it's so thin that it conforms to the object underneath. It's like looking at a snow-covered mountain range. You're looking at the snow, but you're really seeing the shape of the mountain range."

While scientists in other fields use the scanning electron microscope to take extraordinary photographs of the inner structure of the world, Ward usually ends up looking for debris on the nose of a bullet, or studying a particle found on a shirt. Usually he is searching for supportive evidence, but there are times when he can make a case. In a Midwestern rape-murder, for example, a tiny silver spot was found on the victim's blouse. It was much too small to be analyzed by other techniques. A pair of gloves found on the suspect appeared to carry traces of the same silver material. "I tried to associate the spot and the gloves," Ward said, "although I knew it was a long shot.

"We could have performed a bulk composition analysis, which would have determined only what chemicals were present. With the SEM, however, I was able to identify all the particle types present, including their frequency, their size, and their composition. By showing correspondence on that level, I could state that it was likely that those gloves touched that blouse. It wasn't quite so important where that silver material came from or even what it was, as to determine the association."

The SEM can be a means to look into the eyes of a bug or examine life forms found within a raindrop. "There's an extraordinary structural beauty in nature that you can't see with your naked eyes or even through a light microscope," Ward said, "and sometimes when I'm looking at the symmetry of crystals, or the diversity of biological structures, I can't help but admire this world. But the fact that I evaluate traces and change people's lives with the smallest of all evidence constantly fills me with wonder."

To Conan Doyle's Sherlock Holmes, of course, that was elementary.

CHAPTER
- 7 -

The Paper Chasers:
The Document Section

This writing is of extraordinary interest. . . . These are much deeper waters than I thought.

SHERLOCK HOLMES,
in Sir Arthur Conan Doyle's "The Reigate Puzzle"

What can you never do precisely the same way twice?

Who wrote the Bill of Rights?

How did a paintbrush help convict Patty Hearst of armed robbery?

How can you see through a sealed envelope?

And finally, what is the one thing that the vast majority of all crimes have in common—all crimes, from murders to multimillion-dollar bank swindles? Motive? No, crimes are committed for every conceivable reason. Modus operandi? No, crimes are committed in every conceivable way. Here's an important clue: the answer is in your hands.

The vast majority of crimes involve paper. Numerous types of crimes are committed *on* paper: forgery, fraud, counterfeiting, embezzlement, money laundering, swindles, insider trading, espionage. Every crime that requires record-keeping requires paper: gambling, drug trafficking, smuggling, prostitution. Some violent crimes involve paper: kidnappers write ransom notes, bank robbers use demand notes; bombs are sent through the mail; extortionists write down their threats; arsonists use paper matches to start fires. And even the most clever criminals can be traced by the paper trail they leave: receipts for bullets and bomb components, credit card vouchers, car-rental forms, motel registers.

That paper trail can lead directly to a conviction just as certainly as foot-prints in fresh snow. For example, over a holiday weekend robbers drilled into the vault of a Laguna Niquel, California, bank and stole $14 million. They left absolutely no physical evidence at the crime scene. But one as-pect of the robbery was unique: they filled the alarm system with liquid sty-rofoam, which immobilized the system when it hardened. FBI agent Stan Renquist recognized this as the method previously employed by a gang op-erating out of Youngstown, Ohio. Using handwriting samples obtained from gang members during earlier prosecutions as a basis for comparison, investigators learned that the gang had bought plane tickets at a Youngstown travel agency and flown to California. Other handwriting com-parisons confirmed that they had rented cars and a van in Los Angeles un-der assumed names—and in the trunk of one of those cars, agents found a rare coin that had been taken in the robbery. Handwriting comparisons proved that the gang had leased an apartment for several weeks, and when they'd left, someone had forgotten to turn on the dishwasher and their prints were found on glasses and plates. These thieves had traveled, rented cars, and leased an apartment under assumed identities; no one saw them enter or leave the bank, and they left no hard evidence. But the one thing they couldn't disguise led directly to their arrest and conviction: their hand-writing on pieces of paper.

The Document Section of the sci-crime lab includes seven different units, which have responsibility for investigating anything to do with paper, from white-collar crimes to breaking written codes, as well as the machines used to create those documents: typewriters, computers, fax machines, photocopiers, and all kinds of printers; and, by extension, the impressions made by footwear on a surface. Everything about paper is potentially a clue: the paper itself, the ink, the handwriting or typewriting or printing, alter-ations and obliterations, smudges; things that aren't easily seen with the naked eye, such as watermarks, indentions caused by writing on a top sheet, or copy-machine gripper marks; the meaning of words or numbers; even the ragged edges.

From the day the Bureau's crime lab opened in 1932, document exami-nations have been one of the most effective means of linking a suspect to a crime. Probably the first great case in which the lab played a significant role was the infamous "crime of the century," the kidnapping and murder of aviator Charles Lindbergh's baby son. More than two years after the baby's body was found, a man named Bruno Richard Hauptmann was caught after spending some of the ransom money. Substantial circumstantial evidence linked Hauptmann to the crime, but he swore he was innocent. After his arrest, he voluntarily gave authorities a handwriting sample, which Charles Appel, the founder of the crime lab, compared to the writing on the ransom notes.

Testifying before a grand jury, Appel explained that he had examined fifteen hundred different handwriting samples without finding any of the peculiarities that he had found in both Hauptmann's writing sample and the ransom notes. "Remarkable similarities in inconspicuous personal characteristics and writing habits" were found, Appel said, forcing him to conclude that "it is inconceivable that anyone but Hauptmann could have written the ransom notes."

Appel's startling testimony captured the fancy of the public and helped convict Hauptmann of the kidnapping and murder. Although Hauptmann's conviction remains one of the most controversial decisions in American judicial history, Appel's handwriting comparison is considered so strong that it is still used in the training of document examiners.

Handwriting comparison is the most common type of document examination. And it is a very inexact science. Every individual's handwriting is unique. Even you can't write your own name precisely the same way twice. Write your signature on two separate pieces of paper, then lay one over the other and hold them up to a light. They will be close, but one will never exactly cover the other.

Your handwriting is as unique as your fingerprints. No one in the world writes exactly the way you do. Even identical twins will not have identical handwriting. And barring illness, your writing style will be identifiable for the rest of your life.

On occasion you are able to identify a letter writer because you recognize the writing on the envelope. You've seen that writing often enough to recognize its distinctive characteristics. Handwriting comparison works basically the same way. Examiners familiarize themselves with an individual's normal writing by looking at as many samples of that writing as possible, then compare the writing style on a questioned document. The basic tools of this trade are a low-power microscope, a magnifying glass, and various light sources. For more sophisticated work, a camera with various filters will be used.

To make an accurate comparison examiners must have several samples of the subject's natural handwriting. Each person has a normal range of writing characteristics—no one signs a gas-station credit card receipt while standing at a pump the same way he would sign a million-dollar recording contract—and the examiner has to familiarize himself with that range of possibilities. The writing instruments have to be the same; the known document should have been written at approximately the same time as the questioned document; cursive writing has to be compared with cursive writing, and printing with printing. When New York was terrorized by a killer who identified himself in letters to newspapers as Son of Sam, the Questioned Documents Unit in the section had in its anonymous-letter file threatening letters written to a Brooklyn resident by a man named David Berkowitz—later identified as Son of Sam. But because the letters to newspapers were printed while the threatening letters were in script, it simply wasn't possible to make a match.

There's no standard procedure for making a handwriting comparison; it always comes down to a side-by-side comparison of a known document and a questioned document. A person's writing is a combination of class characteristics—the remnants of the type of handwriting he was taught in school—and the individual characteristics he has acquired. A document examiner—there are only about 180 certified document examiners in the country—will look for those individual characteristics and subtleties that make one person's writing different from every other person's.

Using magnification, examiners look at writing skills and style; the slant of the letters; how far above or below the line letters are formed; the size and height of the letters, their angularity, and the way they are connected; the distance between words; the height of the letters, the amount of pressure on the paper, the way in which a word begins when the pen is put down on the paper or is lifted at the end of a word, the way the "i"s are dotted and the "t"s are crossed. They will determine the width of the margins and the length of the indention at the beginning of a paragraph. They will note how much room the writer leaves at the top of a page and how far from the bottom he or she ends. There are no rules to follow, and there is no minimum number of characteristics that must match or be different. The examination is completely subjective, based on the examiner's experience; every examiner has established his or her own set of standards. Examiners have the option of giving a positive opinion, as Appel did in the Lindbergh case, stating that a specific person wrote a specific document; a qualified opinion, meaning that he or she probably wrote it; or a negative opinion. Or he can fail to reach any conclusion at all.

The impossibility of establishing universal standards for all comparisons makes handwriting analysis seem more speculative than scientific, but when Document Section chief Ron Furgerson was asked how many of the 180 certified document examiners would reach the same conclusion in a case as he would, he stated flatly, "All of them."

While handwriting comparison is most often ısed in the cases of questioned documents or to link a suspect to a crime, on rare occasions it has been used to identify a suspect. One of the few cases solved through a document comparison was the 1956 Westbury, New York, kidnapping-murder of a one-month-old baby named Peter Weinburger. The case began with the most horrifying scenario a parent can imagine: the baby was taken from the front porch of his home when his mother went inside to get him a clean diaper. The only hard evidence found at the scene was a hastily scrawled ransom note warning, "Don't tell anyone or go the Police about this, because I am watching you closely. I am scared stiff, & will kill the baby, at your first wrong move . . ." The kidnapper demanded $2,000 and signed the note: "Your baby sitter."

Several phone calls and additional letters were received, and the family agreed to pay the ransom, but the kidnapper failed to show up at the planned payoff location. The largest manhunt in local history began. Because of the nature of the crime and the small ransom demanded, detectives suspected they were looking for a petty criminal.

Lacking any other clues, desperate investigators under the direction of FBI lab document examiners began an exhaustive search of public records in the metropolitan area, hoping to match the distinctive handwriting on the ransom notes. More than two million public documents were examined at municipal offices, schools, public agencies, defense plants, anywhere a large number of public documents was kept on file. And in the U.S. probation office in Brooklyn, New York, an agent noted a strong similarity between the writing on the ransom notes and papers found in the file of a man named John La Marca, who was on probation for making and possessing untaxed alcohol.

FBI document examiners confirmed that the ransom note had been written by La Marca. Confronted with this evidence, La Marca confessed to the kidnapping and led police to the baby's body. Two years later he died in Sing Sing's electric chair. In effect, he had written his own death warrant.

Even the smallest idiosyncrasy in handwriting can be enough to identify a specific person. Weeks before "God's banker," the internationally respected financier Michele Sindona, who handled the Vatican's money, was to go on trial in New York for bank fraud in connection with the failure of the Franklin National Bank—at that time the largest bank failure in American history—he was supposedly kidnapped. Although his family received ransom notes, authorities were skeptical. Many investigators believed that Sindona had arranged this disappearance to avoid trial. Two months later, Sindona showed up in New York just as mysteriously as he had vanished, claiming that he had escaped from his kidnappers.

Prosecutors knew they would have a difficult time making a jury understand Sindona's extraordinarily complex financial dealings, particularly since the key witness against him, an officer of the Italian finance police, had been murdered in Milan. But they also knew that if they could prove Sindona had faked his kidnapping, a jury would be more likely to convict him. If they could prove he had run, the assumption would be that he must be guilty.

Sindona couldn't identify his kidnappers, and he had no idea where he had been held. About the only thing he knew for certain was that he had been transported by automobile; he had never been taken anywhere on an airplane. So agents knew that if they could prove he had been on an airplane his story would collapse.

Information developed in a parallel organized-crime investigation led agents to believe that Sindona had been in Italy during at least part of the time he was missing, and had returned to New York during the same two-week period as several members of the Brooklyn Gambino crime family. Acting on that hint, agents asked the customs bureau to supply all the customs declarations submitted by people traveling from Italy to New York during that period. They suspected that the card they were searching for, if it existed, would be made out in the name of an Italian man in his fifties, probably with a Brooklyn address, probably traveling alone, probably declaring nothing of value. It was a lot of "probably"s, and investigators had only one clue to guide them: Michele Sindona habitually put a small dot inside the bowl of the number 9.

Agent Joe Holliday sat hunched over a small desk at Kennedy Airport for days, examining thousands and thousands of white cards. Meanwhile, Sindona's trial began in Manhattan. As Holliday's search continued, the impeccably dressed Sindona sat impassively in the courtroom, going home each night to his lavish New York apartment, confident of acquittal. Then one afternoon Holliday picked up a card and stared at it—and inside the bowl of the number 9 in an address he saw a dot. Sindona's dot. The card was flown to Washington, where experts in the lab's Identification Division were able to develop a partial fingerprint: Sindona's. Proof that he had been on an airplane, proof that he had been out of the country.

The trial was in session when prosecutors dramatically requested a recess. They presented this evidence to the judge in his chambers. Sindona was immediately remanded into custody. He never spent another free day in his life. The U.S. jury convicted him of bank fraud; two years later an Italian jury convicted him of masterminding the murder of the primary witness against him. He died in prison, claiming with his last words to have been poisoned, but more likely a suicide. One of the most powerful men in the world had been convicted by a dot no larger than the period at the end of this sentence.

Often the crime itself is committed on paper. Frauds and forgeries can be traced back hundreds of years, when criminals would forge the king's seal on documents to give them the full power of the crown. Any writing or printing that gives value to paper, from an ordinary check to Adolf Hitler's diaries, might be forged. And any document that is prepared with the intent to deceive or defraud is considered a forgery.

The most common forgery is a signature. A "freehand forgery" consists of someone signing another person's name in his own handwriting, with no attempt to disguise it. It's very easy to determine that this is a forgery, and it can usually be linked to an identified suspect. A "traced forgery" is made by writing over the actual signature with great pressure, then tracing the indented writing made on the page underneath. A "simulated forgery" is an attempt to duplicate another person's handwriting. It's usually done freehand; the forger simply practices someone else's signature until he or she can simulate it. Sometimes it is extremely well done, and it's very difficult to link a suspect to the forgery because he isn't writing in his own style.

Document examiners usually insist on working with original papers because photocopies help disguise certain elements of forgeries. It's impossible to do an ink examination of a photocopy, or restore erased or obliterated marks, or find an impression in the paper known as indented writing, or develop latent fingerprints. Forgeries can be made by punching tiny holes in a real signature, then simply connecting the dots, which will disappear on a photocopy. Forgeries made with carbon paper will look genuine on a copy. A rubber-stamp copy of a signature can easily be made and used, and on a photocopy it will be almost impossible to determine that the signature isn't real.

But there are several different ways to prove a document is a forgery. Traced forgeries can be detected by comparing the questioned signature to the original from which it was copied. Because no two signatures can be precisely the same, if a signature is completely covered when a second signature is laid on top of it, one of them is a forgery. The Justice Department once asked the FBI lab to examine a document that purported to be a previously unknown seventh draft of Lincoln's Gettysburg Address. Agent-examiner Jim Gerhardt, who joined the Bureau in 1971, was assigned the case. "I discovered that of the six known drafts of that speech, the one that most resembled the document I had was kept in the Lincoln Bedroom at the White House. I went over there with a photographer and we took pictures of that draft; then I did my comparison. The document I'd gotten from the Justice Department matched the White House draft perfectly. When I laid one on top of the other, the bottom copy was not visible. That's impossible; a human being can't function with the precision of a machine. So I knew it was simply a good reproduction of the genuine document."

Proving that Howard Hughes's will was a forgery was slightly more difficult. After the reclusive multimillionaire's death, a previously unknown will turned up, purportedly leaving one-sixteenth of the estate to a Gibbs, Nevada, gas station owner named Melvin Dummar. Agent Jim Lile was asked to examine the document. "The media immediately rushed out to meet Dummar," Lile remembered with a hint of a smile, "and when Melvin heard about this, he fainted. He claimed he had no idea why Hughes had left him this fortune. Of course, when he found out that the will had been sent to the FBI for examination, he remembered picking up an old man hitchhiking in the desert one day. He even remembered somebody giving him this document in an envelope and that he had dropped it off on a desk at the Mormon church.

"I eventually testified for fourteen hours in this case," Lile remembered. "When I first looked at the will I could see it had a lot of problems, but I've been doing this for a long time, and I'd examined a lot of documents in which the writer's style had changed because of age or infirmity or drugs or alcohol or some kind of physical disability. So I couldn't just dismiss this because the contents seemed so unlikely. I still had to do a complete examination. The difficulty I had was that no one knew for sure what the status of Hughes's health was at the time this will supposedly had been written. The only way to solve that problem was to find as many documents as possible written contemporaneously with the will. Because Hughes was practically a hermit, it was difficult to get those samples.

"The State of Nevada eventually provided me with about a hundred pages of Hughes's handwriting. Using them for comparative purposes, I could state positively that the will was a poorly prepared simulated forgery. The first stroke of a pen on paper can either be tapered or blunt, but after that, most end strokes are tapered. The pen is moving when it leaves the paper and flows right into the next word. Between the time most people start writing a word and finishing, the pen rarely leaves the paper. If people do stop within a word, it's usually because they forget how to spell it and pause to think about it. If there is any retouching, it's invariably for legibility. The Hughes will was full of those things I would expect to see in a simulated forgery: blunt endings, retouches as the forger attempted to correct mistakes, illogical stopping places where the forger had to go back and look at the model he was copying, very poor line quality. It was a bad job.

"To prepare a simulation, forgers will create a model alphabet, they'll find all the letters in the hand of the writer and copy them. The difficulty comes in finding examples of the connecting strokes; the way letters are connected is as important to an examiner as how they are formed. *Life* had run a copy of a letter Hughes had written that showed his handwriting, how he made his margins, some characteristics, the kind of paper he used, everything a forger would need to make a model. Using that letter I made my own model to see which letters and connectives were not present, so the forger couldn't know what they looked like. Sure enough, in the will those letters and connectives were totally fabricated—the forger had to fake them—so I was certain that this letter had been used as the model for the forged will."

Ironically, there was no way Lile could prove from the document who had actually written it. Since Dummar was copying Hughes's writing, none of his own writing characteristics were present. But the accumulation of other evidence made it clear who'd forged the will, and Dummar eventually confessed that he had made up the whole thing.

· · ·

On occasion the lab is asked to authenticate historical documents. The only way to prove that a historical document is genuine is to compare the handwriting and the materials to documents known to have been written at about the same time in the same place by the same people. So when the National Archives wanted to establish who had actually written out the Bill of Rights, it sent to the lab a facsimile of that document as well as samples of the writing of William Lambert, a clerk in the House of Representatives when these amendments to the Constitution were adopted. A basic handwriting comparison proved that the Bill of Rights had indeed been written out by William Lambert.

But most historical exams are not that easy. Because there are rarely sufficient handwriting samples to allow a comparison to be made, the materials used to create the document have to be analyzed. Paper is made of fiber, water, and chemicals, but the specific components vary depending on the time and place the paper was produced. By comparing the components in a sheet of paper to what was known to be available when and where the document was purportedly written, examiners can often prove that a document was forged. When diaries supposedly written by Adolf Hitler were discovered, for example, an analysis showed that the paper contained chemical optical brighteners and that the bindings had rayon fibers. Since neither material was used during the period these diaries covered, they could not possibly have been written then.

Almost all written or printed documents consist of ink applied to paper. Since 1969, several ink manufacturers have included a chemical tag in their formulations, allowing investigators to date an ink by the presence of a certain chemical. Prior to that, dating an ink was a difficult process. An enormous variety of natural and manmade stains have been used to write on paper, and identifying the components of an ink can provide vital clues about the validity of a document. Ink changes as time passes: it fades, it chips, it changes color, it reacts with the chemicals in paper, it responds to environmental conditions—and every one of those changes can be used to determine the authenticity of a document.

One of the most ingenious attempted forgeries in recent history was the so-called Salamander Letter. The case began when a Salt Lake City rare-documents dealer named Mark Hofmann, who had previously sold several historic documents to the Mormon church, came into possession of a letter supposedly written in 1830 that contradicted some of the basic tenets of the church and connected founder Joseph Smith with occult beliefs. If this letter was real, the entire history of the Mormon religion would be challenged. Church officials sent it to the FBI to be authenticated. In addition, they sent several other documents from their archives known to have been written by the author of this letter, a wealthy farmer named Martin Harris.

Lab examiners tested the Salamander Letter for the presence of more than one ink; multiple inks might indicate that it had been altered. Only one ink formulation was found. Microscopic examinations revealed no alterations, obliterations, or erasures. The paper and the ink were consistent with the materials available when the letter supposedly was written. The results of the handwriting comparison were inconclusive. While examiners did not confirm the authenticity of the letter, they also did not discover that it was a forgery. That was left to two document examiners in Salt Lake City.

George Throckmorton was Utah's only licensed document examiner, and William Flynn was one of the most respected examiners in the nation. Working with eighty-one contemporary documents provided by the church, they tested everything from the method used to cut the paper to the presence of chemical additives. And they noticed that on some of these documents the ink was uniform, while on others it had developed minuscule cracks and fissures. Something was wrong; all of these documents had supposedly been written at about the same time with the same materials, so it was odd that the ink had aged differently. Throckmorton and Flynn began experimenting, trying to discover if it was possible to create "old" ink in a modern kitchen.

At one time finely ground iron ore was added to ink to make it more permanent, but iron gallotannic ink, like iron, will rust when exposed to oxygen. Over time it will turn reddish brown and eventually flake off the paper. That is what is happening to the Declaration of Independence. But there are means of speeding up the oxidizing process, of making a document appear much older than it actually is. Throckmorton and Flynn discovered that the addition of a substance called gum arabic to ammonia and sodium hydroxide successfully aged the ink—although it also cracked it. In one afternoon they had produced "century-old" ink. They had proved that the letter could have been forged.

But Hofmann had known that the authenticity of this letter might be challenged. And that was the real genius of his plan. His fraud had been years in preparation. Unknown to the sci-crime lab, the sample documents provided to the Bureau by the church as a basis for comparison had *all* been created by Mark Hofmann. He had forged the documents on blank pages carefully removed from old books. Because these documents were of minor historical significance, hence not valuable enough for anyone to go to all the trouble of forging them, they were accepted as genuine. Now the real value of these documents had been revealed. They were created to salt the files, to be used for comparative purposes when potentially valuable documents were offered for sale. And except for those tiny cracks in the ink, Hofmann would have gotten away with his plan, and perhaps changed the history of the Mormon church forever.

In the world of document examinations, seeing is often deceiving. Imagine being able to see inside a sealed envelope or read invisible writing. Forgers often change the monetary value or the designated recipient of a document—a check, for example—by altering numbers or changing the signature. This is done in several different ways: adding numbers in similarly colored ink; erasing; using ink eradicators, bleaches, inorganic solvents, or masking materials such as white-out; even photographing the document, changing features on the negative, and then printing it.

And this is where seemingly routine document examinations get into light physics. Basically, ink consists of a pigment to give it color and a solvent to carry the pigment. When you write on a sheet of paper the pigment remains on the surface, while the solvent is absorbed into the fibers. The visible part, the pigment, can be removed or covered or will fade, but the solvent will remain in the fibers. The trick is to make it visible.

Ink on paper either absorbs or reflects energy to become visible. Lightwaves are measured in nanometers, and absolutely all the light we are capable of seeing with the naked eye measures between 400 and 750 nanometers, not a very large segment of the spectrum. But by adding or subtracting different types of light and filters, it's possible to make the invisible visible—if not to the eye, at least to the camera. There's no real way of predicting how an ink will react to light; it's completely a function of the chemistry of the ink. Ink can reflect light, absorb light, transmit light, or luminesce, meaning glow. Below 400 nanometers, X rays and ultraviolet light will cause some solvents to luminesce, while above 700 nanometers infrared lighting will make others visible. But a camera with the appropriate lens and filters can see light up to 1200 nanometers and display it on a photograph or a screen, thus making something invisible, visible.

The camera will see only what is visible within a desired wavelength and nothing else. Thus it can "see" through white-out, for example, because the correction fluid is not visible at the same wavelength as the ink material beneath it. The camera can even "see" through paper, which makes it possible to photograph documents inside a sealed envelope, or read through the carbon on a charred piece of paper. It's a long way from comparing the way two "t"s are crossed.

So by manipulating lights and filters, document examiners can look at what appears to be an ordinary check and see that the signature has been eradicated and written over, or that the check's value has been changed by the addition of zeros in an ink that appears to be the same color but which luminesces at a different wavelength.

There are ways to protect yourself from forgers. Many signature blocks include "safety patterns," extremely thin decorative lines. While it's possible to eradicate a signature, it's extremely difficult to reconstruct the lines that had been covered by that signature and were removed with it. In fact, document examiners have been able to reconstruct the original name and numbers on a check by closely examining the places where the pattern was broken. "Closely examining" is actually not right—in these cases, the farther away you stand the more discernible the broken pattern becomes.

To prevent your documents from being changed, write on top of as many printed lines on the page as possible, such as the ones underlining the signatures, and use ink of the same color as the printing. Forgers can use filters just as examiners can; if you use blue ink to sign a document that's printed in black ink, someone can easily filter out the blue ink to create a photo of a "clean" document. Using black ink to sign a document printed in black forces forgers to painstakingly remove your entire signature by hand, a tedious and often difficult task.

Writing or printing on paper also makes an impression in the fibers, not only on that page but on several pages beneath it. These impressions are called indented writing. On television, detectives like Columbo lightly brush over a blank sheet of paper with a pencil to fill in the impressions in that paper. That's about the last thing a good detective would do, because it's more likely to cover up whatever image is there than to make it visible. Indented writing can be made visible with oblique lighting or with a fascinating machine called an electrostatic detection apparatus (ESDA).

One of the basic principles of sci-crime investigation is that things that aren't immediately obvious will become visible when the angle of the light source is changed. If you lay a flashlight on the floor or on the seat of a piece of furniture, its beam will illuminate all sorts of hairs and fibers and other objects you hadn't previously noticed. Or if you lay one sheet of paper on another and write something on it, then look at the bottom sheet under normal lighting, you may see some barely perceptible indentions. But if you lay a flashlight at the side of the paper and look at it again, the oblique (or "raked") lighting highlights shadows in any depressions in the paper and makes them readable. So rather than brushing a sheet of paper with a pencil, Columbo should have been looking at it with an angled light source.

Indented writings have provided key evidence in numerous cases. People often destroy the paper on which they have written, but just as often they forget that they have made an impression on the sheets beneath it. In 1986 Jim Gerhardt worked on a Massachusetts murder case in which a woman's ex-lover was suspected of killing her new boyfriend. The victim was murdered on his birthday, his head practically blown off by a shotgun fired at point-blank range. A note found next to his body read, "Happy Birthday, Friend." Local police wanted the Document Section to compare the printing on that note with samples from the ex-boyfriend. They obtained a search warrant; in the ex-lover's car they found an envelope with the woman's name and address printed on it. They submitted it to the lab for comparison with the note.

"My job was to put the note and the envelope side by side and examine the handwriting characteristics," Gerhardt remembered. "It was a basic writing comparison and I had no reason to examine the envelope for indented writing. I was working in an office with a window looking east. I was there about seven o'clock in the morning and the envelope just happened to be lying on my desk. As the sun rose behind me, sunlight streamed into my office at a very low angle. I just happened to glance at the envelope— and I saw that there was indented writing on it. When I looked at it more closely, I could see that the indentions read, 'Happy Birthday, Friend.'

"It was incredible. I had the Special Photography Unit photograph the envelope using oblique lighting, then prepared an overlay for the trial showing that these indentions had been made when the note was written. It's possible that the suspect would have been convicted of murder without this evidence, but we were able to show that he'd sat in his car and written this note, and then had gone inside and killed the victim. That proved this was premeditated murder, and he received the death penalty."

As improbable as it may seem, Gerhardt actually had an even more unusual indented-writing case. After breaking up with her boyfriend and starting to see another man, a young New England woman began receiving neatly typed threatening letters. The eleventh letter warned, "If you don't quit seeing him, you're going to get shot." Soon after that letter arrived, a shot was fired at her while she was driving her car. Local police began surveillance of the woman's former boyfriend, and one cold winter night they saw him go out in his backyard and bury something wrapped in a plastic garbage bag. Several days later the woman received a twelfth note six lines long, concluding with the promise, "Next time I won't miss." And he didn't. As she paused at a stop sign, a rifle bullet ripped through her car door into her spine, paralyzing her for life.

Police immediately obtained a search warrant and dug up the suspect's yard. Buried in the frozen ground they found a manual typewriter, presumably the typewriter on which the threatening notes had been written. It went to Gerhardt for comparison. "Just looking at the typewriter I could see that the type was the same size and design as the letters on the notes, so it seemed probable the notes had been written on it," Gerhardt said. "But to identify a typewriter as the one on which a document was written to the exclusion of all other typewriters, you need some unique identifying characteristics like damaged typefaces or bent type bars or a peculiar alignment of characters, and this typewriter didn't have any of those. I really wasn't sure I could make a positive identification."

Once again, Gerhardt was sitting at his desk very early one morning, the rays of the rising sun coming in from behind him, but in this instance the light illuminated indentions in the rubber platen of the typewriter. "Normally you can't read typewritten characters on the platen because they're continually being pounded on top of each other," Gerhardt said. "But in this case the characters were clearly visible. I put better lighting on the platen and with a bit of magnification I could read six lines that were identical to the wording and spacing of the twelfth note. This was the hard evidence needed to connect the suspect to the shooting. So I made some notes and sent the platen to the Special Photography Unit to be photographed as evidence.

"The next morning I got a call from one of our photographers. 'What do you want us to photograph?' he asked.

" 'The indentions in the platen,' I told him.

" 'There aren't any,' he said. Apparently when I received the typewriter the rubber platen was still frozen from having been buried in the ground. But as it warmed up in the lab the indentions disappeared, and before we could photograph it they were gone completely. The only thing I could do was write a complete report stating that I had seen the impressions on the platen, and that they were identical to the twelfth note. Fortunately, my report was enough. The suspect pled guilty to the shooting."

In fact, the colder the environment, the more likely that indentions will be found in paper. Humidity tends to swell the fibers in paper and make indentions disappear.

The most unusual thing about the electrostatic detection apparatus is that no one can figure out why it works. It just does. The ESDA was developed by the British as a means of enhancing latent fingerprints on paper, but it wasn't very effective for that purpose because indented writing kept showing up and interfering with the prints. The ESDA very simple to use. A sheet of paper that might have indented writing on it is laid on top of a glass plate. A sheet of Mylar is laid on top of that. The lid of the machine is charged with about eight thousand volts of current, and there is a brass plate in the bottom. An electrostatic material, usually copy-machine toner, is sprinkled onto the paper. When the ESDA is turned on, these tiny charged pieces of toner migrate to the places closest to the brass plate—the depressions in the paper—fill in those indentions, and make whatever writing is on the page legible.

That's the theory. But fingerprints will also show up when the machine is turned on, and since fingerprints do not make impressions in paper, the theory doesn't hold up very well. Still, however ESDA works, it does work, and it can be a very valuable sci-crime tool. For example, an Oregon woman with two small children fell in love with a man who didn't like kids. So one night she drove her children to a lonely spot and shot them. One of them died. Although she claimed that a bushy-haired stranger had attacked her family, she was convicted of murder and attempted murder.

Amazingly, she managed to escape from prison. Among the few things found in her cell was a blank notebook. Tiny scraps of paper along the spiral edge indicated she had torn out some pages, so Oregon detectives, who did not have access to an ESDA, rushed the notebook to the FBI lab. Document analyst Joanna Neuman examined the notebook page by page. And on the fourth page down the ESDA magically revealed a roughly drawn map and a street address. Oregon police obtained a search warrant for that address and found the woman hiding there. Within days of her escape she was back in prison.

Being able to prove that a sheet of paper came from a specific notebook has enabled police to link a suspect to crimes in several cases. Bill Bodziak, who joined the Document Section in 1973 with degrees in biology and chemistry, was assigned a Massachusetts murder case in which a man and a woman were accused of killing another woman. "The police had found a map at the crime scene," Bodziak remembered. "It was a diagram of the barn that the victim would go to every night to feed her horses. Each of the stalls was indicated, and the speculation was that it had been drawn by the female suspect to show her male accomplice where to hide in wait for the victim. One of the items I was asked to examine was a blank notebook found among the female suspect's possessions.

"If we could prove that this drawing had come from that notebook we could link the woman to the murder. That kind of paper is usually cut with long knives, and the edges are nicked off in a random pattern. It leaves a pretty rough edge, and if you look at it under a microscope you can see a pattern. In addition, the knives also leave a striation pattern along the side of the notebook. You can't see it if you look at one sheet of paper, but if you look at most notebooks from the side that pattern is visible.

"These pages had been cut at a slight angle. If I put the map in the back of the notebook the edge would protrude ever so slightly. But if I put it between the twelfth and fourteenth pages it fit perfectly, and the striations made by the cutting knives also matched up perfectly. When I looked for indentions on the fourteenth page I found not only the map we had, but evidence that an earlier version of the map had been drawn. So by putting that incriminating map back in her notebook, we proved she'd been involved."

One of the major problems the Document Section faces in dealing with paper is that paper can be easily destroyed. It can be torn, shredded, burned, or crumpled up; it can even be soaked until the fibers separate and it disappears. Part of the Document Section's responsibility is to restore damaged paper documents so that whatever information is on them can be recovered.

Occasionally that becomes a gruesome task. In an Indiana case, an elderly woman was murdered by paper. The killer had stuffed wadded pieces of paper down her throat and in her nostrils, suffocating her. Those wads of paper were submitted to the lab on the slim chance that the killer might have brought the paper to the crime scene with him, and that there was some information on it that might help pinpoint a suspect. Each wad of paper was painstakingly opened and examined, but the paper turned out to have came from the victim's home and had no value as evidence.

Obviously the technique used to restore paper depends entirely on its condition. Wet paper, for example, must be allowed to dry slowly at room temperature or, preferably, put in a freezer and allowed to dry there. Papers burned or charred in a fire might appear to be hopelessly destroyed, but if they haven't disintegrated into ashes, they probably can be restored and read. When a pile of papers burns the pages in the middle are protected because there is little oxygen around them to feed the flames—that's the reason the center of an artificial fireplace log takes hours to ignite. So after being separated they can be read. Even those pages completely charred can be read with infrared lighting and photography, the light allowing the carbon to became transparent and the ink opaque.

Often the difficulty in restoring damaged pages is that when touched they crumble into tiny pieces. To prevent that, at one time each page was placed between two layers of glass. This worked, although each page weighed about a pound. Plexiglas made it a little lighter. But when the Document Section was asked to restore a brittle sheet of paper found glued to the back of a painting recovered from art thieves, a new solution to that problem was found at the Library of Congress. Librarians there had been encasing fragile documents in a remarkably thin polyester film that enabled them to take a brittle sheet of paper and, once it was enclosed, bend it, fold it, crumple it, even bake it without harming the document. The film absorbed the stresses created by movement without harming the paper at all.

Some papers are so badly crumpled that any attempt to flatten them would destroy them. A seemingly magic potion, called parylene, actually rebuilds the paper. Originally developed to give strength and resiliency to extremely brittle materials ranging from thousand-year-old fabrics to spiderwebs, parylene comes in granular form and is baked onto the surface of whatever is to be protected in a special chamber. The process can be thought of as injecting silicone into a butterfly's wings to give them added strength. A sheet of paper that has been crumpled into a ball in a fire can be coated with parylene while still in that shape, then opened and smoothed out and read.

There are no miracle devices when it comes to putting back together torn or shredded papers. Restoring them is like solving an intricate jigsaw puzzle. Someone has to sit at a desk for hours and hours matching up tiny scraps of paper. There are no shortcuts, and the work is as arduous as it sounds. But often the recovered documents prove invaluable.

When a landlord in Portland, Oregon, was cleaning out a house he had rented to a group of college-age kids, a torn scrap of paper drifted to the floor. It looked like a portion of map, and an arrow on it pointed to a local bank that had recently been robbed. The landlord contacted the FBI, and agents began sifting through a large Dumpster near the house. They discovered thousands of tiny scraps of paper, and examiners from the Document Section flew to the site for what they assumed would be a few days' work. Seven weeks later the restored pages provided evidence—and fingerprints—in five bank robberies, the planned kidnapping of the mayor of Portland, and the attempted bombing of an army induction center. Four suspects were identified by name. Three addresses were found that assisted authorities in their efforts to track down the gang. Eventually eight people were arrested in connection with these crimes, and almost every scrap of evidence came right out of the garbage.

Even the most experienced detectives have to piece together scraps of paper the same way they would solve a jigsaw puzzle: they start with corners and edges; they look for matching colors or similar handwriting; they find unusual patterns or smudges or coffee stains; they look for clues in the way the pages have been ripped. They do the work scrap by scrap; there is no easier or faster way.

Some types of paper are made to be instantly destroyed. Gambling and drug records, espionage documents, and records of just about any type of criminal enterprise are sometimes kept on flash paper or water soluble paper, both of which can be destroyed instantly without leaving any trace evidence. Nitrocellulose, commonly known as flash paper, is simply ordinary paper treated with a nitrate to make it highly flammable. Stage magicians use it to make their tricks disappear in a puff of smoke. It's dangerous, unstable stuff. A ream of flash paper has the destructive power of a small bomb. When the sci-crime lab was located in the old FBI headquarters in the Justice Department building, an agent working gambling cases locked a pile of flash paper in his metal desk when he went to lunch. The heat from the sun ignited the papers, blowing up the desk and moving a temporary wall back several inches.

Flash paper should be kept refrigerated. About the worst place to store flash-paper evidence is in the evidence room. Many cases have literally gone up in smoke when a seemingly spontaneous fire broke out in a sealed evidence storage room.

Water-soluble paper isn't dangerous; instead of disappearing in a flash, it instantly dissolves. When dropped into water the paper is transformed into a murky cloud and then disappears, leaving absolutely no trace evidence. Most large-scale gambling operations keep a pail of water on the floor next to each desk so that records can quickly be destroyed. Water-soluble paper is used in a variety of commercial products from laundry-detergent packaging to pipeline cleaners, so that the entire package can be dropped into the water. But blank water-soluble paper has so few legitimate uses that possession of it has been accepted in trials as evidence of participation in a gambling operation.

Whatever the condition of the paper, a lot can be learned about a suspect from the particular words written on the document. Examiners don't rely on any type of graphology—handwriting analysis—because generally it isn't possible to determine, on the basis of handwriting, a person's sex, age, general health, race, religion, educational or professional background, or even which hand they wrote with. (However, there are some indications of handedness in the slant of the letters and the way the "t"s are crossed.) But the choice of words on a document can be used to draw a portrait of the person who wrote them.

Penny Pickett is the lab's forensic linguist. By examining the way writing is structured and the words the writer chooses, a forensic linguist is able to derive a general description of the writer. While there is no way short of a signature or a telltale clue to identify a specific individual, a forensic linguist can give investigators strong clues about the type of person who prepared a particular document. From a friendly letter or a ransom note, a forensic linguist can confidently deduce the writer's gender and age, educational level, racial and religious background, nationality, and sometimes even professional history or military background. Although forensic linguistics sounds like some New Age technique, document examiners in the Lindbergh kidnapping were able to determine from the ransom notes that the person who wrote them was a German national who had spent several years in the United States—an accurate description of Bruno Hauptmann.

As technologies have evolved, the Document Section has had to keep pace with them. The fountain pen was replaced by the ballpoint pen, which in turn was replaced by the felt-tip pen. At one point the only personal writing machine was the manual typewriter. The lab still maintains the largest collection of typewriter samples in the world, and can determine from typeface and spacing exactly what make and model of typewriter was used to produce a document. By focusing on the unique characteristics of the questioned document—bent keys and spacing and type bars—it is even possible to prove that a document has been written on a specific typewriter. As far back as 1933, in one of the very first cases worked by the lab, a woman who had mailed poisoned fudge to a relative in a veterans' hospital was caught when examiners were able to match the typing on the package to the L. C. Smith typewriter she had left in a repair shop.

One of the most controversial cases ever worked by the lab, the Alger Hiss espionage case, turned on a typewriter identification. Examiners proved that negatives found hidden in a pumpkin were photographs of sensitive State Department documents that had been written on Hiss's typewriter. Legend has it that Hiss's attorney tried to have a duplicate typewriter made that exhibited the same unique characteristics as the one used by Hiss—which would demonstrate that it wasn't unique after all—but that proved impossible. Hiss was sent to prison for denying under oath to a congressional committee that he had prepared and hidden those documents.

The once-ubiquitous manual typewriter was replaced by the electric typewriter and the electronic typewriter, which in turn are now being replaced by the computer disk and personal printers. But the machine that has really changed the work of the Document Section is the photocopier. The copy machine has enabled everyone to become a printer. In the early 1970s examiners realized that more and more often the original evidence they had to work with was itself a copy. Just as with typewriting, a technique had to be developed to link copies to the machine on which they had been made.

Try to find copies of two different documents and look at them. Were they made on the same copy machine? If you had to trace them back to the copier on which they were made, where would you start? What would you look for? "People believe photocopies are not traceable," Jim Gerhardt pointed out, "and that's just not true. With a little luck, we can not only prove a document was made on a specific machine, we can determine within a narrow period of time when it was made."

If you look carefully at copies of documents, marks you didn't notice before suddenly become obvious: black dots, thread shadows, dirt, tiny star-shaped smudges caused by cracks in the machine's glass. Idiosyncrasies like these make it possible to prove that a specific document was copied on a particular machine to the exclusion of all other copiers. They are the "fingerprints" of that machine. The combination of the design and location of these marks is unique; no other machine in the world will produce them. The problem is that many of these defects are transient—they disappear when the machine is cleaned—and that new characteristics can be created.

Occasionally a copier's unique characteristics are obvious. In the 1980s an individual who identified himself, in notes left at crime scenes, as "El Condor" exploded small bombs against the walls of several federal buildings, including the FBI office, in the Miami area. The notes were identified as photocopies that had been made on different copiers. Since no two copies were made on the same machine it was assumed the bomber didn't have access to a copier and was therefore using coin-operated machines. Immediately following a bombing, detectives searched the surrounding area for stores with coin-operated copiers. In a 7-11 convenience store, a detective opened the lid of a copier and found a banana peel squashed against the cover. The banana peel appeared as a dark stain on copies made on that machine, and it matched the dark stain found on the note left at the scene of the last bombing. A general description of "El Condor" was obtained from a clerk in the store and eventually he and his partner, "El Tigre," were apprehended.

The illegal copying and distribution of confidential documents has became a major problem in both the business and political worlds, making it very important that a method be found to identify the individual who provided the original documents. Look very carefully at this page. It consists of ink printed on paper. But no two sheets of paper are alike, and copiers will reproduce the unique characteristics of a sheet of paper, enabling investigators to prove that a document has been copied. Mike Noblett, who joined the sci-crime lab in 1976 when photocopies were just beginning to be accepted as evidence, helped develop the investigative methods used in copier examinations. When a major tire manufacturer somehow obtained a copy of a confidential Department of Transportation report critical of its new product, for example, the DOT wanted to find out who had leaked the report. Copies of the report had originally been distributed to ten people; each of these copies, in addition to the copy retrieved from the manufacturer, was sent to the lab. Noblett conducted the investigation. "On one page of one of the original copies I found a single unbleached fiber in the paper," he said. "On the white paper it was just a brown speck, but in exactly the same position on the leaked document I found a black mark. The unbleached fiber was completely random in nature, but it was the finger-

213

print of that page. It enabled me to show that this was the document that had been copied and identify the office that had leaked it."

The quality of color copiers has gotten so good that it's possible to make copies of currency or stock certificates that can pass as originals. In a major stock scam a share of Walt Disney stock was reproduced several times on a copy machine and the forgeries were put up as collateral against a large bank loan. The name and serial number were obliterated before the copies were made, and each copy was numbered and signed as though it were an original. The lab was asked to show that one specific certificate, and no other, had been the source of the copies. What made this one certificate unique was a slight wearing of the ink where the certificate had been folded. Folds or creases are entirely random and no two will match precisely, even if the sheets are folded inside each other. The fold on a particular original certificate was matched to the copies, proving they had been made from that document.

Anything that makes a document different from every other document can be the source of identification: the tiny holes left by the removal of a staple, a fold in one corner, a speck of dirt, even stains will enable a copy to be linked to the original.

The American greenback is the most counterfeited currency in the world, because it is the most easily recognizable; and the twenty-dollar bill is the denomination most often counterfeited because it is the largest one easily passed. Anything larger is very carefully scrutinized. The quality of currency produced on some advanced color copiers is so good that the counterfeit bills can actually be used in change machines, while most other color copiers will produce bills just good enough to be accepted in dark bars or foreign nations. Hold a twenty-dollar bill up to a light. To prevent American currency from being easily copied, a translucent vertical strip has been embedded in each bill between the presidential portrait and the left end of the bill. Printed in microprint on that strip is the denomination of the bill. This security strip has been added specifically to prevent counterfeit bills from being produced on copiers, because even the most sophisticated machines can't reproduce the microprint.

As the nature of crime has evolved, the structure of the sci-crime lab has also evolved to reflect those changes. During World War II and throughout the Cold War, for example, the cryptanalysts had their own section, but now, because codes involve the use of paper, cryptanalysis is within the Document Section's purview. When Ron Furgerson joined the lab in 1971, as many as fifteen people still worked almost full-time on breaking codes in the Cryptanalysis, Gambling and Translation Section. But as the need for code breakers diminished, that section was incorporated into Documents. Currently the two people working codes average about two cases a month. The majority of Bureau cases involve criminal activity rather than espionage, so most of the work once performed by crime lab cryptologists is now done by the CIA and National Security Agency. The spy business just isn't what it used to be.

"We still see a lot of codes," Furgerson pointed out, "because people involved in a clandestine activity, whether it's criminal or espionage, are going to try to protect their communications from law enforcement, and they do this by creating codes. The fact that we still do work in this area makes us unique among crime labs."

A criminal organization is run just like a big business. Records of orders and deliveries and payments and bets and payoffs have to be kept, and most of those records are kept in code. These records can be used to prove ongoing criminal activity, but to have any real value the codes have to be broken. The lab first got into the code-breaking business in the early 1930s, when rum runners violating Prohibition encoded their records. But then and now, most criminal organizations—and most criminals—don't use the ingeniously complicated codes used to transmit military information. They have neither the time nor the need. Rather they use the most basic types of code. And here's your chance to be a code breaker: Decipher the letters AZCGLMQGQI.

The key to deciphering a code is figuring out the key, which is the explanation of what each cipher represents. The most common type of code is the substitution code, in which another letter, an abbreviation, or a symbol is used in place of the actual letter or number. The most basic substitution codes use the first, second, or third letters above the numbers on a telephone dial as substitutes for those numbers, while the two letters that do not appear on the dial, Q and Z, represent the numbers 1 and 0, which are not accompanied by letters on the dial. Hence AZCGLMQGQI is 202-456-1414, the telephone number of the White House.

According to Furgerson, criminal codes are still cracked the traditional way—with a lot of hard work. "Unlike espionage or military cryptanalysis," he said, "we're often working with a very small amount of text. We probably don't even get a complete alphabet, maybe just a few records. If we were trying to break a Russian navy code, we'd have tons of intercepts and we could apply all types of computer techniques to try to break it. But in criminal work the computer is usually of little help."

A basic method used to find the key is to apply mathematical probabilities to the code. Each letter of the alphabet appears in written English with a known frequency. Matching that to the frequency with which ciphers appear in the code might give code breakers a clue to the identity of some of those ciphers. But because criminal codes are generally brief, sometimes just a heading at the top of a column of numbers, the frequencies don't manifest themselves. "It's trial and error," Furgerson said, "assumptions based on experience, some guessing, trying one thing, then trying something else, then trying again. There's a lot of educated guesswork involved, and then, if you're lucky, the guesswork slowly evolves into probabilities until you find that one element that cracks open the door just a bit. Sometimes you can work on something for days and days and days and then in the middle of the night, when you're not consciously thinking about it, the light will go on. It's the most joyous feeling you can imagine."

What makes breaking criminal codes even more difficult is that often the cryptologist is working blind; he doesn't know what the code might be about. If it were that Russian navy code, a cryptanalyst would assume that it had something to do with ships and water and that military terminology would be present. A criminal code can be about almost anything, so one of the first things a cryptologist will do is try to make a comparison between actual events that have occurred and the encoded material. Knowing the type of information that might be contained in a code is extremely important in solving it. After heiress Patty Hearst was kidnapped by the Symbionese Liberation Army, she participated in several robberies. When she was caught, the question arose whether she had been forced to participate in those crimes or had done so willingly. There seemed to be no way to determine a definitive answer to that question.

But among the items found on Patty Hearst when she was arrested was a slip of paper on which were written some seemingly random letters. The importance of that paper didn't become obvious until SLA sympathizers Bill and Emily Harris were arrested and the same letters were found written on a piece of paper in their home. Obviously this was encoded material. But how would you begin to figure out what a line of seemingly random letters means? First, by making some assumptions. "We tried to figure out what information these people would need to carry with them," Furgerson said. "What would they need that they wouldn't want other people to know? Eventually, we realized that they had to have a means of getting in touch with each other if they were separated, a way to regain contact. So our first assumption was that these were telephone numbers. But they were longer than normal phone numbers, so our second assumption was that some nulls, some meaningless letters, had been added to the code. That led us to believe that it was what is called a keyword code."

A keyword code uses as its source a ten-letter word or phrase in which no letters are repeated, with the first nine letters representing the numbers 1 through 9, and the tenth representing 0. "Once we decided these were phone numbers, we looked at the rules regarding such numbers," Furgerson explained. "We knew they didn't start with a one or a zero. We were certain it was a California number so we had some idea what the first three numbers might be. We just worked at it and worked at it until it began to make sense." One member of the SLA was a painter; as it turned out, the keyword for this code was "paintbrush"—ten letters, no repeats, each letter representing a number. The "p" was 1, the "a" was 2, and so on up to 0. When the code was broken it turned out to be a list of phone numbers through which SLA members could safely regain contact with the group if they were separated. At Patty Hearst's trial, the fact that the SLA trusted her enough to give her these encoded numbers was evidence that she had become a willing member of the group and had voluntarily participated in the robberies.

Keyword codes are used frequently in criminal activities because the keyword is easy to remember and the code is relatively simple to decipher. In one major drug case, for example, the memorable keyword was "money talks."

Ironically, while advanced computers have made it possible for governments to create codes that realistically can never be broken, the most difficult codes submitted to the Document Section for decoding are those created by individuals for use by a small group of people. A chemist who was making PCP, angel dust, in his laboratory disguised his notes in a code based on the periodic table of the elements. Many codes are created in prisons to allow inmates to communicate privately with each other. In one case a man killed a police officer, spray-painted the doors of his police car white so he could use it for his getaway, and stole the officer's weapon. When arrested he claimed he had been insane when he committed the crime. Two slips of paper were found in his pocket. On one was written a meaningless series of letters, while the letters of the alphabet with tiny pencil marks below them were written on the other.

Those tiny pencil marks were the key to breaking the code. To an experienced cryptanalyst, they indicated that the person who prepared the code was counting something and that the code had a mathematical basis. It turned out to be what is called an auto-key generation code, in which each letter is determined by the letter that precedes it. When the code was broken the first plaintext word was "rifle." The "r" was in plaintext; it was an "r," and "r" is the eighteenth letter of the alphabet. The next letter should have been "i"; the code's creator began with "i" and counted eighteen letters, so the "i" was represented by the letter "z." "Z" is the twenty-sixth letter of the alphabet; "v" plus twenty-six became "u." When decoded, the note laid out the suspect's entire plan for killing the police officer and escaping. It proved that the killing had been premeditated, and so it destroyed the insanity defense. The suspect ended up pleading guilty.

Usually when police break up a drug or gambling organization, they get to see only a piece of the action: a major drug dealer might get caught holding only a single kilo of cocaine. But his records will show the entire scope of his organization. Knowing that, criminals often try to protect such records by hiding them inside computers. Law enforcement had to develop means to get that information out of the computers. When the first request to break into a computer and retrieve business records came into the lab in 1985, only two people, Mike Noblett and Betty James, knew anything at all about computers, and Betty James was completely self-taught. "We worked two cases that year," she remembered, "and in 1992 we worked a hundred and twenty cases, many of them involving systems consisting of several computers."

The Computer Analysis Response Team, CART, which was enlarged in 1993 to include eleven people, was made part of the Document Section because hard and soft disks generate documents. "The computer is a repository of records," James explained, "an electronic filing cabinet. In the old days an agent would be able to execute a search warrant by opening file drawers and looking through them. Now he sends the computer to us and we open it up for the accountants, who try to make sense out of whatever we find stored there."

Many people mistakenly believe that when data are erased from a computer they're gone forever. In every case the computer unit begins by copying all the data on the hard disk onto a new disk, and all work is done on that copy. As James said, "The one thing we're careful not to do is tamper with evidence. We don't change anything. We just go in there and browse around and then print out whatever we find. We never leave footprints." That also enables the investigators to avoid traps left by clever programmers that will delete information if the wrong command is given.

Most of these programs are password protected, meaning the only way to get into them is either to figure out the password or find a means to bypass it. Figuring out a password is the latest example of code breaking. People, even criminals, often use as a password something that is part of their lives and therefore easy to remember: their nicknames, the name of their pet, the street they live on, or the team they root for. One large drug operation used the password "drugs."

While the vast majority of cases consist of finding and printing out records and spreadsheets, occasionally other crimes will be documented on computers. When paintings worth several million dollars were stolen from a private art museum in Boston, the museum computer that ran a sophisticated security system was sent to the lab. "It was obviously an inside job," Noblett said. "It took us about two months to figure out what the computer was trying to tell us. Finally, we could determine when the alarms were turned on and off, what doors were open at what time, and where the guards were at every moment. By working backwards, we were able to figure out which guard was at the door that was opened when it shouldn't have been, how long it was open, and when he returned to his assigned post. The computer solved that crime for us."

Killers occasionally like to record their crimes. A Virginia murderer kept a chilling computer diary in which he wrote of stalking his victim for more than a year. At the end of this file he wrote that if he couldn't have this woman, no one would, and then he killed her.

Computers have provided the hard evidence in several violent crimes. While most of the computers sent to the lab are IBMs or IBM clones, an old Atari system was submitted in a Midwestern case in which an entire family was murdered. With the help of the manufacturer, Betty James was able to break into the family's system. Among the documents she found was a letter supposedly written by one of the victims and dated weeks before he was killed, in which he approved the transfer of valuable stock options to another man. But computers can't lie; the internal clock on the hard disk proved that this letter had actually been written after the murders. The motive for the killing was right there in black and white. The murderer had broken into the house and killed every member of the family, then coldly sat down and written the letter on the computer, transferring the stock options to himself and making sure to backdate the letter. He never realized that the internal clock would destroy his alibi.

While the use of computers is one of the most advanced methods of tracking a suspect, probably the oldest of all detection techniques is simply following a suspect's footprints. Even now, in a world covered by concrete and tiles and carpets and hardwood surfaces, these lasting impressions will provide surprisingly valuable evidence. Because footwear makes an impression on a surface in the same way as a printer makes impressions on paper, these investigations are assigned to the Document Section. For similar reasons, so are tire impressions.

Bill Bodziak, a compact, dark-haired man who has a ready smile and is the recognized expert on footwear evidence in the sci-crime world, believes that such evidence can be found at just about every crime scene. "The criminal had to walk around to commit the crime," he said. "In homicides and assaults, rapes and robberies, violent crimes of any kind, footwear evidence has been the sole basis for a conviction. And believe me, no pun is intended. Simply, if we can show through a footwear or tire tread impression that an individual was present at a crime scene, that person is going to have to come up with a pretty good reason to explain why he was there. And if that impression is made in the victim's blood, as often happens, then he's got a real problem."

Footwear impressions are made when someone walks on a soft surface, like snow or sand or mud or even dirt, when someone tracks material from a dirtier surface onto a cleaner surface, or simply when someone walks in the dust. Impressions can be made from any material—water, blood, or grease, for example—and they are found almost anyplace you can imagine: on countertops (the prints are made when robbers leap onto a counter and walk on papers); on tiny pieces of broken glass from the windshields of cars (victims push their feet against the glass as they struggle); in blood on concrete steps; even on the skin of a human being.

When a six-year-old Florida girl was brutally raped and murdered,

Bodziak was able to find evidence in the bruises the killer left on her skin. "There was a contusion, a bruise, made by the heel of the killer's shoe when he kicked her," he said. "Normally contusions will give you some detail, but they rarely show the small details, cuts and scratches in the shoe, that enable us to match it to one shoe to the exclusion of all others. But this was unusual. I could determine the size and the design of the shoe, and I could even see evidence of wear. I was able to determine that the contusions had been made by a deck shoe whose heel was worn down, and I could see precisely where the stitching had gone into the heel. Stitching is done randomly; no two shoes are alike. Using the stitching holes, I was able to match the impression on that little girl's skin to the suspect's shoe. It was the footwear impression that really got us the conviction."

Although there are tens of thousands of different shoe types and styles, footwear comparisons can be narrowed down to a specific shoe. Comparisons are based on class characteristics—the design, size, and shape of the shoe—and then on more individual characteristics, which include anything that has been added to the shoe or taken away from it. Such characteristics might be produced by normal wear and tear, a nail embedded in the heel, gum stuck to the bottom, a pebble wedged into the sole, cuts and scratches, the location of the stitching holes—anything that makes that one shoe different from all other shoes. "People often use the phrase 'DNA fingerprint,' " Bodziak said, "meaning it could come from only one person. I'm trying to convince people to say 'DNA footprint.' "

When a footwear impression is found at a crime scene investigators begin by photographing it. Then, if it is a depression, a cast is made using hard dental stone. If a photograph won't provide enough detail and it's not possible to make a cast of the print—for example, if the footprint is made in blood on a tile floor, often that section of the surface is actually lifted up and submitted to the lab. When the young woman who managed a New York City Gap store was murdered, a large slab of concrete flooring and tile was sent to Bodziak, who was able to enhance a barely visible athletic-shoe print that had been made in the manager's blood. That impression was eventually matched to a sneaker worn by a former employee of the store, and led to a conviction in the murder.

"We're one unit that gets everything sent in," Bodziak reported, "including the kitchen sink. We get sent entire countertops, staircases, slabs of concrete. In a Maryland murder case a woman's body had been dumped from a car, and the car then backed up through her blood, leaving three distinct impressions of the tire tread on the road surface. Three large sections of macadam were brought in by hydraulic lift, and from those we were able to enhance some faint impressions and make a positive match to her husband's car."

The most difficult problem with any latent evidence is making it visible. Like latent fingerprints, footwear impressions that aren't visible can be enhanced with chemicals or powder, then "lifted" with tape. Shoeprint impressions made in the dust are the flimsiest of all evidence, fragile enough to be blown away by a soft breeze, yet powerful enough to send someone to prison. This is fate at play; an open door on a windy day might be enough to prevent a killer from being convicted.

Finding and preserving evidence in the dust is the stuff of the finest fictional detectives. The best way to find prints in dust on hard surfaces is not to turn on the lights but to turn them out, and examine the surface with oblique lighting, something as simple as a flashlight laid on the floor. But almost any impression left in the dust can be materialized and preserved by a remarkable instrument, the electrostatic dust lifter, which is one of the really great "toys" of the sci-crime world: a tool to make the invisible visible. Unlike most instruments, which are adapted for sci-crime work from another field, the electrostatic dust lifter was developed specifically to do precisely what it does: transfer impressions made in the dust from a surface to a sheet of paper for preservation. It was invented in the 1960s by a Japanese policeman who worked part-time as a TV repairman. He noticed that dust was invariably attracted to the high-voltage source in the back of the set and realized that this property could be adapted to sci-crime purposes.

It's simple to use. If there is reason to believe prints might be present— if, for example, someone had to move from a dirty surface to a clean one to commit the crime—a sheet of black lifting material is laid down over the surface and a high-voltage charge is run through the material. The material is drawn down tightly against the surface and the dust is transferred to the lifter. The impression is actually made by the dust. The process is nondestructive, and usually enough dust is present to enable several lifts to be made from the same area. And the method works on just about any surface.

In a Wilmington, Delaware, rape case, an impression left on the floor was just about impossible to photograph because the tiles were old and dirty. When Wilmington detectives tried lifting the concrete it broke in small pieces. Bodziak took a two-inch-by-three-inch fragment of tile and, using the electrostatic dust lifter, was able to bring up a portion of an athletic-shoe sole bearing several unique wear marks, more than enough evidence for prosecutors to make a positive, and incriminating, match to the suspect's sneakers.

That's the way footwear evidence is developed and used in an ideal situation; unfortunately, few cases are so straightforward. About the strangest shoeprint Bodziak ever saw wasn't even a print, but rather the negative impression of a print. After a string of armed robberies in convenience stores, on a freezing winter afternoon New York City police got lucky and interrupted a holdup in progress. The suspect started running over snow-covered rooftops and down alleys, just as in the movies. When police finally caught him the gun he had been carrying, the gun that might connect him to several robberies, had disappeared. Investigators retraced the chase route, and in a dry area behind a roof vent they found a gun that was eventually linked to the holdups. The challenge was to find a way to connect that gun to the suspect.

Not far from the gun, police found several ridges of snow in a recognizable pattern. When captured, the suspect was wearing boots with an indented ripple pattern on the soles. During the chase snow had been packed into those indentations; when the suspect bent down to hide the gun behind the vent, his soles bent and the snow popped out, much like ice cubes popping out of a plastic tray. It left an almost perfect negative impression of the boot soles. Although there was not enough detail to make a perfect match between the ridges of snow and the suspect's boots, there was enough to allow Bodziak to testify that the ridges had very likely come from those boots. That testimony connected the suspect and the gun, and it took the jury about twenty minutes to convict him of the series of armed robberies.

Contrary to the plotting of detective fiction, it isn't possible to estimate someone's height by the distance between steps—his gait—because during the commission of a crime, a suspect is usually moving very fast; he is running or backing up or moving sideways or struggling, attacking or defending, even sneaking around. The thing he isn't doing is moving normally. But it is possible to make a good estimate of someone's height from the size of his shoes, and the size of a shoe can be determined from a shoeprint.

Tire tread impressions are almost as useful as shoeprints. There are thousands of tread designs, and every tire wears differently or picks up debris from the road, making it unique and therefore identifiable. Tire treads are made of what are called elements, which are small sections of the tire with a specific design that is repeated over the entire tire. Some tires have as few as three different elements, while better tires have as many as nine. These elements are designed to improve traction and cut down on the noise the rubber makes as it is squeezed against the road surface. Tread design—the size and location of the elements—is what makes a tire identifiable. Sci-crime detectives can not only identify a specific tire from a tread impression, they can often find the portion of the tire that left the impression.

Oddly, anecdotal evidence shows that most violent crimes in which tread marks are found have been committed by people driving older cars with various brands of replacement tires. So even though there are thousands of identical tires on the road, the combination of different tires makes a car unique. For example, Florida police searching for a serial killer knew that he was driving a sedan with two somewhat unusual rear tires, one of them put on backward so that the whitewall faced inward. When Bobby Joe Long was identified as a suspect, a quick examination of the tires on his car proved that it had been used in at least two murders.

As you might suspect, tire impressions are often found on the bodies of hit-and-run victims. But, surprisingly, these are not tread impressions. Rather, as a car runs over a body, clothing wraps around the tire so that the imprint of the sidewall, the part of the tire on which the brand name and model number appear, is pressed into the cloth. Bodziak has worked several cases in which he could read the name of the tire manufacturer on the victim's clothing.

The Document Section will use absolutely anything found at a crime scene to make a match to a suspect—even a match. Since the section has responsibility for anything involving paper, upon request it will conduct cigarette or matchbook examinations—paper matches only; wood matches are examined by Hairs and Fibers. Jim Gerhardt is the lab's matchbook expert. "It's not really much of a competitive field," he admitted, "and I guess I've sort of cornered the market. We only get four or five cases a year, but sometimes these comparisons can be very useful. Naturally, matches are most often found at fires in which arson is suspected. The object is to somehow connect those matches to a suspect.

"Turn a match on its side," Gerhardt explained, "and you'll see little particles sticking out. That's because paper matches are produced from junk filler consisting of everything from rag threads to paint chips. Those particles will fit perfectly with the adjoining matches in a matchbook, enabling us to make a microscopic comparison to prove that a match came from a specific matchbook to the exclusion of all other matchbooks ever made. I can often find as many as thirty different points of comparison in one match."

When burned matches were found near the place where a suspicious fire had started in Los Padres National Forest in southern California, Gerhardt was able to link them to a matchbook found on a suspect by showing that the ragged edges of the burned matches fit together perfectly with the ragged edges in the matchbook.

Matches may seem to be the most common thing in the world, but they are unique enough to provide telling evidence of a crime. When a large Boston building burned down in 1986, police at the scene found a matchbook with all the matches torn out. The property owner was questioned and denied having been near the building. In his pockets police found two unused matchbooks. Gerhardt couldn't link burned matches to the empty matchbook; instead, he was able to show that the matchbook found at the scene had been made between the two matchbooks found in the building owner's pocket. Gerhardt showed that the empty matchbook shared a ragged edge with each of the other two. The owner pleaded guilty to setting the fire to collect insurance on the building.

In years past it was considered important to be able to identify the brand of cigarette found at a crime scene, and the lab maintained an extensive cigarette sample collection. It was rarely used and even more rarely valuable, so it was disbanded. But cigarettes can still make strong evidence. Police found a bloody cigarette butt at the scene of a 1986 murder in Allentown, Pennsylvania, and asked Gerhardt to try to associate it to a pack of cigarettes found on the primary suspect. Gerhardt could show that the butt was the same brand as the pack; that proved nothing. But he also found a filter in the bottom of the pack, and he was able to show microscopically that this filter had been detached from the butt found at the crime scene. It was a simple—and incriminating—association. Apparently the filter had been knocked off the cigarette during the fatal brawl and by chance had fallen back into the pack. It was a one-in-a-million oddity that led directly to a murder conviction, perhaps proving once again that smoking can be hazardous to your health.

While the cigarette collection was one of the first maintained by the lab, it became outdated as more conclusive means of linking a suspect to the crime scene were found. But with the recently developed ability of examiners to make DNA comparisons, cigarette butts, which might contain saliva from which DNA can be extracted and compared to DNA from a suspect, have once again become important pieces of evidence. The world of sci-crime goes around and around.

And finally, the old saying promises that good things often come in small packages. But in the Document Section, the good thing often *is* the package. After a Washington schoolboy found what appeared to be a rock with perfectly rounded edges at the mouth of the Columbia River, it eventually found its way to the Document Section. This "rock," in fact, consisted of hard cash—very, very hard cash. It turned out to be made of calcified layers of currency, $6,000 in twenty-dollar bills that had been compacted over time into a rock-hard substance. When agent Lou Senter pried apart the layers with a tweezer and read the serial numbers of the bills, the "rock" turned out to be part of the $200,000 ransom paid to America's first skyjacker, the infamous D. B. Cooper, who had parachuted out of an airplane with a satchel filled with cash. The money was the first clue to Cooper's fate after he leaped out of that airplane and was never seen again.

CHAPTER
- 8 -

Number One with a Bullet:
The Firearms and Toolmarks Unit

Do you know, Watson, I believe your revolver is going to have a very intimate connection with the mystery which we are investigating.

SHERLOCK HOLMES,
in Sir Arthur Conan Doyle's "The Problem of Thor Bridge"

"The President's limousine arrived back in Washington about six o'clock. Around one o'clock the next morning Cort [Cortlandt Cunningham] and I started sifting through the blood looking for lead fragments. It was tough; it was very tough." Bob Frazier, believed by many experts to be the finest firearms examiner who has ever lived, was speaking for the first time outside a courtroom about the assassination of President John Kennedy. "The yellow roses that Mrs. Kennedy had been holding were scattered all over the back of the car along with Mrs. Connally's bouquet of red roses, and we had to move them, we had to get them out of the way. We'd just reach down into the clots of blood and scoop it up in our hands and let it dribble through. Whenever we felt something gritty, we'd clean it up and if it was lead, we'd save it in a pillbox. We didn't really recover a lot of the lead."

"Guns don't kill people," proclaims the slogan of the National Rifle Association. "People kill people." Actually, bullets kill people: bullets shot from guns, fired by people. This is an unbreakable chain, a chain that can be traced from either end. From a bullet found in a victim, it's possible to determine precisely which gun fired it, and from that gun, the person who pulled the trigger can be identified. In perhaps the classic example, when

227

the bullets that killed Dr. Martin Luther King, Jr., were proved to have the same rifling characteristics as a rifle found nearby, fingerprints found on that rifle eventually led to the identification of the assassin, James Earl Ray.

A bullet makes a fuss. It leaves plenty of information in its wake, and finding and interpreting that information is the basis of sci-crime ballistics. It's the work of the Firearms Unit, and it is one of the oldest applications of science to crime solving.

The proliferation of guns in America is a subject of great controversy. Guns have become the primary means of murdering human beings in this country, and the issue of gun control has become a central focus of American political debate.

Firearms examiners don't take sides in this debate, at least not officially. By the time sci-crime investigators get involved the weapon has already been fired, the victim has been shot. Their work is devoted to answering one question: Who pulled the trigger?

The use of a bullet to connect an individual to a crime dates back to 1835, when a member of London's Bow Street Runners, the predecessor to Scotland Yard, was able to match a ridge found on a bullet removed from a victim's body to a gouge in a bullet mold found in a suspect's home. When confronted with this evidence the suspect confessed to the shooting, and the science of ballistics was born. The first recorded firearms case in America took place in 1879, when a man charged with murder was acquitted after a gunsmith testified that the suspect's gun hadn't been fired in more than a year. In a 1902 murder trial, Judge Oliver Wendell Holmes enlisted the services of a gunsmith to determine if the fatal bullet had been fired from a suspect's gun. The gunsmith fired several shots from the weapon into a basket of cotton, then used a magnifying glass and microscope to show the jury that marks found on the fatal bullet were identical to marks on the test bullets. Thus he proved that this gun had been used in the murder, proof that lead to the suspect's conviction.

Basically, that's still the way firearms examinations are conducted. The equipment has become a lot more sophisticated, but the premise is exactly the same: bullets fired from the same gun will exhibit many of the same unique characteristics. So by comparing a bullet fired in a crime to a bullet fired in a test, investigators can prove that a specific weapon was used in the commission of that crime.

Almost every firearms case handled in what is officially known as the Firearms and Toolmarks Unit begins with the submission of a gun or bullets. Sometimes the bullets have been pried out of a wall or a tree, but many of the ones that reach the lab have been taken out of a body. The Firearms Unit deals almost exclusively in violent crimes, and its examiners have plenty of work.

Generally, the first information that can be gotten from a bullet is the type of gun from which it was fired. A weapon fires a certain size of bullet, a certain caliber, but many different guns fire bullets of the same caliber. What makes each make and model unique is its rifling, the grooves inside the barrel. It was discovered hundreds of years ago that spiral grooves cut into the barrel of a weapon will significantly improve both its range and its accuracy. When a weapon is fired, a tiny explosion caused by the hammer striking a primer inside the cartridge ignites the gunpowder which propels the bullet through the barrel. The grooves in the barrel cause the bullet to spin rapidly, greatly increasing its stability in flight. The raised areas between the grooves are called lands, and as the bullet spins down the barrel, these lands and grooves make an imprint on it. The rifling, the number of lands and grooves, the direction of the "twist"—the spiral that makes the bullet spin clockwise or counterclockwise—and the width of the lands and grooves are the gross characteristics that make it possible to determine what kind of gun fired that bullet.

These microscopic marks left on a bullet were the strongest evidence in one of the most controversial trials in American history, the 1921 murder trial of Nicola Sacco and Bartolomeo Vanzetti. In April, 1920, the paymaster and a guard carrying the $16,000 payroll for a South Braintree, Massachusetts, shoe company were shot and killed in a daylight robbery. Within days the getaway car was discovered abandoned in nearby woods. A man seen in that car was traced to a second car then being repaired in a garage in West Bridgewater. Then this suspect showed up to pick up the second car; police raced to the garage, but by the time they got there the man had grown suspicious and fled on a motorcycle. He eventually escaped to Italy. But two other men who'd accompanied him to the garage, Sacco and Vanzetti, were arrested. A .32-caliber Colt automatic was found on Sacco, while Vanzetti was carrying a .38-caliber revolver. The guard had been killed by a .32.

Sacco and Vanzetti were poor Italian immigrants who spoke little English. But both men were anarchists, members of an international movement that believed that true social justice for the poor and oppressed could be achieved only by the destruction of established governments. In America, anarchists had purportedly been responsible for numerous bombings, among them attempts on the life of John D. Rockefeller and the attorney general of the United States. The government had responded with mass arrests and deportations. So what began as a local robbery and murder case grew into an international political event, and Sacco and Vanzetti were seen as martyrs in the struggle of the downtrodden against the rich and powerful. Throughout the world many people believed that their arrest was simply a crude effort by the ruling class to crush political dissent.

The entire case turned on a single bullet. Six .32-caliber bullets had been taken from the bodies of the victims. The chief of the Massachusetts state police fired fourteen test shots from Sacco's pistol into a box of oil-soaked sawdust, then compared them to the six bullets fired in the robbery. The rifling on the test bullets matched one of the bullets recovered at the crime scene. It was assumed that the other five bullets had been fired from another pistol, perhaps by someone else involved in the robbery.

Although several cartridge shell cases found at the scene could also be associated with Sacco's pistol, the prosecution's case really came down to that one bullet. Had it been fired from Sacco's gun? Two self-taught "experts" testifying for the prosecution said the marks proved it had been; two self-taught "experts" testifying for the defense said it had not.

During their deliberations, jurors requested a magnifying glass so that they might examine the bullets themselves. This rudimentary examination was apparently enough to enable them to conclude that the bullet had been fired from Sacco's gun. Both men were convicted of murder and sentenced to death.

The saga of Sacco and Vanzetti became a major international cause. Millions of dollars were raised in their name. Huge demonstrations were held in Paris and Moscow and cities throughout South America. The French Chamber of Deputies, the British Labour party, and the German Reichstag asked that they be released. American embassies around the world were bombed, and government officials were threatened. Artists drew inspiration from the case, producing books and articles and plays, paintings and sculptures. The convictions became even more controversial in 1925 when a condemned killer claimed that the murders had actually been committed by his gang. Finally, in 1927, Massachusetts governor A. T. Fuller bowed to the pressure and appointed an independent three-man commission to advise him whether or not to grant clemency to Sacco and Vanzetti. In effect, this was a new trial.

But while the case was making headlines around the world, several significant advances had been made in sci-crime ballistics. Phillip Gravelle invented the comparison microscope, which allowed two bullets to be examined side by side; physicist John Fisher developed a microscope that measured lands and grooves and angles with unprecedented accuracy, as well as the helixometer, a lighted "telescope" that could be inserted into the barrel of a weapon to make a detailed inspection of the rifling.

It was during the 1927 hearing that the comparison microscope, which eventually became the essential tool of sci-crime examiners, was first used in a courtroom. Dr. Calvin Goddard, a pioneer in the study of ballistics, examined the bullets and stated that the fatal bullet had been fired from Sacco's gun and that at least one of the shell casings found at the scene had also been fired by that gun. A defense expert who had previously claimed that Sacco's gun could not possibly have fired that bullet peered into the comparison microscope and said, after a long and dramatic silence, "Well, what do you know about that?" He then withdrew from the case.

On August 23, 1927, as millions of people around the world protested, Sacco and Vanzetti were executed. That ended their lives, but not the controversy, which continued to rage through the decades. But even more sophisticated tests conducted by ballistics experts in 1961 affirmed the original conclusion that the questioned bullet had been fired from Sacco's .32-caliber Colt automatic.

Not only do rifling characteristics permit a bullet to be linked to a gun, but because each arms manufacturer uses its own land-and-groove design, it is possible to work backward, to determine from the impressions on a bullet exactly what make and model of weapon has fired it. In the early 1920s a man named Charles Waite traveled around the world recording the number of lands and grooves and the direction and angle of the twist for almost every gun that had been mass produced. So when police recovered a .32-caliber bullet with six lands and grooves and a left twist, they knew precisely what type of gun they were looking for.

That capability helped solve one of the most infamous crimes in American history, Chicago's St. Valentine's Day Massacre. On February 14, 1929, two men disguised as policemen walked into a garage with guns drawn and ordered seven members of bootlegger Bugs Moran's gang to put up their hands and stand against the wall. The gangsters did as ordered, confident that Moran would clear up any problems with the law. But as they stood facing the wall, two other men came silently into the garage and mowed them down. Within seconds six of the men were dead and the seventh was dying. The cold-blooded slaughter horrified—and titillated—the American public and made Al Capone, the man believed to have masterminded the killings, the nation's most celebrated gangster.

More than seventy cartridges found at the scene were identified by firearms experts as having been fired from .45-caliber Thompson submachine guns. The police knew what type of weapons to look for. Ten months after the killings, a policeman in St. Joseph, Michigan, was shot by a motorist he had stopped for a minor traffic violation. The shooter escaped, but his license-plate number was traced. When police broke into the apartment of the man to whom the plates belonged, they discovered a small arsenal hidden in a closet, and among the weapons were two .45-caliber Thompson submachine guns.

Using his comparison microscope, Dr. Goddard proved that these were the weapons used in the St. Valentine's Day Massacre. The motorist, Fred Burke, was eventually captured and, primarily on the basis of Goddard's testimony, convicted of murder and sentenced to life imprisonment.

Goddard's work on the case so impressed two wealthy Chicago businessmen who had served on the coroner's jury that they hired him to establish the first Scientific Crime Detection Laboratory in America. It opened on the Evanston, Illinois, campus of Northwestern University in 1929.

It was the success of Goddard's laboratory that convinced director J. Edgar Hoover that the Bureau of Investigation needed its own crime lab. When the Criminological Laboratory, as it was officially known, opened in 1932, the very first piece of equipment purchased specifically for the lab was a comparison microscope to be used for making bullet comparisons.

While the world of sci-crime has been revolutionized in so many ways since then, bullet and cartridge case comparisons remain as valuable as ever. In the 1980s Jack Dillon, who became Firearms Unit chief in 1988, headed a five-year project that created an updated database of firearms rifling. This database, available on computer software to law enforcement agencies, contains the general rifling characteristics of more than eighteen thousand different weapons. That's not every make and model produced by arms manufacturers, but it does include the weapons police officers commonly encounter.

These class characteristics provide excellent information. In San Antonio, Texas, for example, a federal judge named John Wood came out of his house one morning to discover that his car had a flat tire. As he bent down to inspect it, a bullet ripped into his back and killed him. The bullet was shattered by the impact, but several fragments were submitted to the lab. The class characteristics of these fragments enabled the lab to report that the bullet could have been fired from one of only four different weapons, among them the expensive .240 Wetherby Magnum Mark 5 rifle.

The investigation proceeded on several paths. Judge "Maximum John" Wood, as he was known, had made a lot of enemies by handing out the longest possible sentences, particularly in drug-related crimes. It was eventually learned that a woman named Jo Ann Harrelson had recently purchased a Wetherby Magnum Mark 5 rifle, and she became a suspect in the killing. Gradually other evidence was developed, and her husband, Charles V. Harrelson—the father of actor Woody Harrelson—was convicted of the assassination of Judge Wood. He had been hired by drug dealers who were about to be tried in Judge Wood's courtroom and wanted to ensure that he would never pass the maximum sentence on them.

While rifling enables examiners to state the make and model of the weapon that fired a bullet, it can't be used to prove that a specific weapon fired a specific round. To link a bullet to a particular gun investigators must compare the unique marks found on the inside of the gun barrel with the marks imprinted on a bullet.

Arms manufacturers use a very sharp, very strong tool to cut grooves into the metal barrel of a gun, and just like a knife being continually rubbed against a rock, this tool is worn down. Because it changes microscopically with each cut, it leaves slightly different marks, usually striations, inside the barrel. These marks are unique: no two guns will ever have the same ones. They are the weapon's fingerprint, its DNA profile.

Usage also leaves marks inside a gun barrel. Sometimes these marks are transient, like rust or dirt, but more often they are permanent and will be found on every bullet fired through that barrel. Additionally, other machine-made parts of weapons—the firing pin, the breechface, the extractor, and the ejector—all make contact with the cartridge case and imprint distinctive marks that enable a gun to be positively linked to cartridge cases found at a crime scene.

These unique marks are reproduced every time a gun is fired and they provide indisputable evidence that a bullet was fired from that gun. To make a bullet comparison in the lab, a weapon suspected of having been used in a crime is fired into a water tank. Then the marks made on the test bullet are compared with the marks on the bullet recovered at the crime scene. At least, that's the way it is usually done. "The most unusual case I ever worked took place in the early 1980s," recalled Agent-examiner Bob Sibert, who has spent two decades in the Firearms Unit. "I'd gotten fired bullets and cartridge cases in a case we called Tribal Thumb. That was the name of an extremist group in San Francisco that had assassinated two people who were sitting in a parked car. The bullets were in pretty good shape and I was hoping to determine from the rifling the make and model of the gun that had fired them. We keep as many different bullet cartridge cases as possible, both specimens submitted to us for examination and specimens we've test fired, in a file for comparison purposes. I started going through that file looking for class characteristics, lands and grooves, type of twist, firing pin shape, all types of marks. I pulled out a cartridge case that had been fired during a bank robbery. Some of the robbers had been caught, but they hadn't been tried yet. I looked at this cartridge case, and not only were the class characteristics identical to the cartridge case found at the murder scene, but so were the unique markings. It was very hard to believe; the odds against that happening are astronomical, beyond calculation. I examined the cartridge case under the comparison scope and sure enough, they'd been fired in the same gun. When I made that identification, my jaw dropped so hard it just about left an impression on my 'scope. It was the most incredible coincidence." Sibert's discovery provided the link between the bank robbers and the killings, and resulted in their conviction for murder.

On television, when a detective finds a gun at a crime scene, usually he will very carefully and professionally pick it up by sticking a pen or pencil into the barrel so that he won't mar any latent fingerprints on the gun. In fact, that's about the last thing a real detective would do. The most important information that can be obtained from a gun is inside the barrel, and sticking any object in there may alter or destroy telltale marks. On occasion criminals will try to alter these markings by scratching the barrel with a sharp object or pouring a caustic substance, battery acid for instance, into it. And that will work; it will change the markings enough to prevent that gun from being linked to a bullet fired from that gun. (Incidentally, the proper way to pick up a weapon that might have been used in a crime is to put on cotton gloves, pick it up touching only the scored, or rough, surfaces—usually the grips—and dropping it into a bag. That will preserve any latent prints that might be on the weapon.)

Bullets are a lot more difficult to find at a crime scene—unless they are in the victim. As Agent-examiner Gerald Wilkes, who has spent more than two decades in Firearms, pointed out, "Once bullets start flying, where they're going to end up is almost random and haphazard. Bullets don't follow a predictable path. They do strange things, seemingly for no reason. In an Oklahoma case, I remember, an individual drove a hundred and fifty miles from his house to rob a bank. And lo and behold, the teller turns out to be a girl he went to high school with, and she recognizes him. So he has to eliminate all the witnesses. There were three people in the bank and he took them out back and made them kneel down. He shot the first two in the back of the head. But then he took that same gun and put it against the back of the girl's skull and fired it at point-blank range. It was a .357 Magnum, a very powerful weapon. The bullet entered the back of her skull, took a ninety-degree turn, and went all the way around her head, then exited from her forehead. It knocked her unconscious. He rolled her over and saw the exit wound and assumed she was dead. She wasn't; she wasn't even badly hurt. She suffered no brain damage and was able to testify against the guy in court. That bullet didn't even go into her skull, and there is no one who can tell you why that happened.

"But we had another case in which the victim was shot by a .22 bullet. That's a small caliber, and he was hit in the wrist, which normally is not very serious. But the bullet went into his vein, traveled through the vein up his left arm and into his heart, and killed him. With bullets, you just never know."

In a shootout inside a house in St. Louis, Missouri, a suspect fired five shots, killing FBI agent Doug Abrams and wounding two other agents. Four bullets were quickly accounted for, but the fifth bullet, which had passed through an agent's leg, could not be found. A week later it turned up in six inches of water in the kitchen sink. By comparing damage to the bullet to damage to objects, Firearms examiners determined that the bullet had passed through the agent's leg, gone through an indoor-outdoor carpet in the kitchen, hit the floor and bounced up through the carpet, hit a chair leg, which deflected it upward, bounced off the ceiling, and finally landed in the sink, where it was found. You just never know.

There are many ways to search for bullets at a crime scene. Obviously, if a bullet is in the victim the doctor or coroner will find it. If the shooting took place indoors, the bullet will usually be found embedded in the walls or furniture. But when a shooting takes place outdoors, a flat trajectory can send the bullets absolutely anywhere, and often they're never recovered.

Even in what is certainly the most carefully investigated shooting of all time, the assassination of President Kennedy, the first bullet fired was never found. "From the Zapruder film we knew when the first shot was fired," Bob Frazier, who headed the firearms investigation, remembered. "It obviously missed, and hit the limb of a tree or something. There was a man standing a couple of hundred yards away who said he got hit with a piece of cement and there was blood running down his cheek. Nobody could account for it except that the bullet might have hit the curb and knocked a piece of cement out of it which cut him in the cheek. Nobody ever found that bullet. It could have gone to pieces. But it just disappeared."

Detectives use metal detectors, underwater metal detectors, crime-scene vacuums, even X-ray machines to find spent bullets. They are found embedded everywhere imaginable: in the ground, inside utility poles, inside flattened automobile tires. They are found smashed into fragments next to a brick wall. One examiner received a tree trunk; still embedded in it was a bullet from a murder committed thirty years earlier. In those cases in which bullets cannot be found, the spent cartridges become the best evidence.

One of history's most controlled crime-scene searches took place not far from the lab when John Hinckley attempted to assassinate President Reagan. Gerald Wilkes and Rick Crum were two of the first agents on the scene. "The first thing we had to do was account for all the shots," Wilkes explained. "We wanted to know where each bullet was, which would eliminate the possibility that there was a second shooter. We knew six shots had been fired because there were six fired cartridge cases in the cylinder of Hinckley's gun, and the sound of six shots being fired had been recorded on videotape. We knew that four people had been hit, so that's four bullets. Another bullet had hit the right rear window of the limousine, the fifth bullet. But we couldn't find the sixth bullet anywhere.

"We walked through the crime scene, then we crawled through it on our hands and knees, and finally we went through there with brooms and swept up everything. We collected gum wrappers, bottle caps, cigarette butts, everything. And finally we found that bullet. It had missed everything, gone across the street and hit a second-story window, and shattered. We found tiny bullet fragments on the pavement outside the window and on the floor inside the building. There was only a small hole in the glass.

"Agents at the hospital where the President was being treated gathered up all his belongings and sent them to us so we could do residue tests. Now we believed we really did have everything we needed. In fact, two nights later, I was fast asleep when the assistant director in charge of the lab, Tom Kelleher, woke me and asked, 'You still got all of the President's stuff?' When I told him I did, he asked, 'Did you happen to get a little flat card with an orange band on it?'

" 'Yeah,' I said, 'it's in my locker.'

"I could hear him breathe a sigh of relief. 'Would you get out of bed right now and go to your office, please. Two White House staffers will meet you there.'

" 'Couldn't this wait till the morning?' I asked.

" 'Uh, no,' he said firmly. 'That thing you stuck in your locker box is the encoding card that arms all of our nuclear warheads. You've had it for two days and they'd really like it back.' "

It often requires a great deal of skill as well as luck to find a bullet at a crime scene. When a flight carrying gamblers between San Francisco and Las Vegas crashed for no obvious reason in the 1950s, there was speculation that the pilot had been shot. The lab sent Agent-examiner Bill Magee to the site to investigate the crash. "My job was to go out there and try to find out if a gun had been fired on that airplane. It turned out to be a nightmare. As I discovered, a rivet hole is just about the size of a .38-caliber bullet. And when a plane crashes, those rivets start popping out. I looked at thousands of holes, almost any one of which could have been made by a bullet. When I went back to the lab and reported that I hadn't found any evidence to support the shooting theory, they told me to go back and look some more.

"This time, before I went back, I developed a spot chemical solution that would turn purple when exposed to lead. I knew that when a bullet hits metal it leaves a lead deposit, so I figured this solution might help us find the evidence we needed. I went back there and began demonstrating the procedure we were going to use to the agents who would be helping me with the search. I picked up a piece of metal tubing with a dent in it and applied some of my solution to it—and the damn thing turned purple! I sent this piece back to the lab, and in addition to the lead we found some antimony. Antimony is used in bullet metal to harden it. The piece turned out to be part of the frame from the pilot's seat. There was no question about it, at least one shot had been fired on that plane, at the pilot."

Finding a bullet at a crime scene can also help determine its point of origin. In some instances firearms experts can trace the trajectory of a bullet to find the spot from which it was fired. This can't be done often, because once a bullet hits something, whether a brick wall or a human bone, it changes direction and its path can't be traced. To successfully establish the trajectory of a bullet, investigators need two different surfaces that the bullet has passed through. Then it's simply a matter of lining up the holes, which can often be done by aiming a laser beam through them and seeing where it ends up. Sometimes this is done the old-fashioned way, by sticking a dowel through a hole and determining the angle of penetration with protractors, a carpenter's level, and a plumb line.

When a shot was fired through a window and into the wall of the Israeli consulate in Washington, D.C., government officials feared that it was a terrorist act. Lab examiners aimed a laser beam from the point of impact in the wall through the hole in the window. The beam went straight between other buildings to a spot several blocks from the consulate. An investigation discovered that at the time the shot had been fired, a security guard was chasing a purse snatcher and had, in fact, taken a shot at him. The rifling on the bullet was consistent with the guard's gun. This proof that the episode had been just an unlucky shot perhaps averted an international incident.

In a similar case, Supreme Court justice Harry Blackmun, who wrote the majority opinion in the controversial *Roe v. Wade* case, which established a constitutional right to abortion, was sitting in his Virginia apartment near the Potomac River when a bullet crashed through the window and lodged in his chair. This certainly could have been an assassination attempt.

The first thing examiners noted was that the bullet, which was made of soft metal and should have been badly damaged, in fact was almost intact. That meant it had been fired from a substantial distance and had been slowing when it went through the window and into the chair. By retracing the path of the bullet, the point of origin was determined to have been more than a half-mile away, across the Potomac. That was far too great a distance for a handgun to be fired with any accuracy. Although the gun from which the bullet had been fired was never identified, some police officers in Georgetown admitted they had been shooting at an opossum at just about the time the bullet went through Blackmun's window, and it is probable that this was the source of the stray shot.

A popular misconception about bullets is that the angle of incidence— the angle at which a bullet strikes an object—will equal the angle of rebound, as it does when a ball is thrown against a wall. If that were true, experts would be able to plot the path of a bullet even after it struck an object. But when a bullet hits something, its shape is altered; and that change in shape will cause it to deflect at a different angle. In fact, if someone is shooting at you, about the worst thing you can do—contrary to TV or the movies—is lie on the ground or hide behind a car, because when a bullet strikes the ground it will generally rebound or rise only about a few inches and travel close to the surface. So if you're hiding behind a car, all the shooter has to do to hit you is aim at the ground directly in front of you.

The first thing that happens when a gun arrives in the firearms lab is that an examiner or technician looks inside the barrel. When a gun is fired, a small but very powerful vacuum, the blowback, draws anything close by into the barrel. On occasion blood, hairs, or fibers from the victim are found in the gun barrel. In a double homicide case in Florida, the killer tried to muffle the sound of the gunshots by shooting through a pillow. When a suspect was arrested, parts of a feather were found in the barrel of his gun—a feather that Doug Deedrick of the Hairs and Fiber Unit could positively associate with the feathers in that pillow.

Once the barrel has been cleaned the gun is test-fired. Just about every gun that comes into the lab is fired twice, to produce two bullets and two cartridge cases which can be used for comparisons. In the FBI lab guns are fired into a water-filled steel tank four feet wide, five feet deep, and ten feet long. The water makes the bullet decelerate and drop to the bottom of the tank, which is painted a light color to make it easy to find the bullet. Water is the ideal medium to use to slow down a bullet, because it won't affect any of the microscopic markings. Historically, firearms examiners have test fired bullets into boxes filled with cotton or oil-soaked sawdust, fifty-five-gallon drums, even a ten-foot-long row of telephone books. While those materials might stop a bullet, they are not particularly efficient; it can take a long time to find a small bullet in a big box of cotton.

Guns arrive in the lab in every conceivable condition, and sometimes have to be repaired before they can be test fired. In some cases, this has to be done despite great difficulty. In December 1987, a Pacific Southwest Airlines commuter flight from Los Angeles to San Francisco suddenly dove into a hillside, killing all forty-three people aboard. Initially National Transportation Safety Board officials suspected the plane had been destroyed by a bomb. But one of the cockpit tape recorders picked up several screaming

239

voices and what sounded like gunshots seconds before the plane crashed. And in the debris police found an airsickness bag on which someone had written, "Hi, Ray, I think it's sort of ironical that we end up like this. I asked for some leniency for my family, remember. Well, I got none and you'll get none." Among the people killed in the crash were an airline supervisor named Raymond Thompson and a passenger named David Burke, whom Thompson had fired three weeks earlier for purportedly stealing $69 from cocktail sales. Speculation began that Burke had shot Thompson and the pilots, causing the plane to crash. The bodies of the victims were so badly mutilated that it was impossible to find evidence to support that theory. But FBI agents located one of Burke's former co-workers, who admitted loaning him a .44 Magnum pistol and twelve cartridges a month earlier.

"In the crime scene we found a .44 Magnum broken into two pieces," explained Agent-examiner Robert Murphy, firearms expert with more than two decades' experience in the lab. "The barrel had been broken off the frame and the pieces were found about a hundred yards apart. The frame was beyond repair; it was twisted and distorted. The cylinder had frozen into the frame and we had to pound it open to see if there were fired cartridges in the chambers. There were; all six cartridges had been fired.

"So we had a gun, but we didn't have any bullets. While the gun and the note and the cockpit recording were strong circumstantial evidence that some event had taken place aboard the aircraft just before it crashed, we really couldn't prove anything."

Eventually a member of the search team found a copper bullet jacket in the wreckage and gave it to Murphy. "I looked at it," he recalled, "and sure enough, it was a .44 Magnum bullet jacket. We knew that if we could positively link that jacket to the gun, we could prove bullets had been fired on the plane.

"But the gun was mutilated, there was no way we could fire it. Fortunately, the barrel was intact, and the barrel was the critical part, the part with the markings. I thought that if we could put the barrel on another gun and somehow fire it, I might be able to make an identification and close this thing out.

"Every day we receive guns for disposal, guns that were used as evidence in court cases that weren't returned to the owner, guns that were confiscated from criminals, guns that have been surrendered or just turned up somewhere. A few of these weapons are added to our gun collection, but most of them are taken up to a steel plant and melted down. I looked through the disposal collection and found a Smith & Wesson .44 Magnum revolver. Our armorers at Quantico fit that barrel onto the frame for me. From that point on it was just a routine examination: I test-fired the gun into the water tank, then examined both bullet jackets under the comparison scope. The markings were so good it took me just a few seconds to make a positive identification. There was no longer any question about what had caused that airplane to crash."

Most of the guns submitted to the lab for examination are pretty common weapons, but occasionally unique specimens will turn up. They are usually handmade guns taken from prisoners, and while they may not be very sophisticated, they are as deadly as the best store-bought weapons. They are made of wood and pipe fittings, rubber bands and elastic. Nails become bullets. One particularly ingenious prisoner constructed the barrel of his gun out of paper. For safety reasons, homemade guns are always fired into the tank by remote control.

Silencers are also submitted to the lab. A silencer is any device that, attached to the end of a gun, will muffle the noise when the gun is fired. Even a poorly made silencer can be effective, as every six-decibel reduction will cut the sound of a gunshot by half. So if a silencer reduces a gunshot sounding by twelve decibels, it cuts the sound by 75 percent.

Many years ago a sport called parlor shooting—target shooting in the living room—was a popular pastime. At that time silencers could be legally purchased—presumably so as not to disturb the neighbors—but since then they have become illegal. With the exception of soldiers and police officers, no one can legally possess a silencer. That means silencers can't be bought; they have to be made. And they can be made very easily, out of basic household products ranging from plastic bottles to lawn-mower mufflers. Among the most popular materials are two-liter plastic soda bottles.

Silencers work by containing, then gradually dissipating, the gases released when a gun is fired. One of the most unusual—but still effective—silencers submitted to the lab was made out of a plastic baby bottle filled with rubber nipples. When the gun was fired the plastic expanded; after the bullet exited the plastic contracted, while the nipples caused the gases to slowly dissipate.

A silencer can also be used to link a bullet to a weapon. Anything through which a bullet passes, especially a silencer, will leave its mark, and these traces can be used exactly like barrel markings. Probably the most importance case in which silencer marks provided decisive evidence was the murder of Alan Berg, a very controversial radio talk-show host in Denver, Colorado. Berg had received several death threats from the right-wing groups he regularly attacked on his show; one night, as he got out of his car in front of his home, he was gunned down by an automatic weapon. As many as fifteen shots were fired in a few seconds. A neighbor who heard the firing said it hadn't sounded like gunshots, but rather like a muffled chain being dragged off the back of a pickup truck: an apt description for the sound of a silencer.

Berg's murder went unsolved for several months. Then an informant told police that members of the Silent Brotherhood, a right-wing white supremacist group in Washington State, were responsible for the killing. An investigation eventually narrowed down the numbers of suspects, and search warrants were obtained. Among the weapons found in one house was a .44-caliber automatic with a silencer welded to its barrel. It was sent to the lab, where Bob Murphy examined it. "I think we were a little surprised when we found this weapon," Murphy said. "Why they didn't just get rid of this gun I have no idea. The only thing we could figure out is that they were so enamored with guns that they couldn't bring themselves to get rid of it.

"When I got the gun the silencer was still attached to the muzzle. It was a homemade silencer made out of a grease-gun tube. Truthfully, it was the strangest-looking weapon I've ever seen. It looked just like a submachine gun with a grease gun welded to the front. But it reduced the sound level almost twenty-four decibels, which meant that the gun made only about ten percent of the normal sound. A portion of the silencer made contact with the bullets when they were fired, and it left some very rough, very coarse striations. Anyone with experience would have known immediately that the marks were too rough and too haphazard to have been made by the barrel. No barrel is rifled that roughly. So the marks had to come from an external source, and there was that big thing stuck to the end of the barrel. When I test-fired bullets through the silencer, I was able to duplicate those marks and make a positive identification. There was no question about it, this was the gun that had been used to kill Alan Berg."

Four members of the Silent Brotherhood were eventually convicted of crimes associated with Berg's murder and received sentences of up to one hundred years.

Of course, even after a bullet has been linked to a gun, the gun has to be linked to a suspect. That can be done in many different ways, including fingerprints, but as Bob Sibert pointed out, "Whoever is caught holding the gun is the guy with the problem. It's either help us link it to the person who fired it or be indicted as a co-conspirator. And if he doesn't want to help, he might end up facing the whole rap by himself."

The Firearms and Toolmarks Unit works about eleven hundred cases annually, many of them involving multiple weapons. After a disastrous fifty-one-day confrontation with the Branch Davidian religious cult in Waco, Texas, ended in the deaths of four federal agents and at least seventy-five members of the cult, for example, the unit examined more than three hundred weapons. The majority of these guns are eventually destroyed, but a few of them are added to the Bureau's weapons collection, the most complete and fascinating collection of weapons anywhere in the world. It includes more than five thousand handguns and shoulder arms of just about every conceivable type, from miniature revolvers to sawed-off shotguns and grenade launchers, and almost every one of them has been used in a crime. The collection includes common weapons, like the two-dollar Liberators the Allies air-dropped to guerilla fighters by the tens of thousands during World War II, and unusual weapons, like the seven-shot cylindrical revolver used in the Wild West and a survival weapon in which all the parts fit into a floating stock. It even includes historical curiosities like the guns used by John Dillinger and Ma Barker and a shotgun that Pretty Boy Floyd unsuccessfully tried to convert to an automatic weapon. Examiners use the collection to identify parts of weapons recovered at crime scenes, to familiarize themselves with weapons they will be examining or testifying about, and simply to see how certain weapons work.

While the best piece of evidence in a shooting is always the gun, much useful information about the crime can be learned from the bullet. A common misconception is that the bullet is the thing that's put into the gun and fired. Technically, a bullet consists of a cartridge case that holds everything together, plus a primer that is struck by the weapon's firing pin to cause a tiny bit of explosive powder to burn and drive the projectile— the bullet—through the air. It's the bullet that causes the damage.

The first thing examiners try to determine from a bullet is its class characteristics, which identify the type of weapon that could have fired it. If all bullets arrived in the lab in pristine condition this would be a very simple examination, but they don't. The function of a bullet is to hit something, and when it does so it's going to be damaged. The examiners in the Firearms Unit are among the most expert in the world, but with more than fourteen thousand different types of ammunition available, sometimes even they can't readily identify a bullet from a few shattered fragments. And when John Hinckley attempted to assassinate President Reagan, their inability to quickly identify the type of bullets he fired almost proved fatal.

The bullet that hit President Reagan had ricocheted off the presidential limousine. It was a million-to-one shot. The bullet had gone through the tiny opening between the open rear door and the car body; it was deflected by the frame and struck the President under the arm. "When I got the bullet that night," said Gerald Wilkes, who did the examinations, "it was as flat as a dime. It had been flattened when it hit the car. One side was completely caved in, while the other side was intact. The hole in the President's garment was more of a little slit than a bullet hole. We didn't know it at first, but the fact that the bullet hit the car the way it did may have saved the President's life.

"This bullet had limited marks on the undamaged side. They weren't the greatest, but they were enough to allow me to link it to bullets I test-fired from Hinckley's gun.

"A second bullet had hit Press Secretary James Brady in the head. That one was in a million pieces. All that was left of it was the very bottom portion of the base. My first thought when I looked at it was that I'd rarely seen that type of mutilation. There was no way we could make an identification on that bullet. There just wasn't enough of it left.

"The third bullet had struck Secret Service agent Tim McCarthy. It had been damaged but we were able to identify it. The fourth bullet had hit DC Police Officer Thomas Delehanty. It had lodged so close to his spine that doctors had decided it was too risky to operate, that he could live with it in his body, so we couldn't identify it.

"Two days after the shooting we got a box of ammunition that had been found in Hinckley's hotel room. As soon as I opened the box I got this terrible feeling in the pit of my stomach. These bullets were called 'Devastators.' They carried a tiny explosive charge in an aluminum canister in the nose—and they are designed to explode upon impact. That's why there was so little left of the bullet that hit Jim Brady. It had exploded in his brain. In each case the soft nose had been flattened, and the lead had folded over the canister, preventing me from seeing this.

"Right away I knew we had two serious problems. First, we needed to know what the explosive charge was. That stuff is potentially poisonous. And if some of it had leaked into the President's body, it was possible he was being slowly poisoned. And second, we had a police officer with a bullet in his body that could explode at any moment.

"We immediately informed the doctors at Bethesda Naval Hospital that they had a serious problem to deal with. Then we sent agents to Norcross, Georgia, where these bullets were made, to learn as much as possible about them. We didn't know if they were heat sensitive, shock sensitive, we didn't know anything.

"It didn't take us too long to find out that they were dangerous. One of the examiners in Neutron Analysis, Rod Asbury, was very carefully dissecting a Devastator with a scalpel under his microscope when the bullet exploded. The microscope shielded him from serious injury. He had some cuts and the scope was ruined, but he was very lucky. That told us for certain we were dealing with a very unstable explosive.

"We learned from the manufacturer that the explosive charge was lead azide. It doesn't take much to cause azide to explode. The obvious question was, Why hadn't the bullet that hit the President exploded? No one will ever know for sure, but there were probably two reasons. First, these bullets needed to be traveling more than nine hundred feet per second to develop enough force to detonate, and when the bullet glanced off the limo it had slowed down. Second, the nose had been flattened when it hit the car, sealing the canister inside. We weighed the amount of azide remaining in the bullet removed from the President's body and compared it to the weight of an unfired Devastator. The weights were almost identical—none of the azide had leaked into President Reagan's body.

"But when we told Officer Delahanty's doctors what kind of bullet they had in there, they accused us of inventing the story so we could get the bullet as evidence. The situation really got pretty nasty. Finally, I told the doctor, 'You do what you want to do. It's your call. I'm just telling you what's in the guy's neck.'

"The doctors wanted answers we couldn't give them. 'All I can tell you,' I said, 'is that this stuff is very dangerous. There's a real danger to your hands and eyes. It's possible that if you touch this stuff with a metal tool it'll explode. We just can't rule out anything.'

"The final decision was left to Delahanty, who wanted them to operate. The operation took place in an isolated wing of the hospital, and it was performed by volunteers. Everyone wore special glasses to protect their eyes, and although it was an intricate and complicated procedure, the bullet was removed without incident and the patient was fine."

The fact that bullets can be flattened or smashed on impact often makes it impossible to link them to the shooting weapon, but there are situations in which that damage can actually be beneficial. When a bullet passes through a substance it picks up and carries with it microscopic particles of that substance. Pieces of bone, hair, dirt, drywall, brick and mortar, paint, glass, fibers, even blood are found on bullets and can be very helpful in figuring out the path of a gunshot. In the St. Louis shootout in which Special Agent Doug Abrams was killed, a bullet found in a hallway had a fiber impression that matched Abrams's pants. Another bullet carried paint and drywall, confirming it had bounced off a wall.

When a Pennsylvania police officer was charged with killing an innocent motorist, he faced the almost impossible task of proving the death had been a terrible accident. The officer claimed he had tripped and his gun had gone off, striking the victim, but there were no witnesses, just one scared police officer and a body. Then an examiner found microscopic bits of cement and glass embedded in the nose of the bullet. This evidence supported the officer's story that his gun had accidentally discharged, and that the bullet had ricocheted off the pavement, through the car window, and into the unfortunate victim.

When a bullet's nose is distorted, it may lock materials and fibers inside; by prying it open, investigators can see, in order, every substance that bullet passed through. This kind of evidence can be particularly useful in determining whether victims have been shot in the front or back, which is sometimes very difficult to figure out from their wounds. In another St. Louis case, when Doug Deedrick in Hairs and Fibers opened up the nose of a bullet he found fibers from the victim's jacket and jacket lining—and, to his surprise, orange fibers that didn't match the victim's shirt or T-shirt, and a tiny piece of a feather. Deedrick realized that this meant the victim had been wearing a down vest, a fact that hadn't appeared in any police reports because the vest didn't look damaged. But when police took a more careful look at it, they discovered a small rip on the seam—which changed their reconstruction of the position in which the victim had been standing when he was shot.

When a bullet is too badly damaged to be linked to a weapon, or if the bullet is in good shape but a gun is never recovered, a strong case can still be made by linking the elemental composition of the fired bullet to the composition of unfired cartridges found in a suspect's possession. All arms manufacturers uses their own mixtures when making ("loading") ammunition, and that mixture changes with different batches. Antimony is used to harden metal, and bullets will consist of between one half of 1 percent to 2½ percent antimony, depending on the manufacturer. The fact that a bullet recovered at a crime scene has the same composition as bullets that can be associated with a suspect makes strong circumstantial evidence. The odds that two people randomly purchased the same type of ammunition made by the same company in the same batch are statistically very slight.

Linking crimes committed by the same person in different jurisdictions has long been a basic objective of law enforcement agencies, but except for the sensational cases headlined by the news media, they have never been able to do it on a regular basis. Incredible as it might seem, even if the same weapon was used in murders in jurisdictions as close as Washington, D.C., Virginia, and Maryland, there was absolutely no way for police departments in those areas to associate the killings. To help local departments link crimes committed by the same person, in 1992 the Firearms Unit initiated its Drugfire program. Originally started to connect drug-related shootings, Drugfire was expanded to include all crimes in which a weapon is fired.

The only way to link shootings is to compare the markings on recovered fired ammunition components, and until recently that meant physically examining all the specimens that might have been fired by the same weapon under a comparison microscope. That rarely happens. But a new computer process has made it possible to create a digital image of the marks on the surface of a cartridge case and to characterize them in detail by means of numbers. When a computer matches the digital image of two or more cartridge cases, these images can be transmitted between different sci-crime labs, and if they still appear to be similar then the specimens will be physically examined.

Drugfire enables investigators in different jurisdictions to enter the description of fired ammunition components in a shared database, in which they are stored until matched to items recovered in other crimes. In the program's first, experimental year of operation in the Washington, D.C., and Maryland area, seventy pairs of cases that previously would not have been associated were found to involve the same weapon. This allowed different departments to pool their resources in their investigations.

"I know I'll never forget the first hit we got because it was so strange," remembered Bob Sibert, who was instrumental in setting up the program. "One day we were training some officers from the Metro Washington police department. There were a limited number of cases in the system. So to show them how the thing worked, we put in the description of a cartridge case that had been recovered from a homicide that had taken place in March—and the computer matched it to a cartridge case that had been test-fired from a firearm that had been recovered in January. Well, it looked like we had our first problem with the system. How could a gun that was in police custody in January have been used in a homicide two months later?

"It was a very good comparison. I called over one of our managers and told him that I'd been looking at firearms evidence for twenty years and if that wasn't an identification I'd eat it. So we called the Metro Washington police department and asked them to pull the cartridge cases from evidence and physically compare them. They did, and agreed it was an ident. Then we asked them to get the gun out of the property room. And that's when we found out the gun was missing.

"They discovered that a number of firearms had been stolen from the property room and had found their way back onto the street. Internal Affairs jumped all over this and eventually arrested an individual for stealing guns out of the property room and trading them for drugs."

Drugfire is one of the very few technological breakthroughs in firearms identification since the development of the comparison microscope in 1925. "As the program expands regionally," Sibert said, "local police departments are going to be able to associate shootings, and that's going to save time and money. And cause a lot more dangerous people to be taken off the streets."

While the best evidence in a shooting is still a smoking gun, sometimes the smoke is enough. Residue, smoke, can be used to show that someone has recently fired a weapon and, more significantly, it can also be used to approximate the distance between the victim and his assailant.

When a weapon is fired, two metals present in the primer, barium and antimony, survive the burning process and are often found on a shooter's hand. Often, but not always: the shooter might have been wearing a glove; the residue might have been blown away by the wind or washed away by rain; the weapon might not have left any residue because of the way it was held; the shooter might have rubbed off the residue by putting his hand in his pocket or by washing his hands. Or, for a reason no one can explain, in some instances there isn't any residue. Even in ideal conditions residue rarely remains on a shooter's hands longer than a couple of hours. So lack of residue isn't exculpatory evidence—not finding it doesn't prove that a subject wasn't near a gun when it was fired. But finding it is a strong indication that he was.

This invisible residue becomes particularly valuable when it can be used to refute an individual's claim that he wasn't near a fired weapon. In a South Carolina homicide, a woman denied being in her home when her husband was shot to death. But when primer-residue tests on her hand turned out positive, she collapsed and confessed that she had shot him.

The traditional method used to detect residue after a shooting was to wipe the back and side of a subject's hand with a cotton swab which would then be chemically tested for the presence of barium and antimony. But barium and antimony are also found in fertilizers and paper products and other sources of environmental contamination. In fact, at any time about one percent of the general population would test positive for these metals. So defense attorneys would argue—sometimes successfully—that the presence of these metals had no meaning at all. But several years ago it was discovered that primer residue is actually composed of microscopic particles, little balls, containing these elements, and that they can be seen under an electron microscope. More important, barium and antimony combine this way only in primer residue, so finding them in this form is considered strong evidence that an individual was near a weapon when it was fired. The microscopic particles put the shooter at the scene.

For a long time the presence of primer on a body was considered the best way of determining if an individual had committed suicide or been murdered. No more—not since it has been shown that a shooter may have no primer on his hands, while victims shot at close range may well have a measurable amount on their bodies.

Suppose two people go into the woods and the one who comes out claims that the other person was shot during a fierce struggle and that he had fired in self-defense. Or suppose a dead person is found gripping the gun that killed him. It looks like suicide but no note is found and some valuables are missing. How do you figure out what really happened? Gunshot residue. It's different from primer residue in that it's found on the victim rather than the shooter. And it can be used to approximate the distance between the weapon and the victim; that's often the key piece of evidence in a claim of self-defense or a questioned suicide.

When a bullet passes through any material, an invisible residue, consisting mostly of lead, is deposited around the bullet hole in a very specific pattern. If the area around that hole is treated with chemicals that react to lead, a residue pattern emerges as a purple stain. It makes good evidence because its size varies according to the distance from the weapon to the victim. Imagine that you're throwing a handful of powder against a wall. The closer you are to the wall, the smaller the area the powder will cover; the farther away you are, the larger the pattern. Residue patterns are produced exactly the same way. If the gun is fired within a few feet of something a small, dense pattern will be left on it; beyond a certain distance, about ten feet, there won't be any residue at all. Because the size of the pattern will be the same every time the same weapon is fired with the same ammunition from the same distance, it's possible to figure out how far the shooter was from his victim by reproducing the pattern in test firings.

This is evidence that can destroy a defense. In one early-1980s case, a woman and her boyfriend were camping out in Yosemite National Park. It was just the two of them, the stars above, and a high-powered rifle. The seemingly distraught woman claimed that her boyfriend had been cleaning the rifle when it accidentally went off, striking him in the chest and killing him instantly. One survivor, one story. The rifle, several rounds of ammunition, and the victim's clothing were submitted to the lab. Chemicals were applied to his shirt, and a gunshot residue pattern developed. On a firing range, the rifle was fired at a similar shirt from various distances to try to produce a similar residue pattern. Repeated tests proved that a pattern of the size found on the shirt could have been created only if the weapon was fired from between five and a half and six feet away. No one can clean a rifle from six feet away. That evidence proved the woman was lying, and a jury convicted her of murder.

In many cases a shooter claims that the gun went off during a struggle. This happens, though it happens most often on television. Without witnesses, it's a very difficult claim for a prosecutor to disprove. But a bullet fired at almost point-blank range will leave several clues. For example, a contact shot will actually melt certain types of cloth fibers around the edges of a bullet hole, and that melting can easily be seen under a microscope. A contact shot may also leave powder burns or deposits of unburned gunpowder.

Gunshot residues are far better at proving that a weapon was fired within a few feet of someone or something than they are at proving that a shooter was several feet away. The lack of residues really doesn't prove very much. Residues are pretty easily blown away or washed away, or they just aren't left when a shot is fired from a long range. The residue of a given shot might even have been deposited on some intervening material—a curtain, a piece of glass, a car door. But when police find a compact residue pattern, powder burns, or unburned gunpowder on a victim, that victim was shot at close range, and could have been shot during a struggle or committed suicide.

Many shooters claim that their gun fired accidentally: They were cleaning it, and somehow it went off. They tripped, and it went off. They dropped it, and it went off. As Rick Crum said, "We're asked quite often, 'Could this weapon have been fired accidentally?' The answer is always yes. Any weapon that can be fired can be fired accidentally. But what they really want to know is, 'Was it fired accidentally?' And there is almost no way we can answer that question."

The first thing lab examiners will do when a shooter claims his gun fired accidentally is try to reproduce the action. They will drop it and shock it and bang it and try many different ways to make it go off. Even if the gun doesn't fire, the strongest conclusion the lab will report is that they were not able to make this weapon discharge, but they can't eliminate the possibility that some external force caused it to fire.

A Georgia man accused of shooting a friend in the head claimed that the victim had been twirling the cocked weapon Western style when it went off. The victim had survived, but had no memory of the incident. "We tried it in the lab," Crum remembered, "and we found that it's extremely difficult to make a weapon fire by spinning it by the trigger guard. To keep that gun spinning, your finger can't be on the trigger, it has to be on the trigger guard. The force is being exerted downward, not forward. So we reported that it was difficult to make this weapon discharge in the direction of the person spinning it by the trigger—but once again we couldn't rule out the possibility."

Generally, other evidence has to be used to either support or disprove a claim that a gun fired accidentally. In a Florida retirement community, a seventy-year-old woman was shot to death by a single blast from a shotgun as she sat in her rocking chair. Her distraught husband claimed he had found her body when he returned from a fishing trip, but detectives noted that he appeared to be drunk, and they questioned him carefully. Not buying his alibi, they arrested him and charged him with his wife's murder. The shotgun and a shell casing were submitted to the lab.

Two days later the man changed his story. This time he admitted that he had killed his wife, but he claimed it had been a terrible accident. As he walked into the kitchen, he said, he tripped on the edge of the rug; the shotgun went off, killing his wife, who was sitting on the other side of the room.

One survivor and one story, but the evidence spoke for the victim. The kitchen door and the edge of the rug were approximately thirty-five-feet from the rocking chair. The wound in the woman's left cheek was about an inch and a half in diameter. By test-firing the murder weapon with the same type of ammunition the husband had used, examiners were able to prove that the only distance from which a wound that size could be produced was five feet. The husband's alibi was destroyed and he was convicted of murder.

All the information that can be learned from guns and bullets and residue is put together in the reconstruction of a crime scene. Few of the other units in the lab ever go to a crime scene; even firearms examiners rarely see a body, but they do often visit shooting scenes to try to reconstruct the crime. "What we try to do," explained Rick Crum, an expert in such reconstructions, "is determine what happened, how it happened, the sequence of events, and the location of the shooters in relationship to each other. And we do this by applying just about every firearms technique we use."

In 1988, a polygamist clan known as the Singer-Swapp family bombed a Mormon church in Marion, Utah, then barricaded themselves into a house on the family farm. The standoff lasted thirteen days, and when the shooting started, Utah Department of Corrections officer Fred House, a dog handler, was killed, an FBI agent was shot in his bulletproof vest, and Adam Swapp was wounded. After this shootout the family surrendered.

Crum was assigned to go to the site to try to reconstruct the shooting. "We began by walking over the whole scene. The shooters had been in the main house. A second house, seventy-five yards away, which we called the greenhouse, was where Officer House had been killed. The neighbors, the

Jepsens, lived in the third house, which was a hundred and fifty yards from the main house. Timothy Singer admitted being the shooter, but he claimed that he had been firing at Fred House's dog, which was about twenty feet in front of the officer, and that the killing was accidental. The question I had to try to answer was whether Timothy Singer was aiming at Fred House or the dog.

"The people on the scene gave me a good idea of what they thought happened. Eyewitnesses aren't completely reliable, because people don't necessarily try to remember things when the shooting starts; they try to keep themselves from getting shot. A total of ten shots had been fired from the main house. Four shots had gone through the door where Fred House was standing, each of them between waist to neck high and lodged in a wall. A fifth shot had struck him in the side and killed him. Two more shots passed through the open doorway, traveled through the house and out through a rear window, and hit the Jepsens' garage.

"Initially we believed that Timothy Singer had done all the shooting. But when I positioned myself in the window from which he reportedly had fired the shots that hit the Jepsens' garage, I couldn't see the bullet holes. I thought that was pretty strange." Crum requested a survey team be brought to the site to determine if the shots could have been fired from that window. The team reported they could sight an area about six inches to the left of the holes, but the holes themselves were blocked by a corner of the greenhouse. This was the first indication that there might have been a second shooter. Crum knew he had to find out where those shots had been fired from.

"Two bullets had gone right through the Jepsens' garage wall, across a three-foot storage space, and into a second wall," he explained. "I took some steel rods and stuck them through the holes, right across the storage area. I could have used a laser beam, but it would have been difficult because these holes were so small. I could tell the bullets had traveled straight through the walls, because the rods were not bent. Using a protractor I could very accurately measure the angle of penetration of each shot. Then I asked the surveyor to project these angles backwards in the direction of the shooter. Very surprisingly, these holes projected backwards through a broken window in the greenhouse, through the doorway in which Fred House had been standing, to a position at the corner of the main house. This told us that Timothy Singer could not possibly have fired these shots.

"It had snowed heavily since the shootout, and more than two feet of snow was on the ground, but using metal detectors we recovered several cartridge cases from that position. There had been a second shooter. Lab tests confirmed that the shot that had killed Officer House had been fired from Timothy Singer's .30 carbine, but that three bullets had been fired from a second .30 carbine. Eventually the people in the house admitted that Jonathan Singer was the second shooter.

"One of the determinations we had to make before the trial was whether or not these rifles hit where they were sighted. Could the shooters have been firing at a target twenty feet in front of Officer House and accidentally hit him? When I test-fired these rifles I found nothing that would have caused a shooter to miss by that wide a margin. I fired these weapons with the sights in every possible position, and they always shot just about where you aimed them.

"None of this told us whether Timothy Singer had been shooting at Officer House or the dog—I couldn't put myself in his mind—but during the trial the jury had to wonder, could it possibly have been a coincidence that two shooters using two accurate firearms had fired at the same time, and that their aim had been so bad that seven of the ten shots had passed through the doorway in which Officer House had been standing at waist to shoulder height?" The jurors convicted four of the people in that house of homicide and other charges.

The most significant firearms determination, that a recovered bullet was fired from a specific weapon, is made possible by the fact that each time a hard object strikes a softer object it leaves a characteristic impression. Tools act precisely the same way: they mark objects, making it possible to prove that a specific tool was used to perform a certain task. Firearms examiners conduct toolmark examinations pretty much the same way they link weapons and ammunition.

Toolmarks may seem mundane, but toolmark evidence can be found in just about every type of crime. Bombs are made with tools; safes are broken open with tools; people who poison consumer products open packages with tools. Toolmarks rarely provide enough evidence to make a case without additional proof, but they can make a significant contribution toward a conviction.

Like every firearm, every tool is unique. Every hammer, every screwdriver, every tool has some sort of defect in its striking surface, cutting surface, or bit; these defects are produced when the tool is made or result from wear. Some of these marks are transient, but others are permanent and will appear every time the tool is used. These marks don't affect the quality of a tool—most of them are not even visible to the naked eye—but they can be identified under a microscope. And they can be used to connect an individual to a crime.

When a tool is found that may have left identifiable marks on evidence, an examiner will use it on a piece of metal or wood, then compare the marks it makes to the marks left on the evidence. Just as in firearms, the proof is in the re-creation. For example, in 1982 a California highway patrolman named George Gwaltney reported finding the body of a woman, later identified as Robin Bishop, who had been shot and killed by the side of the highway. There was no sign of a robbery, just a body with a bullet hole in it. Inside the woman's body medical examiners found semen they could characterize as having come from a man who had once had a vasectomy but later had a second operation to have it reversed.

Eventually, key evidence was submitted to Jim Cadigan, who had joined the Firearms and Toolmarks Unit in 1976 and had worked briefly in the lab with his father, who spent thirty-seven years there as a documents examiner. "What made this case difficult was the fact that there didn't seem to be any motive," Cadigan said. "But a police officer remembered seeing a highway patrol car in the area at just about the time of the murder. As a precaution, homicide detectives decided to examine the service revolvers of all the highway patrolmen on duty at that time. Everybody turned in their weapon except George Gwaltney, who claimed he'd left it at home. The detectives followed Gwaltney to his house, but he beat them there and by the time they arrived the gun was gone. Gwaltney told them it'd been stolen. So these detectives, not being dumb, got a search warrant, and in a locked box in his truck they found the frame of his service revolver.

"Somebody had tried to destroy the gun," Cadigan continued. "The cylinder and barrel had been ripped out of the frame, and without the barrel, it was almost impossible to prove the fatal bullet had been fired from this weapon. A local crime-lab examiner identified some toolmarks on the frame, especially a deep cut that looked like it might have been made by a screwdriver blade, but he was unable to associate any tools found in Gwaltney's house with the marks. Gwaltney was twice tried for murder in his hometown, and both trials ended with a hung jury. Federal prosecutors took over and charged him with violation of the victim's civil rights, and we finally got involved in the case."

The evidence against Gwaltney was all circumstantial. For example, he had had a vasectomy, which had subsequently been reversed. But lab investigators knew that if they could prove he'd destroyed his own service weapon, he'd have a real problem explaining the fact. Innocent people don't do things like that. The case against Gwaltney was built in the lab. Robin Bishop had been found lying face down; Gwaltney claimed he hadn't touched her body. But Alan Robillard in the Hairs and Fiber Unit was able to match a few tiny strands of fur found on her stomach with the fur collar of Gwaltney's uniform jacket, proving he was lying about that. Rick Crum was able to associate Gwaltney with the bullets found in the victim's body by matching machine marks, made on the base of the bullet itself during manufacturing, to other bullets in his possession. Cadigan did the toolmark exam. "The marks on the frame hadn't been made by a screwdriver at all," he said. "They weren't pressure-type marks; they were gripping marks, the kind that might have been made by a tool holding the gun tightly while the barrel was unscrewed. I decided it was a vise or a pipe wrench.

"Among Gwaltney's tools we found a pipe wrench with a broken tooth. I tested it on a piece of metal and it left a very similar mark. Using that mark for orientation, I was able to positively identify other marks found on the gun frame with marks made by other teeth in the pipewrench. I could show exactly how the wrench had held the frame, and the broken tooth gave us the unique mark we needed to prove it had been held by this particular tool. The jury had to wonder why he'd taken the gun apart and then lied about it. With the additional evidence we were able to develop in here, the prosecutors finally got a conviction on the third attempt. Gwaltney was sentenced to ninety-nine years in prison."

Toolmarks can be large scrapes in the ground made by a shovel, or tiny nicks on a bottle cap. Toolmarks can be impressed into any kind of material; wood and steel and even human skin and bone. Pliers, for example, have been identified from marks left on nipples. A knife was identified from marks left on an esophagus. After Milwaukee police arrested the serial murderer Jeffrey Dahmer, they submitted parts of several human skulls, in which holes had been drilled, along with a set of drill bits found in Dahmer's home, to see if examiners could make a comparison. Not all tools leave marks; saw marks are almost impossible to identify because the edges are continually cutting and ripping, which destroys individual marks. Occasionally drill bits can be matched to holes if those holes do not completely penetrate a material. In the Dahmer case the holes went through the bone, and the best the lab could do was report that the holes drilled in the skulls were consistent in diameter with the recovered bits. That type of class evidence has very little value, because Dahmer's were standard-sized bits that might have been found in any tool collection.

Toolmarks examiners are also qualified to make fracture matches, to testify that at one time two pieces were part of the same object. For example, several Virginia bank robberies in which thieves used crowbars, screwdrivers, and hammers to pull out night-deposit drawers were positively connected through toolmarks found in the debris. But from the type of crime and the method they used, that was pretty obvious anyway. And it didn't help identify the gang. After one of the robberies, however, detectives found the broken tip of a screwdriver at the scene. It didn't seem like much, just a tiny piece of broken metal. But eventually several suspects were identified and a search warrant was obtained. In the suspect's possession police found several broken screwdrivers, and toolmark examiners were able to positively link the broken tip to one of the broken blades. That tip connected the thieves to that specific robbery, and other toolmark evidence connected that robbery to several others. Primarily on the basis of toolmark evidence, the entire gang was convicted of bank robbery.

Throughout history people have set out to make their marks in the world, but when weapons or tools are concerned, marks have often led to their undoing.

In the Singer-Swapp family case, Rick Crum proved there had been an unseen second shooter. But in the most controversial crime in American history, the assassination of President John Kennedy and the wounding of Texas governor John B. Connally, Jr., the conclusion reached by the lab's Firearms Unit that there was one assassin has been challenged and debated for more than three decades. This was probably the most extensive firearms investigation in history. The official determination of the commission chaired by Supreme Court chief justice Earl Warren was that a single gunman, Lee Harvey Oswald, firing a C2766 Mannlicher-Carcano rifle from a window in the Texas School Book Depository, had killed the President. Al-

257

most immediately, though, that conclusion was challenged. The possible existence of an unseen second shooter became the basis for countless conspiracy theories. Since that time much of the evidence has been questioned, dozens of books have been written, additional hearings have been held, and a majority of Americans continue to believe that there existed a conspiracy to assassinate the President.

Bob Frazier, then chief of the Firearms Unit, and examiners Cort Cunningham and Charles Killion conducted the original investigation. And while the crime was sensational and the result heartbreaking, the procedures the men followed were relatively routine. "We worked exactly the same way we did in every other case," Frazier remembered, "except it was decided that in this case there would be three examiners—myself, Cort Cunningham, and Charles Killion—and each of us would do his own work. All three of us came out with the same results, and those were the results that were furnished to the Warren Commission."

The actual investigation was divided into two phases: the initial firearms comparison and the crime-scene reconstruction. "We heard about it at noon," remembered Frazier, who in a career that began in 1943 has conducted more than twenty thousand firearms investigations. "That evening we got the rifle from Dallas. I think we received two cartridges at that time, and we got a third one later. We also got a loaded round that came out of Oswald's rifle. Between the time of the assassination and the time we got the rifle, we were looking for the same type of ammunition [Oswald had used]. It was Western 6.5 millimeter and we got three different lots of it. I don't know if this came out or not, but I think the CIA furnished Italy with three or four million rounds of this ammo. Italy didn't use it, so it was sold back to the U.S. on the open market. Believe me, holding that rifle was emotionally upsetting, 'cause we knew it was the rifle that had been used. I know it affected me and it still does, it still does."

Practically the first thing Frazier and Cunningham had to do was recover as much of the fired ammunition as possible from the President's limousine. "We didn't really recover a lot of the lead," Frazier said. "One bullet went through his head, caught him behind the ear. It blew out a large piece of skull that was found in the gutter. And two big pieces of that bullet came out the top of his head; one fragment hit the chrome above the front window on the windshield, and the other one hit the windshield. It definitely hit it because we found lead on the glass."

"They appeared to be two pieces of one bullet," added Cunningham, who also did the firearms investigation of the revolver Oswald had used to kill Dallas police officer J. D. Tippit.

"What happened," Frazier continued, "I think probably in the confusion when they got to the hospital, everybody jumped out of the car and if there were lead fragments on their clothes or in their pockets or anywhere else, they fell on the ground and were just trampled on and that was the end of it. But we found core fragments that accounted for practically all of the bullet that hit the President in the head. The other bullet that was found [lying on a stretcher in Dallas] was the one that went through the President and through Connally . . . That was the one they called the pristine bullet, but it wasn't pristine at all. The commission came up with that term, 'pristine,' meaning it was undamaged. What they meant was that the nose hadn't been mutilated like the one that hit the bone and broke into pieces. But this one was flattened; if you'd taken a hammer and hit that bullet on the side, you could have flattened it just like it was flattened."

As soon as the lab received the evidence, the rifle was test-fired and the unique markings on the test-fired bullets and cartridge cases were compared to those on the bullets and cartridges recovered from the shooting. "We had a long cotton-filled box that we fired into at that time," Frazier said. "One very interesting thing about the microscopic marks is that in one of the groove impressions there was a defect to the extent that it produced a little deeper groove in the bullet. The muzzle might've had a little tick in it or something. That particular groove was later used by an outside examiner to say that in all probability Oswald had also shot at General Edwin Walker in April that year. A bullet recovered from that shooting had that one groove on it. He found other marks that he said probably came out of this gun. We did not. We felt there weren't enough marks on it to reach any conclusion at all in the Walker shooting. Bureau policy has always been if it's not positively identified it's no conclusion."

On the basis of microscopic rifling marks, the examiners were able to conclude that the whole bullet, the bullet fragments, and the cartridge cases had come from the rifle, found in the book depository, on which Dallas police had identified Lee Harvey Oswald's fingerprints. The firearms examination proved that this rifle and no other was the one from which the fatal shots had been fired. "And when it comes to the firearms part," Frazier pointed out, "there have never been any changes."

The investigation's conclusions, rather than being the end of the case, were the beginning. Almost every other aspect of the assassination scenario has been challenged. Among the many claims made by skeptics are that a second shooter fired from behind a grassy knoll, that more than three shots were fired, that Oswald could not possibly have fired his rifle three times within the necessary time frame and certainly not with enough accuracy to hit a moving target, that one bullet could not possibly have wounded both Kennedy and Connally and ended up in Connall 's knee, and, finally, that Kennedy's movements when shot prove that the fatal shot had come from in front of him, rather than behind.

In this crime-scene reconstruction, the FBI examiners had the advantage of a home movie of the shooting, taken by a spectator named Abraham Zapruder. Cunningham said that the crime-scene reconstruction began with that film. "We kept going over and over and over the film. Once we started looking at it, we watched it a hundred and fifty times if we watched it once."

"I remember the first time we looked at it," Frazier said. "There were about six or eight of us watching. That first time was pretty rugged because the President's head just explodes. The room was absolutely silent. Then we discovered that there was information on the Zapruder film we saw that didn't appear on the screen when the film was projected. The frame is eight millimeters, and another two millimeters is film that's exposed in the drive wheel— and you can actually see the rest of the picture. You'd be surprised how much information is out in the perforated edge. We had eight-by-tens printed of every frame. In prints you can see a woman standing on the steps of the School Book Depository who doesn't show when it's projected. Or it will show somebody over on the other side taking a picture at a certain point. The way the reconstruction was handled, we got together all the pictures that had been taken that could be located, and using the Zapruder film for timing, we triangulated the car in a particular place at a specific moment. We were trying to pick out when the bullets were fired, where the car was hit, the direction the bullets came from, everything."

Frazier and Cunningham did not investigate the possibility of a conspiracy. They simply examined the evidence they had, and from that reached their conclusions. As for the second assassin supposedly shooting from the grassy knoll in front of the President, Frazier explained, "All this talk about someone seeing a puff of smoke, what they forget is that the charge used in bullets is smokeless powder and the word 'smokeless' means smokeless; it doesn't produce a puff of smoke. It produces a little dark residue possibly, but not like you would take a puff on a cigarette and blow it out."

Key evidence for those people who believe that someone fired at Kennedy from the grassy knoll is the fact that on the film the President's head seemed to jerk backward when he was shot, rather than being driven forward as would seem logical if he was shot from behind. "There's no doubt where the bullet struck the President in the back of the head," Cunningham said. "That frame can be pinpointed."

"And the fact that his head moved backwards can be explained by the jet effect of all the liquid leaving his skull," Frazier continued. "It was like a jet effect created by the material leaving. . . . People say, Well, the motorcycle people behind were all covered with blood and brain tissue. Of course they were. They were moving forward at fifteen miles per hour; this material went up in the air and they drove underneath it. You can look at the President's car and find blood and brain sprayed all over the front windshield and even on the hood of the car."

When President Reagan was shot, a videotape with audio made it possible to prove how many shots had been fired. Zapruder's film did not have sound, and the number of shots witnesses heard was disputed. "They had people who practically heard a machine gun going off," Frazier said. "But there were three people in the Book Depository building on the floor right under Oswald and they said definitely they heard three shots, and they definitely heard cartridge cases hit the floor. And when the shots went off, the floor shook and little particles of sawdust and cement fell down, so they knew where the shots came from.

"Some people [standing outside] underneath the shots said they heard three or four or five shots, but what they were hearing was the crack of the bullet going overhead because it was traveling faster than the speed of sound. They heard the sound of the bullet going overhead and then a half second later, boom, they heard that same shot going off back there in the building. If you hear that second shot, it means you haven't been hit by the bullet. Later, investigators returned to Dealey Plaza and fired a weapon and people heard echoes off the grassy knoll, off the stone work, the railroad embankment. They were hearing reverberations. Eyewitness testimony is not the most accurate there is, and earwitness testimony is even worse."

According to the Zapruder film, the three shots had to have been fired in a minimum time span of 4.8 seconds if the second shot missed, or between 7.1 and 7.9 seconds if either the first or third shot missed. Many people believe that Oswald's rifle simply could not be fired three times within that time span. Frazier and Cunningham disagreed. Frazier, Cunningham, and Charles Killion test-fired the rifle for speed and accuracy within days of the assassination. The examiners proved it was easy to fire three aimed shots from Oswald's rifle within any of those time frames. "We fired that gun several times," said Frazier. "Cort fired it, Killion fired it, and I fired it. The minimum amount of time it took me to fire three shots was four point six seconds; the maximum time was six point five seconds. And I wasn't familiar with that gun. The problem with most people is that they forget the clock starts running when you fire the first shot. The cartridge is already in the rifle, you don't have to load it. You're really only loading two shots while you're firing the three. Those two shots had to be fired in a minimum of four point eight seconds, which is twice as long as it takes to shoot carefully aimed shots."

As for accuracy: "This is something that just about every expert has ignored," Frazier said. "The scope of the rifle had been taken off by Dallas police to search for latents, and when we got it, it was loose; we had to tighten the screws down. I think there were shims under the scope when it was used and the Dallas police lost them when they took it off.

"Cort and Killion and I went down to the range and fired at fifteen-yard targets and twenty-five-yard targets and later at hundred-yard targets. At twenty-five yards you could cover our shots with a quarter; at a hundred yards we were within two inches, and the longest it took was six point five seconds. When we tightened the scope we found that it was arranged so that it was shooting a little bit high and to the right. The car was moving, so if you aimed right at the President, then the car would actually move right into the line of fire. If you aimed right at him with the first shot you'd hit low, but with the car moving, the second shot would have hit him the way it did."

Finally, the so-called magic bullet, the "pristine" bullet. This bullet supposedly passed through the President, passed through Governor Connally, hit him in the wrist, and then penetrated into his leg. More than any single piece of evidence, it is the damage attributed to this one bullet that raises doubts about a single shooter. "There's no such thing as that magic bullet," Cunningham said flatly. "Bullets are not predictable. I remember I testified in a case in Baltimore where a man sitting in a bar got into an altercation with someone else, who took out a .22 and shot him right between the eyes. A police officer arrested the shooter and called the ambulance to remove the body. Halfway to the morgue the victim sat up and started complaining that he had a hell of a headache. This bullet struck his skull, went under his scalp and over the top of his head, and ended up in the back. The doctors took it out, patched him up, and he went back to the bar where the same astonished officer saw him later in the day.

"But you have to understand that in the Kennedy assassination we're talking about military-type bullets which have a solid nose, a jacketed nose, and they're crimped around the base of the bullet. That makes it much stronger, and you get much more penetration with it."

"When the Zapruder film showed the President had been shot," Frazier said, "he was sitting straight up in the car. He'd been waving and he'd just lowered his hand when he got shot in the back. The reason the bullet was squashed was because it went through the President's body and came out through the buttonhole area of his shirt. It just nicked his tie. It didn't hit anything hard next to the backbone, but the pressure would've damaged the central nervous system. That caused the President to jerk up his hands in front of him. In the films you could see he was frozen in that position.

"Connally had been facing forward. When the bullet came out of Kennedy, it was traveling sideways, because the wound in Connally's back was an elongated hole. So the bullet was tumbling when it hit him and it went through him still tumbling, knocked a piece of rib out and came out of his chest. Then it went through his wrist backwards. It had to be backwards because the bullet didn't mutilate and there was lead found in Connally's wrist. And then it buried itself in his leg, still traveling backwards, because when they X-rayed him they found a couple of pieces of lead there. None of this was unusual. It got squashed flat and slowed down. That's why it didn't completely shatter his wrist bone. At the instant of the shot, Connally was facing just exactly right for the bullet to follow a straight line through the President, through Connally's body, to hit his wrist and go into his left leg.

"When we hear this called the magic bullet, we kind of laugh."

Neither Frazier nor Cunningham has ever doubted the conclusions they reached in the days after the assassination. "At first I got angry when I heard these stories," Cunningham said, "but now I just shrug. They start out with a false premise or a 'Let us suppose,' and three pages later, it's no longer 'Let us suppose,' it's a fact. I mean, it would send a logic professor to his grave. It's the most ridiculous thing."

"Same with me," Frazier agreed. "You know they don't have their facts straight, but I'm not going to straighten them out. I almost wrote Walter Cronkite once because he twice made a serious mistake about the amount of time it took to fire three shots—they developed a big TV program on that basis—but if they want to do that they will, regardless of what I say."

"I don't mean to be insulting to people," Cunningham added, "but these people are not taking the facts into account, because if their story isn't sensational, it doesn't sell books."

Neither man has seen *JFK*, director Oliver Stone's movie based on numerous conspiracy theories. And the investigators have read very few of the dozens of books on the subject. "I had to read the first few," Frazier admits, "because Mr. Hoover said, 'Read these books and tell me whether they're right or wrong. Go through it and write in the margins." So I wrote a memo saying, 'He's wrong here, he's wrong here, he's wrong here,' and then I forgot about it. That's the way we handled the controversy."

And finally, when asked the seemingly obvious question—"Was this the greatest case of your career?"—Frazier smiled and said, "When you're dealing with firearms cases, you get a case of a lifetime every week."

CHAPTER
- 9 -

Frame-ups and Downright Lies:
The Special Photography Unit, the Video Enhancement Unit, and the Polygraph Unit

"I am immensely indebted to you. Pray tell me in what way I can reward you. This ring—" He slipped an emerald snake ring from his finger. . . .

"Your Majesty has something which I should value even more highly," said Holmes.

"You have but to name it."

"This photograph!"

SHERLOCK HOLMES,
in Sir Arthur Conan Doyle's "A Scandal in Bohemia"

We are a world of picture takers. In the United States more than two billion still photographs are taken annually—pictures of weddings and parties and parades, beautiful pictures of the Grand Canyon and historic monuments, pictures of family and friends and lovers, and pictures of accidents and tragedies and rapes and assaults and bank robberies, pictures of mutilations and decapitations and simple murder. We record what we do, the good and the bad. We make a permanent record, on film and on videotape, of the most beautiful and horrific moments of our lives. The FBI's Special Photography Unit works mostly with the horror.

While photography and, by extension, video are generally believed to be modern crime-fighting tools, in fact photography is one of the oldest. Within years of the invention of photography in France in the 1820s, da-

265

guerrotypes, photographs printed on silver plates, had replaced branding as the preferred means of identifying felons. The problem was that the pictures could not readily be reproduced, and criminals would change their expressions while being photographed, making it difficult to positively identify them. In 1885 Alphonse Bertillon, the creator of the Bertillon Method of identification by body measurement, insisted that all French prisoners be photographed from the front and in profile, under good lighting and from the same distance. Bertillon thereby invented the mug shot.

A photograph was first used as evidence in an American trial in 1859, when it was used to prove that a property title was fraudulent. The first traffic-accident photo was entered as evidence in 1875, when a plaintiff tried to prove that he had been forced to drive his horse and buggy off an embankment to avoid a deep mud hole. When technology finally made it possible to reproduce photographs in large quantities, almost every major American police department established its own "rogues' gallery," as photofiles of wanted criminals were known. Today, the very first thing that happens at a crime scene, before anything is touched, before the body is examined, before prints are developed, is that it is photographed. A permanent record is made to be used in the investigation and perhaps as evidence.

In 1935 the FBI set up its Photographic Operations Unit, which was eventually split into the Photo Processing Unit, which mass-produces almost four million documents annually, and the Special Photography Unit—the picture detectives.

Special Photo, which officially is part of the Document Section, has management, service, and investigative responsibilities. The unit purchases and maintains the four thousand Nikon camera bodies and eleven thousand interchangeable lenses used in field offices, photographs all the evidence submitted to the lab and conducts all of the esoteric photo work—including surveillances, aerial photography, and the placement and supervision of concealed cameras. But its day-to-day investigative function consists of trying to squeeze every last bit of information out of a photograph. The photographs submitted to the lab for examination are often overexposed or underexposed; they're out of focus; the subject is partially out of the frame or is too far away to be identified or is even obscured by reflections. Special Photo's task is to overcome these problems so the people or objects in the picture can be identified.

There's often a wealth of information to be found in photographs that is too small to be seen with the naked eye. What time is showing on the victim's watch? Can that bracelet be identified as part of the stolen property? What's the license-plate number of that truck? Is that a man crouching behind the bushes on the grassy knoll?

In sci-crime photography, bigger is much better, so photographs are either enlarged or are examined under magnification. But there is a limit. A photograph is actually a mosaic. It consists of thousands of minuscule grains of light-sensitive minerals. When these minerals are exposed to light, they get darker; the more light they're exposed to, the darker they get. A negative simply regulates the amount of light hitting the grains. Different films consist of different amounts of grain; the more grains there are, the better the quality of the print. But when you enlarge a photograph, you will eventually see each of these grains, as well as the white spaces between them. Enlarging or magnifying a photo doesn't produce additional information, it just makes it easier to identify what's already there.

A lot of crucial evidence is developed just by making a portion of a photograph larger. In a 1984 case, for example, a suspect indicted for producing and distributing child pornography freely admitted he had made the films, but claimed to have made them more than seven years earlier. If this was true, he was protected from prosecution because the statute of limitations would have expired. The films were sent to the lab to see if that claim could be challenged. In the lab a persistent technician went through the films frame by frame until he found a sequence in which several books were visible in the background. He enlarged those frames and looked at them under a high-magnification lens, then enlarged them again. And again. And finally he was able to identify a 1979 J. C. Penney catalogue. In 1984, the year of the indictment, that catalogue was only five years old. The statute of limitations on those frames hadn't expired, and on the basis of that evidence the suspect was successfully prosecuted.

In a Fort Lauderdale, Florida, murder case, a coroner apparently misidentified the bullet he removed from the victim, stating that its caliber differed from that of the bullet entered as evidence against the known shooter. The defendant's attorney moved for a dismissal, claiming that someone had tampered with evidence to frame his client. All that stood between a murderer and freedom was a photograph taken during the autopsy, in which the fatal bullet could be seen lying on a tray. "A bullet is a bullet," explained Gerry Richards, who served as unit chief from 1985 until his retirement in 1993, "and generally you can't see the striations because there isn't enough resolution in the photo. But we started blowing up the frame, we magnified it as far as it would go before it started falling apart, and I noticed what appeared to be random spots on the bullet. Some kind of stains. We couldn't do a firearms comparison, there wasn't that much detail, but we could see that the relationship between the stains and lines and grooves on the bullet were exactly the same as we saw on the bullet in custody. That enabled us to show that the coroner had made a simple mistake. It was the right bullet all the time."

Perhaps the most extensively examined blowups in history are those made from the Zapruder film of President Kennedy's assassination. One particularly controversial frame has been interpreted by some people as showing a man mysteriously crouching behind bushes on the grassy knoll overlooking the scene. Other viewers see nothing more than innocent shadows. The lab has looked at the Zapruder film several times since 1963 as photo enhancement technology improved, but as Richards said, "Often making it bigger isn't the answer. What's behind that bush is a lot of skepticism. In many cases this kind of work is like cloud writing. You look up at a cloud and if you wait long enough you can see anything you want to see. You look through those leaf patterns on the Zapruder film and people are convinced that things are there, and in their mind they are. But they're not."

Because people tend to believe things they see with their own eyes, photos are often doctored, or changed. Enlarging and magnifying are among the tools used by photo examiners to help determine if a picture or a document is genuine. The examiner will look for the unusually sharp edges produced by cutting; differences in contrast or brightness; differences in proportion or scale between people or objects; differences in the direction of shadows; background information; even changes in the dot patterns. In perhaps its most controversial case, the lab was asked to determine whether a photograph printed in a Russian magazine in the late 1980s was genuine. It seemed to show two American airmen who years earlier had been listed as missing in action in Vietnam. If the picture was real, it would prove that Americans were still alive and being held captive more than two decades after the war had ended. A private sci-crime lab concluded that the photograph was real. "That was a tough one," Richards admitted. "A lot of people wanted it to be true, but there was no way that could be determined from that photograph. It was a really bad photograph to begin with; it had obviously been copied many times and then it was badly printed in the magazine. We looked at the shadow detail, we looked at the edge detail—they were very sharp where they should have been soft. We looked at clothing patterns. But there was no way we could give a definitive answer. The best we could say was that in all probability the photograph had been altered, but it was so poor we really couldn't say much of anything." Several years later researchers found the original photograph from which the doctored version had been produced, finally proving that the questioned photograph was fraudulent.

Digital photography, in which images are generated by a series of numbers that can be changed by computer, has made it possible to doctor photographs without leaving any traces. Want to sail a boat in the desert? The computer can make it look real. But this same technique, digital image processing, has also made it possible for the lab to rectify problems with contrast, brightness, even focus. "It doesn't work all the time," said Dick Swing, a mathematician with an expertise in optics who was fifty-five years old when he joined the lab in 1983 and has since become the oldest person working there. "It doesn't even work most of the time, but when it does, there's usually no other way to solve the problem. It's us or nothing."

Special Photo began adapting digital image processing to sci-crime work in 1979. The technique is based on technology created by NASA and the Jet Propulsion Laboratory for the space program, and it's actually a simplified version of the process used to clear up the blurred photos taken by the Hubble Space Telescope. The computer divides a photograph into more than 300,000 tiny squares called pixels, meaning picture elements: 480 in a row, 640 in a column. Every one of the squares is considered to be a shade of gray measured on a scale ranging from 0, which is pure black, to 250, pure white. If there isn't enough contrast, the pixels will be bunched within a relatively narrow range. So 166 on the scale will be slightly lighter than 163, but much too close for the human eye to detect any difference. By manipulating the gray scale with the computer, one can make desired portions of a photograph lighter or darker, thus creating contrast between different areas and making selected images stand out from the background. The result isn't going to be a very pretty picture, but suddenly small details like the license plate number of a truck in the distance become visible.

In a Cayce, South Carolina, murder case, the killer stole his victim's ATM card and code number and began making withdrawals. ATMs routinely photograph each person making a transaction. The photo of the killer was taken in poor light by an old camera on sixteen-millimeter film; it was so dark that local police weren't even sure there was an image on the film, but they submitted it to the lab anyway. As Swing remembered proudly, "We tried all the photographic techniques and we could see that there was something there, we just couldn't see what it was. The picture was badly exposed and badly processed, but the focus was good. We could see there was a man's face there, but we couldn't make an identification from it. And we could see that the picture had all kinds of garbage on it, things like scratches and dings and marks. We used a computer program we have called an eraser in which the computer averages the gray marks of the pixels around the marks and uses that number to correct the damage. After we cleaned it up, we stretched the contrast as much as we could and we began to see a face. Eventually we got an identifiable image; we could see the person who used the victim's card.

"Cayce police had developed a suspect. Apparently when he saw this picture, he rolled right over. He claimed that his brother had actually committed the murder, but admitted that he and his wife had been accessories. Our ability to turn that mud into a usable photograph made all the difference."

Digital image processing is also used to take out a blur or correct the focus. The problem with most criminals is that they refuse to stand still long enough to allow sharp pictures to be taken by a surveillance camera. So their images are blurred. What the computer does, in essence, is push everything back into focus. It squeezes the image together. But to do this, it needs to find a single point of light.

After John Hinckley shot President Reagan, the lab received a series of badly blurred photographs purportedly showing Hinckley shooting at the President over the top of a limousine. But the pictures were so blurry it was impossible to even be sure the shooter was a man. The point of light was a reflection on the limousine's bumper. And while in actuality it was a point, on the blurred film it appeared to be a line. The computer "knew" that the amount of blur in the picture was equal to the length of that line, so when the line was compressed back into a point, the rest of the images also should become sharp. And that was precisely what happened. Even with this process Hinckley couldn't be positively identified—faces are very difficult to identify—but it was clear that the shooter was a man, and many of his features could be distinguished. In other cases digital imaging has allowed investigators to read license-plate numbers, logos on bank robbers' caps and shirts, and parts of documents.

• • •

In the sci-crime world a photograph isn't art, it's evidence, and it's only as valuable as what it can be used to prove. The strongest possible connection between an individual and a crime is a picture of that person committing the crime. But even when a criminal act is captured on film, from a distance the criminal will look enough like many other people to create a reasonable doubt. Making facial identification even more difficult is the fact that most photographs taken by surveillance equipment are terrible. While it isn't unusual for a camera to take as many as a thousand photographs, or a long roll of video, during a robbery, rarely are more than a few frames usable. The lighting is bad; the robber is wearing a disguise or never looks at the camera; the image is too small; the lens is scratched; or the roll of videotape has been reused so often that the metal oxide on which the image is produced has worn off. The lab actually got a request to examine and return a video of a bank robbery in progress as quickly as possible, because the bank didn't want to have to buy another roll of tape.

The few physical identifications that can be made from photographs are made on the basis of unique characteristics. Everybody's got a head; that's a class characteristic. But a tattoo is different; it's a unique characteristic. Examiners look for permanent, unique characteristics that can be used to pick out one person from everyone else in the world, and the more of them someone has—the more scars and tattoos and freckles and birthmarks and missing teeth examiners find—the stronger the identification will be.

Marks found on any part of the body can serve as the basis for identification. Killers and rapists often take photographs of their victims so they can relive the excitement of the crime. When Baltimore police raided the apartment of a man suspected in several rapes, they found his photograph collection. Although he had carefully hidden his face from the camera in pictures taken with his victims, the lab was able to positively identify him from moles and birthmarks on his leg.

But the great majority of identifications from photographs are made by clothing comparisons. This is a real art. The shirt or blouse you are wearing may have been mass-produced—thousands of seemingly identical garments may have been made—but the clothing you are wearing right now is unique. No matter how carefully a garment is made, different garments will never be identical at the seams. Seams are random, and while great care may have been taken to ensure that, for instance, stripes on a shirt pocket are aligned with the stripes on the shirt's body, manufacturers aren't as careful at the shoulders or in the back, places that aren't easily seen, and variations at these spots generally supply the basis of the easiest clothing identifications. The more intricate the pattern the easier it is to make an identification. The results of wear—stains, tears, loose threads, damage of any kind—are also unique and make an excellent basis for comparison.

To make a comparison between a garment seen in a photograph and a similar garment that can be associated with a suspect, Special Photo takes its own photographs of that garment being worn by a member of the unit. They will try to match the crime-scene photo as closely as possible, recreating the lighting and posing the model in the same position. Then an examiner will compare the two photos. Finding a single unique characteristic in one garment but not in the other is enough to conclude that they are different; and while there are no specific parameters, examiners usually want to find at least three identical, unique characteristics before making a positive ident. All the stripes have to come together at the seams in precisely the same way, the rip has to be just *there*, the same scuff mark has to be on a shoe. An examiner once positively linked a suspect with an ordinary dark-blue wool cap that had been worn as a mask in a bank robbery, by counting the number of rows of threads between two holes cut for eyes.

Clothing identifications are most often made in robberies, but they have also provided significant evidence in several murder cases. After a young Indiana girl had been kidnapped, tortured, and finally strangled with a strip of cloth, police developed a suspect but had no hard evidence to connect him to the crime. They needed something, anything, that would link him to the victim. They eventually found a photograph, taken weeks before the murder, in which the suspect was standing in front of an unmade bed in a motel room. The sheet on the bed looked a lot like the strip of cloth used to strangle the girl. The photograph was blown up so the sheet could be examined in detail. The way the pattern met at the seam was identical in the photograph and on the piece of cloth recovered with the body. The murder weapon had been the sheet seen in the photograph. This comparison was just about the only hard evidence against the suspect, but it was enough to lead to his conviction.

• • •

Years ago the legendary photographer Alfred Stieglitz reportedly told Pablo Picasso, "I don't understand your paintings. They don't look like anything." With that he showed the artist a photograph of his wife, the painter Georgia O'Keeffe. "This is my wife," he continued. "This is exactly what she looks like."

Picasso looked at the snapshot, then replied politely, "Small, isn't she?"

Among the most important clues that can be extracted from a photograph is the size of a person or an object. This is particularly good lead information in bank robberies. Sometimes a bank robber's height can be established simply by putting a height marker precisely where he stood, then photographing it with the same camera and doing an overlay, but most often it requires the use of a technique called photogrammetry. The science of photogrammetry, making measurements from photographs, was born in 1859 when a French army colonel mapped the terrain of a battlefield from a hot-air balloon. Topographic mapping is still the primary use for photogrammetry—the U.S. Geological Survey uses it, exclusively, to map this country—but Special Photo began adapting it to crime fighting in 1979 and is the only lab in the country providing this service.

Most photogrammetry is done with stereoscopic photography, in which two pictures are taken at the same instant from slightly different points. But no one ever takes stereoscopic pictures of crimes in progress, so Gerry Richards and several co-workers in the unit pioneered the use of single-image photogrammetry, which allows measurements to be taken from a single photograph. While you see objects in all three dimensions, a photograph captures only two dimensions. The result of that is perspective: for example, railroad tracks that are actually parallel appear to converge in the distance. To determine the height of a person in a photograph, examiners have to know the exact sizes of several other objects in that photograph, including at least one object that's vertical and touching the floor. In a bank, for example, the known object might be the counter, which can be measured accurately after the robbery.

Photogrammetry uses complicated geometric formulas and permits the height of a person or object to be calculated within an inch. And that inch can mean the difference between freedom and years in prison. After a Los Angeles bank was robbed, the tellers described the robber as very tall, and police subsequently charged a six-foot-eight-inch man with the crime. He was positively identified by the tellers, none of whom was taller than five foot three. The problem was that in the photographs taken by the surveillance camera, the robber appeared to be no taller than six feet. The LAPD insisted it had the right man, but Gerry Richards insisted just as vehemently that the man seen in those photographs was only six feet tall. Eventually he flew to Los Angeles to take a new set of measurements and check his calculations. "And then I told the police, if the guy you got in jail is six-eight, he's not your man," Richards said. "He may be a bad guy, but he didn't do this one. I finally told the prosecutor, 'If you put this guy on trial, I'm going to testify for the defense.' Finally, and reluctantly, they decided to let him go."

Photogrammetry played a supporting role in the *Twilight Zone* case, in which actor Vic Morrow and two young children were killed when a helicopter crashed during the filming of a scene in which a Vietnamese village was being bombed. Director John Landis was indicted for criminal negligence for ordering the helicopter to hover too close to the explosions, but in fact no one really knew how close to the ground the helicopter had been before it crashed. The National Transportation Safety Board asked Special Photo to determine where the helicopter was at all times and whether the crash had been caused by debris from the explosion flying into the rotor, delamination of the rotor (in which the several layers that make up the rotor come unglued due to excessive heat), or simply a faulty rotor.

"Let me put it this way," Richards remembered. "After we got done laughing, we told them it was impossible. Then we started figuring out how to do it. The techniques we normally use to make photogrammetric measurements depend on having manmade objects that are straight and level and either vertical or perpendicular. Here we were dealing with round thatched huts. There was nothing straight, nothing level. We eventually figured out that the only thing in the pictures that we might be able to use were the helicopter's landing skids. They weren't square, but they were parallel to each other. We also had about twenty known factors: the camera speed, the size of the frame, the focal length of the lens, the distance between the skids, and so on. By combining all of this information, we were able to draw rays, or vertical lines, from the ground to the helicopter, and we plotted its position as each explosion went off. We figured out that it was about twenty-four feet above the ground and its tail rotor was directly over the fourth and fifth explosions when they went off, and that's when they lost control.

"Was that too close to the ground? There's no legal definition of that, but the jury decided there was no criminal negligence. Could we isolate the cause of the crash? No. The prosecutors wanted me to testify that bamboo flying up from the hut had hit the rotor and caused it to detach. When we enlarged the film and slowed it down, we could see all sorts of junk flying up there. I said it looked like bamboo and it was shaped like bamboo, but there was no scientific way of concluding that it *was* bamboo. The only thing I could say was that there was a lot of garbage flying around after the explosion, and in one frame the rotor was there, and then it was gone."

Another difficulty often encountered in working with still photographs is that they are still: they have been taken from one position, sometimes the wrong position. But in some cases it's actually possible to change that position after the photograph has been taken. The technique is called warping, or rubber sheeting, and it's done to eliminate the distortion caused by perspective. At many crime scenes the photographer stands in the doorway and shoots the entire room, meaning everything in that room is distorted. And later, when examiners inspect the photographs, they may find something that had been overlooked—a shoeprint in dust under a television set, for example. Potentially there's a lot of good lead information in that print, but it's only valuable to investigators if it can be seen at actual size, as if it had been photographed from directly overhead so that it might be accurately measured. Two methods are used to rectify the image, to make it look as if it had been photographed from above in what is called an orthographic, or "true," projection.

A special rectifying enlarger, which works by tilting both the lens and the image, can be used if the angle to be corrected is less than fifteen degrees. But if it's greater than that, and it almost always is, then the work has to be done by computer. The computer rotates the image of the shoeprint, recalculates its size on the basis of the degree to which it had to be stretched or compressed, and then fills in the missing areas. This is a sort of futuristic trick photography, and it turns dust into evidence.

Valuable clues can also be found in shadows. Special Photo receives photographs from local police departments that want to know when the photos were taken. In fact, one of the tests given to photo examiners in training is to determine from a picture the time of the day and the day of the year it was taken. Shadow analysis, which is used by military intelligence to decipher aerial photographs, can often answer those questions. Shadows move with the sun, so there are only two days each year during which a person or an object in a specific place will cast exactly the same shadow. If an examiner knows where a photograph was taken, he can figure out the latitude and longitude, and from that determine on which two days a shadow would have a given length. Other clues in the photograph—the type of clothing worn, whether the trees are bare or the flowers are blooming—allow it to be narrowed down to a specific date. If the relationship of the shadow to true north is known—if it is known which way the camera was pointing—it's relatively simple to determine from the length and the angle of the shadow what time of day the photo was taken.

Conversely, shadows can be used to determine where a photograph was taken if you know when it was shot, although obviously the real key to figuring that out comes from the images in the picture. When a known terrorist was arrested in Washington, D.C., several photographs of the city were found in her possession. From the view, it was obvious they had been taken from the dome of the Capitol. This is a restricted area, with very limited access; whoever took those pictures shouldn't have been there. Since it could be determined when the pictures were taken, finding exactly where they were taken might lead to the associate of the terrorist who took them, or at least to the person who provided access to the area. An examiner taped a negative inside a camera so he could see it when he looked through the viewfinder, then walked around the dome until he found the exact spot where he could align the negative with the view. The photo had been taken from a walkway on the second level, and by checking security logbooks agents learned who had been in that area when the picture was taken.

One of the Bureau's most important responsibilities is covert surveillance. It secretly watches bad guys: spies, members of organized crime, drug dealers, money launderers, crooked politicians, and anyone else conducting illegal activities in this country. Such surveillance often requires the use of specialized cameras, lenses, and film, some of which were developed by the military for intelligence work. The FBI "air force" includes several small airplanes equipped with high-resolution aerial cameras capable of both daytime and nighttime surveillance. Long lenses are used to photograph objects from as far as a quarter mile away. When inmates rioted and took control of Talladaga Prison in Alabama, photographs taken from a great distance provided vital information about the location of the hostages, the types of weapons the prisoners had, the weak points in their security, even the way the doors opened and how they were hinged.

"Concealments"—hidden cameras—were once limited by the size of the camera required to produce usable photographs, but technology has made it possible to hide cameras just about anywhere. Concealments can be as small as a pinhole in a wall or as large as the entire wall. Special Photo has built cameras into books and briefcases and heating ducts and lamps and light fixtures; it has put them in tie clips and gift-wrapped packages. For one bribery investigation a camera was built into a hand-carved wooden state seal that eventually hung in the office of the state treasurer.

The ideal place to hide a camera is somewhere that will cause people to stare right into the lens. Television sets make excellent concealments because people look directly at them. In a New York City undercover operation being run out of a bar, a camera was hidden behind a painting of a beautiful nude woman hung in a back room; the sensible assumption was that every man coming into that room was eventually going to take a long look at that painting. When a nurse in a Virginia veterans' hospital was suspected of stealing from patients, a camera installed behind an exit sign above the door caught her in the act. Concealed cameras are capable of operating for months without being serviced, and can shoot as many as sixteen hundred pictures on a single roll of film. The shutter can be triggered manually, by remote control, or even by sensors set off by the subject.

Among the special equipment employed by the lab is a thermo-camera, or thermoimager, which enables investigators to photograph differences in temperature. These cameras produce an image on a monitor, rather than a traditional print. They are often used in searches to find hiding places. Walls are heated, usually with a hair dryer; because recesses hold heat longer than the rest of the wall will, they show up on the monitor. Electronic thermo-cameras are used to locate wall safes, for example, but an imager was also used to search the apartment of a Dallas, Texas, serial killer who was believed to have hidden a jar filled with his victims' eyeballs in a recess in a wall. That jar was never found.

Infrared and ultraviolet filters and lighting enable investigators to see through things, to read documents through sealed envelopes, to read writing that has been obliterated, and to see other things that can't be seen under normal light with the naked eye. The human eye sees only a portion of the entire light spectrum; in that visible portion, four things can happen to an object. It can reflect light, in which case it will appear white. It can absorb light, and appear black. It can reflect some of the light and be visible as a color. Or the light energy passes through it, so it appears transparent.

Alternate light sources—X-ray, infrared, and ultraviolet—make it possible for human beings to see portions of the light spectrum not normally visible. The importance of this to detectives is that different objects, among them inks, respond differently to the various forms of light. Some will get lighter, some will get darker, and some, because they are not visible at that portion of the spectrum, will become transparent. They will just disappear. While alternate light sources and filters are most often used in document examinations, they have also proven valuable in a variety of applications. After a San Diego woman was brutally beaten and raped, police sent the FBI lab the filthy paisley blouse she had been wearing. Her attacker had left a muddy shoeprint or palmprint on the blouse, but the multicolored fabric made it impossible to see the print clearly. When the blouse was photographed using infrared lighting and filters, the fabric seemed to disappear, leaving a clear photograph of the muddy shoeprint.

When the battered body of a Des Moines woman was found on a lonely gravel road, police searched the home of the man last seen with her. Although he claimed that she was alive when he dropped her off, in his home police found burnt fragments of what seemed to be the strap of a woman's pocketbook, and a few charred pieces of a photograph. With infrared lights the camera could see right through the blackened crust coating the photograph, and the victim's relatives identified it as a picture of her niece. Presumably, the photo had been in the victim's pocketbook. The fact that it was found in the suspect's possession was enough for a jury. The suspect was convicted of second-degree murder and sentenced to fifty years in prison.

The lab's permanent setup for photographing evidence under alternate light sources is the only one of its kind in regular use. The camera provides high-quality resolution and a very permanent record—you get the hard evidence that can be used in a courtroom—and with a time exposure the camera can take a good picture of a very weak image. This became important when the body of a Texas woman was found clutching a ballpoint pen. Police, discovering some marks on her hand, believed that before she died she had written the name of her killer on her hand. But the printing was too faint to be read. At the suggestion of an examiner, the police severed the victim's hand, packed it in dry ice, and sent it to the lab. Under alternate lighting some writing could be seen, but still not clearly enough to be read. Then examiners tried photographing the hand with night scopes, which are extremely light-sensitive. While that made the printing slightly more legible, it still couldn't be deciphered. This was terribly frustrating; the killer's name was right in front of the investigators, but they just couldn't see it. Finally, they used the night scope to make a time exposure; they left the lens open for hours, which allowed the faint light emanating from the writing to "burn" an image into the film. After several hours they were able to read the name the woman had written on her hand in the final seconds of her life, providing a vital clue for investigators. They had successfully photographed something that didn't seem to be there.

The Video Enhancement Unit, seven people working in a $4 million broadcast-quality studio located in the basement of the headquarters building, began in the early 1980s as part of Special Photo and became an independent unit in 1990. "What sets us apart down here," said unit chief Don Brager, who joined the Identification Section in 1978 as a clerk and eventually became the first non-agent to head a lab unit, "besides the fact that we're down here, of course, is that we're all young, we're all ambitious to the point of being aggressive, and we run our unit like a committee. There's great teamwork and camaraderie elsewhere in the lab, but I think we go further than anybody else. We're certainly the most informal unit in the lab. We dress nice when we have to, but mostly we're crawling around running cables, so generally we're pretty informal."

In the early 1980s video cameras cost as much as $10,000, well beyond the budgets of most police departments, but as the equipment became affordable, the world of Special Video changed drastically. For the first time accidents and crimes were being taped as they happened, creating a new kind of hard evidence. Video enhancement specialists, or analysts, as the members of this unit are officially titled, are responsible for converting videotapes into usable evidence, and that can mean restoring it, enhancing it, interpreting images, or adding information like time codes or subtitles. Occasionally, they even produce tapes.

Tapes arrive in the lab in every conceivable condition. They have been burned and scratched and scraped and stretched and twisted and cut into pieces. They have been erased and flushed down toilets and retrieved from plane crashes and garbage dumps. In some cases the only request is to try to find anything, even one frame, on the tape. "We do a lot of things in here that no one else has tried," said Bob Keller, a TV and radio major at Ball State University who started in the Bureau's office of public affairs. "Basically, we find that there's a need to do something unusual, then we try to figure out how to do it. There are really no textbooks to go to; our best sources are the people who manufacture this equipment. We had a case in here in which a military aircraft flew into a mountain, and no one had any idea why. The pilots gave no indication that they had a malfunction; they just ran into the mountain. There was a three-quarter-inch video recorder in the nose of this plane that records what the pilot is seeing on his radar screen. The military came to us with some mangled tape that had been retrieved from the wreckage and asked if there was anything we could do with it. I didn't think there was. I mean, this stuff looked like strands of spaghetti.

"One of the things we're proud of in here is that we never say no. This whole area is still so new even we're not sure what's possible. The tape looked awful, it had kind of shriveled up in the fire, but experts from the 3M Corporation advised us to try putting a wet cloth over it and then iron it. We did, and it spread out somewhat. It turned out that the tape wasn't as damaged as it originally appeared to be and we were finally able to play it. I didn't know what I was looking at, but there were two military pilots working with us, and as soon as they saw this thing, they knew exactly what had happened. And basically, it turned out to be pilot error. They saw one mountain; unfortunately, they never saw the other one."

Sometimes tape damage isn't accidental. Sometimes people realize that a tape they have made could put them in prison, and try to destroy it. For example, a Baltimore, Maryland, crack addict calmly set up a tripod and taped himself raping a young girl in her living room. Then he killed her mother. Later, when he realized that the police were closing in on him, he dowsed the tape with lighter fluid and burned it. A few fragments were recovered by police and delivered to the FBI lab in a plastic bag. Most of the magnetic oxide, the part of the tape that carries the image, had been burned off. But examiners were able to develop partial images on a few frames; these showed the rape in progress. It wasn't very much, but it identified the suspect clearly, and when these bits of tape were shown in a courtroom, they were enough to convict him of rape and murder.

While most of the units in the lab deal with brutality and death on a daily basis, only the people in Video Enhancement actually see people dying. As camcorders have become ubiquitous in society, it's no longer rare for a deadly accident or a murder to be recorded. In a typical case, two teenaged boys taped themselves on an all-day drinking spree. They were having a great time; they were laughing, mugging for the camera. But the tape ended abruptly in their car when they crashed head-on into another vehicle. The crash resulted in the death of three people. The lab got the case because police wanted to know how fast the boys were driving when they lost control of the car. The Video Unit reconstructed the tape, then enhanced it so as to be able to read the speedometer just before the impact, and reported the car was approaching ninety miles per hour.

Another tape showed a happy family on their small boat, out on a lake for a summer afternoon of waterskiing. Over the shoulder of a child on water skis, another boat can be seen coming toward them. That tape also ends suddenly and tragically: that other boat, being driven by a drunk boater, crashed into the family and killed everyone except the skier. Three months after the accident, the tape was recovered from the lake bottom; when the lab restored it, the details of the fatal accident became chillingly clear.

"It's really sad sometimes," Brager said softly, "really sad. You just have to learn to separate yourself. We see things in here . . . A guy robbed a convenience store, we see him on the surveillance camera. The security guard comes out and the robber shoots him in the head. You're actually seeing the gunshot on tape. You see the guard's body reel back, you see him collapse on the ground, and he's huddled against a wall. Just sitting there, and then his body goes limp. You just saw a man die. It's not TV or the movies; it's not easy to watch. Sometimes I try to make myself believe it isn't real, that it was just a TV show."

Police investigating that murder wanted the lab analysts to enhance the video, to see if they could produce a clear picture of the killer or determine what kind of gun he used. The video unit, like Special Photo, can use several techniques to improve the quality of a tape. They can lighten or darken it; the image can be sharpened or enlarged; a small section of the image can be isolated; the speed of the action can be changed; and much of the "noise," the graininess and scratches caused by the metal head of the recorder grinding off bits of magnetic oxide, can be reduced. While the unit was able to produce a better picture of the convenience store, there just wasn't enough information on the tape to lead to the gunman.

The unit was a lot more successful in helping Garrison, Texas, police solve the 1991 murder of Constable Darrell Lunsford. After a suspect apprehended by Lunsford in a drug-smuggling case was released by the court because of a lack of evidence, Lunsford mounted a video camera on the dashboard of his patrol car so he could record his arrests. The camera was running the night he stopped three men who appeared to be driving recklessly. As videotaped in the headlights of his patrol car, Lunsford started to open the trunk of the other vehicle—which was later found to have contained forty thousand dollars' worth of marijuana—when the three men grabbed his gun, pushed him into a ditch, and shot him in the head. While the actual shooting was not on tape, the initial struggle was recorded. Lunsford's body was found in that ditch; his video camera was still running.

Although the three men couldn't be seen clearly enough in the dim light to be positively identified, the video enabled police to develop a general description, and the men were arrested within the next few days.

The first thing that happens when a tape arrives at the lab is that copies are made. Original tapes are evidence; they can't be changed in any way. Working on the copies prevents defense attorneys from claiming that someone has tampered with the evidence. In the Lunsford case, the unit was able to substantially improve the contrast, eliminate much of the "noise," and sharpen the focus. The three men, who could barely be seen on the original tape, were clearly identifiable on the enhanced tape. There was little other hard evidence to link the three men to Lunsford's murder. No weapon was found, and there were no witnesses. There was just this videotape. The jury watched it in complete silence, then convicted all three men of murder.

There have been several well-publicized cases in which the unit has been asked to make an identification from a poor-quality tape. In 1989, when terrorists announced that they had hanged Marine Lieutenant Colonel William Higgins in retaliation for the Israeli kidnapping of a Shiite Muslim clergyman, they released a badly blurred video of a man hanging from a rope in a prison cell. From that video it was almost impossible to be certain the body was really that of Lieutenant Colonel Higgins. The Defense Department wanted two questions answered: Was that Higgins's body in the video? And if so, when had he been killed?

Certain clues seen on the tape made it likely that the victim had been killed long before the video was released, before the clergyman was kidnapped. Although supposedly hanged in midsummer, the victim was dressed in winter clothing. Also pathologists noted that the body did not exhibit the usual results of hanging: open mouth, bulging eyes, protruding tongue, darkened eyes, loosened bowels, and elongated neck. This indicated that the man had been killed earlier, and not by hanging, and that his body had been preserved until the tape was made.

Proving that it was the body of Lieutenant Colonel Higgins was more difficult. Unit analysts decided to try to compare Higgins's facial features to those of the victim. They began by making a video of the last known photograph of Higgins ever taken. "We wanted to do an overlay," Bob Keller explained. "But because the body was in a different position in the two videos we had to change its position. We can do that with a video image. We can move a video frame on its axis. We can turn it and twist it and flip it. It's just as if you were holding a photograph in your hand; anything you can do with that photograph we can do with a video frame. They do it all the time on television. But we can't create information that isn't there. If you turned over a photograph you'd see a blank side. We can't turn an image around and look at the other side."

When the figures in the two videos were about the same size and in the same position, lab examiners created an overlay and slowly went back and forth between the two images, using what is known as a wipe pattern. Starting at the very top of the head, a horizontal strip from the photograph was superimposed over the video. Then a second strip, then a third . . . As the strips moved down the screen, it became obvious that the facial features were just about identical. Everything matched: the recession of the hairline, an indentation in the forehead, the depth of the eye sockets, the ear orifice and the nose. The figure in the terrorist video had tape over his mouth, so that was as much of a comparison as could be made. But it was enough to allow the FBI to announce, "A positive identification could not be made, but numerous observable characteristics were noted indicating that the person in the videotape was Lieutenant Colonel Higgins."

In a somewhat similar case, when the body of an American airman supposedly washed up on a beach in a hostile country, the State Department obtained a videotape and asked the lab to confirm that it was one of two men listed as missing in action over that nation. It was an almost impossible job because the body apparently had been floating in the ocean for quite some time: it was bloated and decomposing. "When you look at something like this tape you just sigh and go to work," Bob Keller said. "We did some research and found out that there's only one part of a body that doesn't swell up in the water, and that's the ear, which is basically all cartilage. We also learned that while most facial characteristics change through life, the shape of the earlobe remains the same. So we wondered if we could do an ear comparison.

In Higgins's case that wasn't possible because not enough of the victim's earlobes were visible in the original video, but in this case the position of the victim's head allowed this comparison to be done. After obtaining recent photographs of both of the missing airmen, Keller remembered, "We decided to try to do an overlay. We wanted to lay the ears in the photographs right over the ear visible in the video. We were able to turn the body slightly; it was enough. Once we'd put the ears in about the same position and made them about the same size, doing the layover was pretty basic. We just dissolved back and forth between the video and the photo. Now, this might not have worked if we'd been asked to identify the ear on the video from millions of others, but we didn't have to. It was just whether or not it was one of two known airmen. And when we did the comparison, we could be almost one hundred percent positive that it was."

In addition to enhancing the quality of a tape, the Video Unit will use basic technical means to make it easier for a jury to understand what it is seeing. During surveillance of a drug operation, for example, Washington, D.C., police taped two men passing a briefcase filled with cocaine, but the exchange was made so smoothly and so quickly it was hard to really see it happening. Video normally runs at 29.9 frames per second, but when the tape was slowed to a few frames per second, it was very easy to see the briefcase being passed. When one of the suspects saw himself on the tape, he immediately confessed, and implicated other members of the drug organization.

Perhaps the most famous homemade video in history was a very badly lit, grainy, black-and-white tape showing Los Angeles policemen brutally clubbing a man named Rodney King. Solely on the basis of this tape, the officers were indicted for assault with a deadly weapon. When the tape was submitted to the lab, it was copied onto high-grade broadcast tape, which preserves the quality far longer than most commercially available tapes, and then a time code was added, enabling jurors to see exactly how much time elapsed between blows and how long the entire attack lasted. It was a routine job and probably didn't affect the outcome of the case at all. The first trial resulted in a hung jury, a decision that sparked the devastating riots in South Central Los Angeles, and in the second trial, a federal trial, the officers were convicted of violating King's civil rights.

The Bureau's audio work—planting microphones and enhancing sound-tracks—is done by a unit in the Information Resources Division, but as videotape generally carries an audio track, these two units often work together. More than a year after $7 million was stolen from Wells Fargo in West Hartford, Connecticut—at that time this was the second-largest robbery in U.S. history—agents from the San Juan office planted a microphone in the apartment used by members of a Puerto Rican pro-independence group believed to have participated in the heist. As several members of the gang, Los Macheteros, watched a Boston PBS documentary about the unsolved robbery, they made incriminating comments that were picked up by the bug. They were arrested and Video Enhancement was asked to synchronize this audiotape with the documentary, so a jury would understand the meaning of their comments. But the gang members had been speaking in Spanish, and what really made this tape valuable to prosecutors were the English subtitles added to it, then synchronized with the action. It suddenly became very clear to the jury what one of the suspects meant when he said, as he watched a dramatization of the crime, "Remember that?"

A videotape contains much more information than immediately meets the eye—if an examiner knows what to look for and how to use it. Far in the background of a tape made by a security camera during a Dover, Delaware, bank robbery, an examiner noticed, was a car parked in front of the bank. The car remained there throughout the robbery, and when the robber fled, it disappeared. Police weren't even aware of this getaway car until it was spotted on the tape, and it subsequently became an important lead in their investigation.

In a case that required the video unit to use almost all of its technical capabilities—enhancement, comparison, the addition of information, even production—three blurry frames shot by an ATM time-lapse videocamera were turned into the hard evidence needed to convict a man named Robert Auker of the murder of his wife.

On May 24, 1989, nineteen-year-old Lori Ann Auker simply disappeared from the face of the earth. The next day her car was found in the parking lot of a Northumberland County, Pennsylvania, mall, where she worked in a pet shop. She had gone to work, but she never got there. Nineteen days after she was last seen alive, her body was found at the bottom of an embankment. She had been stabbed at least seven times. Her estranged husband, with whom she was involved in a custody suit over their child, immediately became the prime suspect. But for more than a year police were unable to find enough evidence to link him to the crime.

As it turned out, there had been a silent witness to her abduction. A time-lapse video camera hidden in an automated teller machine outside the Northern Central Bank in the mall took a photograph in which a specific section of the parking lot could be seen in the background. Although the bank had several surveillance cameras, they were all connected to a single video recorder which alternated between the different cameras, so the image seen by this camera was recorded at ten-second intervals. The tape had been reused so often that most of the oxide had been worn off. It was almost transparent, so a Northumberland detective brought it to the lab to see if it could be enhanced and examined. Regular video shoots almost thirty frames a second, but time-lapse video, which is used in place of still photography, shoots only one or two frames a second. So there might be a week's worth of information on a two-hour tape. Bob Keller watched the blurry tape with the detective. "The police were interested in seeing what was on this tape because they'd found her car in the parking lot," Keller remembered. "They wanted to know if we could see anything unusual. Maybe she'd been taped pulling into the lot or walking toward the bank. They were looking for any leads.

"When the detective and I watched the tape we didn't see her pull in, but he pointed out to me where her car had been found. We looked at the few frames they wanted me to see, and in the last frame I saw a blurred person way in the distance—it might have been a woman—walking toward the camera. For some reason the police hadn't associated this person with the victim. So I decided to watch a little more of the tape than they had. Three frames in particular caught my attention. In the first frame I saw a figure coming toward the bank. In the second frame, taken ten seconds later, a car had backed out of a parking spot and the door on the passenger side was open. The figure was just barely visible. But ten seconds later both the car and the figure were gone. That was really strange, I thought. Logically, within that time frame the car might have been gone, but we still should have seen that person coming closer. The probable explanation was that the person had gotten into the car. I told the detective, 'It looks to me like whoever was driving that car is the person you want to speak to.'

"The problem we had was that the quality of those frames was awful. When a tape is playing in a time-lapse mode, or when it's on pause, the metal heads just grind against the oxide. So you get very few plays in the time-lapse mode. In this case the images were just barely visible. An ATM camera is focused on the person using the machine; that's who the bank wants to get a good look at. We were looking beyond that into the parking lot, so the image was out of focus, it was blurred, and the oxide was just about worn off the tape. In fact, there was a potentially important frame that we saw only once; then the last of the oxide fell off and we never could get it back again."

Although the car was visible on only one frame, it was identified from the taillight assembly as a Chevy Celebrity made between 1982 and 1985. Robert Auker's father owned a 1984 Chevrolet Celebrity, and he admitted that his son had been using it the day Lori Auker disappeared.

The day after Lori Auker's disappearance, the car had been sold, and subsequently had been resold several times. By the time the police found it, it was owned by a Pennsylvania state trooper. This was a long time after the murder; although the car was thoroughly searched, all police found were a few hairs and a little bit of blood, nothing that enabled them to associate the car with either the suspect or the victim.

"The police were sort of out of ideas," Keller continued, "So I told them, 'If you think the car in the video is the car you have in custody, why don't you recreate the video using the same ATM machine. Put the car in the same spot and try to recreate those three frames. That way you'll have a known and a questioned, then you can do a comparison to see if they really are identical. That's the way we work in the lab.' "

At that time Video Enhancement did not have some of the more sophisticated video equipment available, so Don Brager contacted Al Teitjan, a video expert who had done most of the video enhancement work for NASA after the space shuttle *Challenger* exploded. Tietjan agreed to help produce the reconstruction. After the second video had been shot, someone realized that the car mistakenly had been put one parking spot farther away from the ATM machine than the questioned car, a problem Teitjan corrected by enlarging the image to make it appear closer.

Before making the comparison, Teitjan used computerized digital enhancement—the same method used by Special Photo—to remove some of the blurriness and improve the contrast in the original video. He divided the image into pixels and changed selected gray levels to make the person and the car stand out from the background. After that Teitjan and Brager did a wipe, just as had been done in the Higgins case, replacing the car seen in the questioned video with the known car. As Keller recalled, "We put

287

one on top of the other and you could see the similarities were very great. And we never had to say it was the same car. The jury saw this tape and made that determination for itself."

There was additional circumstantial evidence against Auker. He claimed to have been at a store in another mall when his wife was abducted, yet clerks in that store testified they hadn't seen him that day. He had taken out a life insurance policy on his estranged wife just weeks before her murder, but had tried to backdate it. The jury deliberated slightly more than an hour before convicting Robert Auker of kidnapping and murder, then took just a little longer in the penalty phase to recommend death.

While you may not realize it, your picture is probably being taken several times every day. Due to the availability of inexpensive camcorders, point-and-shoot cameras, and throwaway cameras and to the increasing use of security cameras, surprisingly good evidence has been provided in many cases. To take advantage of this new source of hard evidence, the FBI is currently considering establishing regional imaging centers at many of its field offices. These computer-based systems will enable agents to enhance, focus, or sharpen potential evidence right on the spot rather than being dependent on the lab. The Video Enhancement Unit, like Special Photo, will manage and support these systems as well as actively participating in the most sensitive cases.

Another small unit in the Document Section, the Polygraph Unit, does that right now. In addition to maintaining quality-control responsibility over the fifty-one field agents trained to conduct polygraph examinations, the unit performs the most important tests itself. The polygraph, popularly known as the lie detector, may be the most misunderstood of all sci-crime instruments. Most people believe the polygraph is used almost exclusively to determine guilt or innocence, that it can be "beaten" by sociopaths, and that information obtained in polygraph examinations isn't admissible in court.

Not true. The lab uses the polygraph as an investigative tool to help develop leads and evidence and to verify information; only on occasion is it used to help determine guilt or innocence. According to Document Section chief Ron Furgerson, who previously ran the Polygraph Unit, "We're never testing for ground truth. We're testing what the subject believes to be the truth, which is very different. Anybody who believes he is telling the truth is going to pass this test." For this reason, anybody—sociopaths, psychopaths, schizophrenics, the toughest prisoners, experienced espionage agents—can be tested, and the results may prove useful in the investigation. And while the results of a polygraph exam are permitted to be introduced in a trial only by prior agreement of both the prosecution and the defense, a confession made during the test is admissible as long as the polygraph exam itself is not discussed.

Rudimentary versions of the modern polygraph have been used by various cultures for thousands of years. Lie detection is based on the fact that people worry about being exposed when they lie, and that fear or anxiety causes measurable physiological changes.

The ancient Chinese made suspects chew dry rice, then spit it out. Fear causes the digestive system to slow down, producing a dry mouth, which in turn makes it difficult for guilty people to generate enough saliva to spit out the rice. Arabs would put a donkey with a greased tail in a darkened tent, then would warn suspects that when the donkey's tail was pulled by a guilty man the animal would bray. Those who emerged from the tent without grease on their hands were presumed guilty.

The very first lie-detecting machine, the hydrophygmograph, was invented in 1895 and measured changes in the pulse rate and blood pressure of a subject being questioned. In 1921 John Larsen developed an instrument that continuously recorded changes in blood pressure, pulse rate, and respiration during questioning; he named this instrument the polygraph.

For a time it was believed to be infallible. It caused banner headlines in the early 1930s when Bruno Hauptmann, the accused kidnapper and killer of Charles Lindbergh's baby, failed a crucial polygraph test. But in 1938, when lie-detector tests given in a Florida kidnapping-murder indicated that an innocent man was guilty and that the person who later confessed to the crime was innocent, FBI director J. Edgar Hoover ordered agents to "throw that box into Biscayne Bay."

The Bureau continued using it on an occasional basis—after Jack Ruby shot Kennedy assassin Lee Harvey Oswald at point-blank range on national TV, he demanded a lie-detector test to prove he did not know Oswald—until 1964, when Hoover banned it from the FBI completely. That proved embarrassing in 1971 when, directed by President Richard Nixon to find the source of leaks of sensitive material from the State Department, the Bureau was forced to borrow polygraph equipment from the New York City police department. That episode rekindled interest in the polygraph, which, ironically, proved its value two years later when tests given to White House aides Jeb Magruder and Gordon Strachan helped expose the Watergate cover-up.

The sci-crime lab's Polygraph Unit was established in 1978. Since then the lie detector has proved to be an extremely valuable investigative tool. It's a tool, not the answer, and that's the key to its use in the lab. "We interview and obtain information from a wide variety of sources," explained Jim Murphy, the tall, distinguished-looking chief of the Polygraph Unit. "This information needs to be corroborated, and the polygraph is a very cost-effective way of doing that. We know it's not perfect, it's not equal to the truth; but, for the most part, it's a reliable indicator of the truthfulness of what someone says. Simply put, it's an effective way to get a confession from somebody or develop information that's going to solve a crime for you. We need people to tell us what happened."

The success of a polygraph examination is directly related to a subject's fear of detection. Sometimes the test isn't even necessary. After four guards were killed during the attempted robbery of an armored car in Denver, thirty-six of the thirty-eight company employees who had the insider's knowledge required to plan the holdup agreed to take the test. In the belief that innocent people have little to fear from the machine, police immediately focused their investigation on the two men who refused to be tested, and within a short period of time they developed enough evidence to charge one of those men with masterminding the crime.

People's beliefs about what the polygraph is capable of doing are sometimes more valuable than what it actually can do. After three American nuns and a lay worker had been raped and murdered in El Salvador, the U.S. State Department put tremendous pressure on that country's government to allow Salvadorian National Guard troops known to have been in the area to be tested. Special Agent Sinecio Gutierrez conducted the tests in Spanish. The guardsmen were understandably nervous, and the test was set up to magnify that fear. Gutierrez began by warning them that the machine would know when they were lying. To prove this, he conducted what's called a stimulation test. He had the men write down a number between 10 and 20 and hide the paper in their pocket. When the test accurately determined the number they had picked, the troops were convinced of the machine's powers. Four of the guardsmen confessed to their participation in the crime, implicated high officers, and told agents exactly what had happened. Their fear of being caught lying was enough to trigger their confessions.

Often the Bureau relies on the machine to determine the value of a subject's information. "When an FBI agent was murdered in Kansas City," Jim Murphy said, "a fifty-thousand-dollar reward for information was offered. So we had a lot of people coming forward with information. Obviously, they wanted that money. We could have wasted a lot of time tracking down all those leads. Instead we put them all on the machine, which enabled us to determine the value of their material. We had one woman who came in with very detailed information. She claimed to have been with the men who killed the agent; she even drew a diagram. Well, we really thought we had something. But after reluctantly agreeing to take a polygraph test, she failed it. And then she admitted that she'd made up the whole story to collect the reward." The killers were eventually caught by other investigative means, but the polygraph played an important role by eliminating suspects.

At the very beginning of New York State's Tawana Brawley case, in which a black teenager claimed to have been kidnapped, sexually assaulted, and otherwise abused by four white men, a woman said she had seen Brawley climb into the plastic trash bag in which she was found, the bag Brawley later said she had been forced into by her tormentors. When the woman voluntarily took a polygraph test and passed it, the Bureau began to question the teenager's tale, and other evidence was developed that disproved it.

In 1992, Haitian army captain Stagne Doura, a former commander of the national penitentiary, claimed that deposed Haitian president Jean-Bertrand Aristide had personally ordered him to kill a prisoner named Roger Lafontant. Lafontant had been a member of dictator Jean-Claude Duvalier's cabinet. Doura said that Aristide had threatened to kill him if he failed to carry out this order. Lafontant was murdered that night. This was a very sensitive case because the U.S. government was actively trying to restore the democratically elected Aristide to power. The U.S. State Department asked the FBI to administer a polygraph test to Doura. The Bureau reported that the tests showed "no attempt at deception." Doura was telling what he believed to be the truth: Aristide had ordered a summary execution. Even though his claims were probably true, the State Department took no further action in this case.

But sometimes, however, polygraph screenings unexpectedly reveal crucial information that does lead to prosecution. One day a woman named

Barbara Walker contacted the Boston field office and claimed that her ex-husband was a Soviet spy. She hadn't lived with the man for more than a decade, and she seemed to have some personal problems, so initially agents were quite skeptical. But certain parts of her story were too detailed to have been made up. Only after she volunteered to take a polygraph test—and passed it—did the Bureau begin to take her acc sations seriously. As a result, they were able to smash a major espionage operation, and John Walker was convicted of spying for the Russians and sentenced to life imprisonment.

But the polygraph test that provided the most stunning result began as a simple confirmation of an FBI agent's sworn statement. After a young woman in Pikeville, Kentucky, disappeared, her relatives told police that the last person known to have been with her was an FBI agent named Mark Putnam. Putnam had worked in the Pikeville office for several years before being routinely transferred to Miami. During that time, the woman had been one of his informers. She had disappeared at about the same time Putnam was back in Kentucky testifying in a trial. Putnam admitted that the woman had worked for him, but denied her relatives' claims that they had had an affair. He gave a sworn statement to investigators in which he said he had no knowledge about her disappearance.

To prove to Kentucky authorities that the FBI had conducted a thorough investigation, the Bureau's Office of Professional Responsibility, Internal Affairs, asked Putnam to take a polygraph test. It was routine, perfunctory, the kind of test given every day. Except on that day, to everyone's astonishment, the examination results indicated that Putnam had indeed had an affair with the woman and had probably killed her. When told that he had failed the test, Putnam broke down. He admitted that he had had an affair with his informer, had panicked when she became pregnant, and had strangled her to death. Because the only evidence against him was his own statement, which was compelled by the results of the polygraph exam, his lawyer was able to arrange a plea bargain, and he was sentenced to only eight years in prison.

The fact that Putnam confessed after failing the test wasn't unusual. A complete examination consists of three phases: a pre-test interview, the exam, and the post-test interrogation. If the results of the post-test interrogation indicate that the subject has not been truthful, the examiner will explain that and give him the opportunity to talk about it. At that time, according to statistics, more than half the people who have failed will either confess or change their story. That's precisely what happened when Special Agent Salvador Escobedo tested an employee of the DuPont Plaza Hotel in San Juan, Puerto Rico, after a deliberately set fire killed ninety-six people and caused $10 million in damage. After the employee had failed the test, Escobedo gently asked him if he wanted to talk about it. He broke down, admitted starting the fire, and named the two other men who had been with him. Eventually all three men confessed and received prison sentences of a minimum of seventy-five years.

A polygraph exam is not nearly as dramatic as it's made to be in movies. When possible, it's conducted in a small, quiet room with nothing hanging on the walls that might distract the subject. "The atmosphere's created to give us every possible psychological advantage," explained Murphy. "When a subject comes in, we start by talking to him about the facts of the case, and we take down his statement or alibi. But right at the beginning, we warn him that if he doesn't tell the truth he's going to fail the test. I always suggest that if he's going to lie to me, he shouldn't waste my time or his time. He should just get up and leave. And I don't care who it is, no matter how guilty that person is, he never leaves. Never. He knows that leaving at that point would be an admission of guilt. So now I've got a captive subject.

"We try to be natural and sincere and friendly. I usually tell them that my job is to help them get through the test, but that to do so they're going to have to cooperate with me. One case I had, a Washington, D.C., man was accused of having committed a rape about six months earlier. In the pre-test, he denied it completely, but he remembered exactly where he'd been that night, which I thought was unusual. I mean, how many people can tell you where they were on a particular night six months earlier? When I actually conducted the exam, I asked him if he'd been at the place he mentioned on the night of the rape, and he answered yes. I took a deep breath, a loud deep breath, and told him, 'Look, I want to help you get through this, but that alibi just isn't going to work. You're going to have to give me a better one.' So he said, 'Okay, let me try this one. . . .' Gradually I was able to get him to admit that he'd had sex with the victim, but he insisted it was consensual, that she was accusing him of rape to get even with him for something. But he was the rapist and eventually he was convicted of the crime."

Before the examiner begins the test, he will rehearse with the subject the questions he is going to ask. He will go through the questions one by one and explain exactly what they mean. Every question will be answered yes or no. Exams generally are limited to ten questions, which are repeated two or three times in order to collect enough physiological data to draw a conclusion. Several control questions are asked, and questions like "Are you wearing shoes today?" enable the examiner to establish a normal baseline with which to compare the subject's reaction to the pertinent questions. Examiners never ask surprise or trick questions, although they may vary the order in which they ask the questions.

The modern polygraph is a long way from a greased donkey's tail. The subject wears a blood-pressure cuff on his arm, rubber tubing around his chest, and electrodes on the ring and index fingers of his left hand. The polygraph records the responses of the autonomic nervous system: his blood pressure and pulse rate; his breathing; and changes in his galvanic skin reflex, which is his resistance to electricity. In a 1987 study conducted to assess the accuracy of polygraph exams, the Bureau's Inspection Division compared test results with subsequent investigative developments. After looking at more than twenty thousand tests, the evaluators determined that less than one percent were probably wrong. And in the ninety-one cases in which the polygraph results were eventually proven wrong, only twenty-seven involved exams in which people who were lying beat the machine.

When used by an experienced operator, the polygraph can provide a great amount of information. After World War II, for example, polygraph tests were given to Nazis in an attempt to locate art treasures stolen from Paris. Even when subjects refused to respond, their physiological reaction often provided the answer. While the machine is rarely used to pin down a location, in certain instances it can be very effective in doing just that. It was used that way when a Newark, New Jersey, woman claimed her baby had been kidnapped, but told a story that made little sense. Once she was hooked up to the machine, the examiner began "searching" for her baby. When the woman was asked if the baby was in New York State, she replied that she didn't know, but the polygraph indicated she was lying. Working slowly and methodically, the examiner eventually narrowed the location to somewhere in New York City, but couldn't get any more specific. The test reversed the focus of the investigation from kidnapping to abandonment, and the subject finally admitted that she had left the baby in a Macy's washroom. Macy's had turned the baby over to the city's child welfare department, and she was found quite safe.

A polygraph exam is always voluntary. No one can be compelled to take the test. But refusal to take a test does cast doubt on an individual's credibility. When Arkansas state troopers claimed that they had arranged sexual encounters for President Clinton, they offered to take a lie detector test. But when a New York newspaper made arrangements to take them up on that offer, they quickly changed their minds. While the effects of their charges lingered, the story quickly dropped out of the headlines.

Conversely, the fact that a subject voluntarily takes a polygraph test does lend credibility to his or her claims. When figure skater Tonya Harding's estranged husband, Jeff Gillooly, was arrested and charged with plotting an assault on Harding's rival Nancy Kerrigan, prior to the 1994 Winter Olympics, Gillooly decided to make a deal with prosecutors by implicating Harding in the plot. As a prerequisite for any agreement, the prosecutors wanted Gillooly to take a polygraph exam. The questions focused on whether Gillooly was telling the truth when he said that Tonya Harding was aware that there was going to be an assault on Nancy Kerrigan and had approved the plan. When Gillooly passed the test, the focus of the investigation shifted to Harding, who eventually confessed her involvement in the bizarre plan to keep Kerrigan out of the Olympic games.

While the question-and-answer phase of a polygraph test is always straightforward, examiners have been known to use a variety of techniques to convince subjects to tell them the truth. When two suspects in the same crime are being interviewed in separate rooms, for example, the examiners will often play them against each other. They might have a pizza delivered to one room and nothing to the other, and let the second suspect draw the obvious conclusion from that. Or they might use bits of information obtained in one interview to convince the second suspect that they know more than they really do. And finally, they might simply say, "We really don't need to spend any more time here. Your partner told us that he got the watch and the wallet, but that you did the shooting. So we're going to take a statement from him." It's all legal, as long as the subject is not coerced into making a statement, or told what to say. Then it's up to the machine to determine if he is telling what he believes the truth to be.

The roster of cases in which the polygraph has been used to verify information, develop investigative leads, or clear innocent people reads like the history of crime in modern America. One of the most dramatic exams in recent history was that given to Jack Ruby, the man who shot and killed Lee

Harvey Oswald before Oswald could be questioned about the assassination of President Kennedy.

Oswald's murder is the pivotal point in just about every Kennedy assassination-conspiracy theory. According to many of these theories, Ruby knew Oswald and killed him to prevent him from revealing details of the plot to kill Kennedy. Ruby vehemently denied this until the day he died of cancer, and demanded the opportunity to prove, by taking a polygraph exam, that he was telling the truth. The Warren Commission charged with investigating the assassination finally acceded to Ruby's pleas, and Special Agent Bell Herndon was assigned to conduct the test. The test took place in Dallas, Texas, on July 18, 1964. "I'd been working right along on various aspects of the assassination; just about everybody in the lab was," Herndon recalled. "Oddly enough, what I remember most were the President's shoes. They were very old and very worn, they'd probably been resoled several times, but they were so well polished. So by the time I interviewed Ruby, the exam was just another aspect of the case.

"I prepared the questions with several people, including Arlen Specter, later to become a senator from Pennsylvania but then a lawyer working for the Warren Commission. We formulated questions for Jack Ruby to see if we could get to the crux of the matter. Did Ruby know Oswald? Was Ruby involved in a conspiracy? Was there premeditation on the part of Ruby and Oswald to get together to do something about President Kennedy? Was Ruby possibly linked to an organized-crime element out of Chicago and paid off to silence Oswald? Was there a conspiracy? Was Ruby paid off by the Mafia? Was Ruby a member of the Communist party? We were aware of all the theories going around and we tried to cover them all in my interrogation.

"The test was very lengthy, which I objected to, and I do think there came a time when Ruby was desensitized. He was showing some fatigue. When the test began I tried to establish a rapport with him. I felt like I had the best chance with him if I treated him very respectfully, if I was very sympathetic, if I didn't make him feel like he was a subject, but rather just an individual trying to clarify his involvement in the assassination. I didn't want to be the heavy, which is sometimes necessary when you're sitting down with a hardened criminal and you have to dominate the situation.

"I think I was probably correct, because Ruby was cooperative. He seemed to understand the intent of the questions, he didn't move, he didn't fidget, and he answered the questions as he was instructed. I think that Mr. Ruby felt that by taking this test, by being candid and cooperative, he could convince the world that he shot Oswald because he was so mad that Oswald had killed our beloved President. The one question I never asked him was, 'Did you shoot Lee Harvey Oswald?' because that was pretty well resolved. He'd done it on national television; it just was beyond being a relevant question.

"I've always considered the polygraph to be a scientific interrogation technique, but there's more to it than the machine. The Bureau's position is that subjective impressions by the interrogator are just as valuable as what the chart or pen tracings show. I always look for body language, eye expressions, nervousness, whether he's deliberately trying to defeat the machine by flexing his muscles or by moving, clearing his throat; it's all part of an innate sense a good interviewer gets after conducting years of exams.

"I believed Jack Ruby when he told me he did not know Oswald and that he was not part of a conspiracy. I had asked him several control questions where I knew he was not telling me the truth, but I didn't see that same kind of reaction to the relevant questions that I asked him. There was also a question of Ruby's mental stability. His doctor was present because I had been warned that maybe Ruby was not quite what we would call fully sane. But he appeared to be physically fit to me, and he wasn't under any medication.

"My conclusion was that he was a valid subject. I felt that although maybe he had some mental aberrations, and who wouldn't in his situation, I thought that there was no indication of deception to relevant questions. But I also stated that if a doctor said that this man was a manic-depressive, I wasn't going to be foolish enough to contradict him. And if that were true, then I would have to render my conclusion nonconclusive. But on that day, I felt he understood the intent of my questions, that he was not divorced from reality and he was fully cooperative, and that he was telling the truth as he believed it to be."

Is it possible to beat the machine? To get away with deception? Absolutely. The Russians, Cubans, Bulgarians, and other former Eastern bloc countries had extensive programs in which they taught their agents and military officers various ways of handling a forced polygraph exam. Because Eastern bloc nations did not commonly use the polygraph, our government did not have such a program. But in one instance an American operative moving freely between West and East Germany was accused by the East Germans of working for American intelligence and given a polygraph test.

297

He failed the test, and was ordered to return the next day for a retest. This operative could easily have returned to West Germany and safety, so when he voluntarily returned the following day the East Germans decided the polygraph could not possibly be accurate and ignored the results.

Some people are untestable because of their physical makeup or diminished mental capacity, in which case examiners will not get consistent specific and significant responses and the results will be inconclusive. And some people do attempt to beat the machine by using drugs. An experienced examiner can usually read that in the charts, which come out flat as opposed to going up and down. In those cases the examiner may request a urine sample to test for the presence of drugs.

And finally, there is one foolproof way to beat the machine. A man from the hills of West Virginia was suspected of involvement in a bank robbery and was tested in the Fredericksburg, Virginia, field office. During the test he denied that he had robbed the bank. At the conclusion of the test, the examiner looked him right in the eye and told him, pointing to the polygraph, "I have proof right here that you did it!"

With that, the subject ripped the chart off the machine and ate it.

I guess you can say law enforcement officials have come a long way since the days of Sherlock Holmes and his magnifying glass.

—NORTHUMBERLAND COUNTY DISTRICT ATTORNEY ROBERT SACAVAGE,
at the conclusion of the Robert Auker murder trial

ACKNOWLEDGMENTS

Exploring a new world requires guides and helpers, and I was extremely fortunate to have many of these in the preparation of this book. I cannot sufficiently express my gratitude to the men and women of the FBI crime lab who welcomed me warmly and gave of their time and expertise. I hope the recognition they receive from this book in some small way repays them for their efforts in my behalf. I hesitate to name any of them for fear I won't name all of them, but they have my appreciation as well as my admiration.

This project began at dinner one night with my friend FBI Special Agent Joe Pistone, better known as "Donnie Brasco." I value his friendship, as I do that of Lou DiGiaimo, the motion picture casting director who introduced Joe and me and helped create this project.

I would not have been able to embark on this endeavor without the efforts and sacrifices of my literary agent, Jay Acton, a man of many talents and remarkable understanding, and I am grateful to him. My editor, Fred Hills, was unfailingly supportive, in addition to being an extraordinary editor and a very good guy. Of course, he had the benefit of his superb assistant, Laureen Rowland, who helped speed the process with professionalism and strong doses of good cheer.

I needed an enormous amount of assistance in the preparation of my research materials, which included 180 hours of interviews. I was so terribly lucky to find Ann Bartlett and the people she enlisted, Grace DiCamillo and Mary Ann Rebori, and I hope they know how grateful I am for their efforts. It's impossible to enumerate the many tasks accomplished in my behalf by Laura Vertullo, but each of them was done with expertise and enthusiasm, and I thank her for that work. Every author needs help in stepping back from his work when the shaping process begins, and at that time I was fortunate to have had the help of two friends, the best-selling author Berry Stainbeck and editor Ellie Kossack, and for their assistance and the way it was offered I will be forever appreciative.

In a long process such as this one any writer needs friends willing to put up with him, or more specifically in this case, to put him up. I am so lucky to have such friends in Iris, David, and Jordan Kai Burnett; and Trish, Paul, and Jessica Reichler.

And finally, a very special note of appreciation to Margarey Tremblay of the FBI Office of Public Affairs. Marge Tremblay, who recently celebrated her thirtieth anniversary with the Bureau, was the finest guide any adventurer could wish to find, and she does the FBI proud. For those taxpayers who complain about government waste, I offer Marge Tremblay. Believe me, with her we're getting our money's worth.

DAVID FISHER

INDEX

ABOUT THE AUTHOR

DAVID FISHER is the author of many books of fiction and nonfiction about a great variety of subjects. Among his best-sellers are *Gracie* with George Burns, *The Umpire Strikes Back* with Ron Luciano, and *Killer* with "Joey Black." He created and coedited the reference book *What's What*, which is currently being published in nine bilingual editions. He lives in New York City.